INDIAN WATER POLICY

IN A CHANGING ENVIRONMENT

INDIAN WATER POLICY

IN A CHANGING ENVIRONMENT

PERSPECTIVES ON INDIAN WATER RIGHTS

Published by
The American Indian Lawyer Training Program, Inc.
1982

Publisher, Executive Director
Richard Trudell

Editor
Patricia Zell

Editorial Consultants
Robyn Brode
Christine L. Miklas

Design
L. & W. Bonnett

Cover Illustration
Kazuhiko Sano

Back Cover Photograph
© Sue Bennett

Typography
Burch & McElroy

Printing
Paragraphics

The American Indian Lawyer Training Program, Inc., founded in 1973, is a non-profit, tax-exempt Indian owned and administered organization. AILTP's primary goals are to provide access to the increasingly vast and complex legal developments that affect Indian tribes and their members; to contribute toward the proper development of Indian law through publication of resource materials which focus on those areas of the law most vital to the Indian community; and to promote tribal sovereignty and Indian self-determination through training programs designed to develop the skills of members of the Indian legal community. Inquiries about the American Indian Lawyer Training Program should be sent to its principal office, located at 319 MacArthur Boulevard, Oakland, California 94610 (415) 834-9333

ISBN 0-939890-05-4

CONTENTS

"MANAGING THE RESOURCE"
Panel Presentation and Discussion

"STRATEGIES FOR CLARIFYING AND PROTECTING INDIAN WATER RIGHTS"
Panel Presentation and Discussion

FOREWORD

It has often been said—frequently in frustration and anger—that no aspect of American law can be more complex and susceptible to uncertainty, obscurity, and unpleasant surprises than water law. The American people generally have grown up with an image, nurtured by novels and films, that western water law is established and enforced largely with fists and guns. Most westerners and lawyers know better, but it is patently true that the field is perplexing, full of rancor, and ever-bedeviled by changing interpretations and conflicting decisions.

Until recently, the non-Indian water user and his legal advisers, as well as the organs of state governments, paid little or no attention to the water needs of the various Indian peoples and their reservations, much less to their rights to water. Because the federal government was so often either derelict in protecting the rights and property of the tribes or, indeed, collusive in dispossessing the Indians of what belonged to them, injustice was rampant and numerous tribes and their peoples suffered great poverty and unspeakable hardships. But among the non-Indians, the indifference bred illusions. The conflicts of water law, confusing as they might be, with only rare exceptions were perceived as those of the non-Indians alone, and water law itself was fashioned essentially for the white man and his interests.

The situation has now changed. The Indian, with his needs and rights, is at last in the arena as a recognized competing interest for water, and the shock of his appearance and quest for long-ignored justice has been great. If the field of water law was agonizingly convoluted before, it is now more so, for the previously existing maze has been overlain with an evolving Indian case law based on special and unique legally established relationships between the tribes and the United States government. Consider, for example, as at least one of the papers in this volume points out, the legal broken-field running that must be done to harmonize the traditional and constitutional pattern of the federal government's exclusivity in dealings with the tribes and, at the same time, the long-standing Congressional deference to a state's right to authority over water use within its boundaries.

In the decade of the 1980s, and undoubtedly beyond, no issue perhaps will be more important to most Indians, particularly those in the West, than water. It is, as another contribution to this book makes clear, not merely a matter of rights, but one of justice, including the safeguarding of homelands. If the ends are clear to Indians, however, they are not necessarily so to all non-Indians, nor even to those whites, such as states' attorneys general, who must cope with the tribes' assertions. Even less clear, not only to whites but to Indians and their legal representatives as well, are the nature and character of the mazes through which contesting parties are only just beginning to thread their way.

Each and all of the various papers in this book—delivered as addresses to the landmark Symposium on Indian Water Policy in a Changing Environment at Oakland, California, in November 1981—goes a long way toward helping to clarify what lies ahead. Their presentation of objectives and points of view, no less than their identifications of points of friction, and procedures and methods that offer possibilities for satisfactory solutions and the attainment of justice, provide hope that this book will be useful for a long time to come to everyone, Indian and non-Indian, who is interested in, or affected by, this intricate, but vital, subject.

ALVIN M. JOSEPHY, JR.
President, National Council
Institute of the American West
Sun Valley, Idaho

"There has been a lot said about the sacredness of our land which is our body; and the values of our culture which is our soul; but water is the blood of our tribes, and if its life-giving flow is stopped, or it is polluted, all else will die and the many thousands of years of our communal existence will come to an end."

Frank Tenorio
Governor, San Felipe Pueblo
1978

Images from

"Water: The River of Life"

by John Running and Sue Bennett

The Salt River in its transit from mountain brook in the high country figuratively passes through a staggering array of court decrees, state laws, acts, and treaties.

In the face of increasing demands for diminishing water supplies, Indian people must be aware of the economic, political, and legal forces working to determine water allocations today.

*Water, this country's most precious resource,
is managed on a scale that nearly defies imagination.
Great aqueducts and tunnels reroute entire rivers
and slice through mountain ranges.*

Water rights and fishing rights are inseparable issues. Ownership of the riverbeds and lakes, control of water quality and of the environment are all crucial considerations.

The way in which Indian water rights are resolved may well determine the future of the western United States.

When a thirsty nation demands more water than the rivers and rains will supply, then water becomes more than life; distribution of water becomes economics, control of water becomes politics, and water politics becomes bitter business.

PREFACE

As the demands on limited water resources increase in this country, the controversy attached to Indian water rights intensifies. State governments, as well as certain special interest groups within the private sector, question Indian entitlement to water, and although the federal government recognizes rights to water reserved for Indian use, federal water projects have primarily benefitted non-Indian users. The failure of the federal government to support the exercise of Indian water rights has significantly frustrated tribal efforts to attain economic self-sufficiency.

To understand and appreciate the complexity of the issues and conflicts which surround Indian water rights, one must study the full context of non-Indian competition for limited water resources, the legal basis for Indian water rights and the state and federal policies which either hinder or promote Indian use and regulation of water resources. This book provides a brief summary of disputes concerning Indian rights to use and regulate water resources in thirteen states, a primer on Indian water rights, an update on recent decisions affecting Indian water rights and perspectives of tribal leaders, attorneys, representatives of federal and state agencies, and academicians on how Indian water rights should be protected, evaluated and used. Their perspectives were presented and discussed at a symposium on *Indian Water Policy in a Changing Environment* sponsored by the American Indian Lawyer Training Program in November 1981.

If Indian water rights are to move from legal abstraction to actual, beneficial use, it is imperative that both non-Indian and Indian policymakers understand the water needs and priorities of Indian tribes. Historically, tribal governments always recognized that water was a vital resource to protect, conserve and manage for the maximum benefit of all water users. The challenge of the future, however, lies in governments working together to bring about equitable solutions to the present conflict over water. We hope that this book promotes a better understanding of and appreciation for Indian entitlement to water, so essential to Indian self-determination and economic self-sufficiency, and that it stimulates constructive discussions and actions designed to assist tribal governments respond to and resolve the issues and problems surrounding water resources planning and management.

RICHARD TRUDELL
August 1982

ACKNOWLEDGMENTS

The American Indian Lawyer Training Program (AILTP) owes a debt of gratitude to the many people who helped make this book possible. The cooperation and support of the speakers, moderators and panelists who participated in the symposium on *Indian Water Policy in a Changing Environment* is greatly appreciated. Their perspectives on how Indian water rights should be protected, evaluated and used provide the basis for this book.

I wish to express my deep appreciation to those intimately involved in making this book a reality: Patricia Zell for her editing, proofing and coordinating the preparation of the manuscript; John A. Folk-Williams, Charles N. Estes, Jr., Barbara Fritzemeier and Alvin Josephy, Jr. for their writing contributions; Joseph A. Myers for his invaluable perceptions and insightful editing; Christine L. Miklas for her excellent editorial comments and preparation of the overview section; and Linda Bonnett for her sensitive design expertise and patience with our preparation of the manuscript. A very special thanks goes to Patricia Zell and Deanna Martinez for their dedication and invaluable assistance in coordinating the symposium. Sincere thanks are due the AILTP staff for their patience with me and their unwaivering commitment to excellence. It is difficult to measure the dedication and support these individuals gave to the production of this book. A final note of thanks is extended to Ann R. Roberts, the Akbar Fund, the Rockefeller Foundation, the Cummins Engine Foundation, the Field Foundation, the Columbia Foundation, Gulf Oil Corporation, the Atlantic Richfield Foundation, and the Ford Foundation for their financial support of our work in this critical area of Indian affairs. Their interest in the general welfare of Indian people is deeply appreciated.

Throughout, the resilience and pride of Indian people inspired our work on this book. Their vision and attachment to the land has enabled them to endure and survive the encroachments by those who do not appreciate the harmony and beauty of our land.

RICHARD TRUDELL

OVERVIEW

For nearly two hundred years Indian tribes in the United States have been subjected to federal controls and policies which have frustrated the development of tribal institutions. Historically, the intensity of this frustration has been determined by the non-Indian appetite for Indian resources. When this appetite becomes strong, the federal government imposes additional limitations upon the powers of tribal self-government. Over the years the objects of non-Indian interests in Indian country have included land, oil and gas, coal, and other energy resources. Today it is water.

In the western states we are experiencing today what certain commentators term a cultural war, a conflict between agricultural, industrial, urban, and Indian interests concerning the use of precious water. In certain regions of the West the demand for water far outweighs the supply.

The non-Indian focus on Indian water rights has become increasingly intense. There is legislative talk of tribal relinquishment of water rights for non-use within a certain time frame. There is also pressure being brought to bear on Indian tribes, by both the federal and state governments, to quantify Indian water rights.

Historically, Indian tribes have turned most frequently to the federal courts to protect their water rights, and, in fact, the legal case history affirming Indian water rights is nearly as old as this century. Due, however, to a complex array of competing economic and political concerns, the translation of paper water rights into wet water for actual Indian economic development has lagged far behind the hopes inspired by the landmark *Winters* decision in 1908. Although that decision recognized that Indian tribes have reserved rights to water sufficient to transform each reservation into a permanent homeland, conditions of water scarcity, particularly in the thirsty western United States, have forced Indian tribes to become involved in complex and expensive efforts of litigation, legislation, and negotiation in order to actually claim and use the water to which they have reserved their legal rights. *Indian Water Policy in a Changing Environment* documents the experiences and philosophies of Indian and non-Indian water development and management experts assembled by the American Indian Lawyer Training Program to share their concerns, identify problems, and discuss strategies for developing and managing the water resources so vital to the survival and economic advancement of Indian peoples.

From state to state the issues and conflicts pertaining to Indian water rights vary. John A. Folk-Williams, who has recently written a book-length study of Indian water issues entitled *What Indian Water Means to the West,* summarizes here, in excerpts from that study, the specific water problems that confront Indian tribes in the western states of California, Arizona, Colorado, Idaho, Montana, Nevada, New Mexico, Oregon, Utah, Washington, and Wyoming. He concludes by discussing the water situation in North and South Dakota, where plans to divert upper Missouri Basin water out of the states make clarification of water rights for the Dakota tribes a process that will have important consequences for other Indian and non-Indian water users throughout the entire Missouri Basin.

Because of the scarcity of water in the West, in that region the *Winters* Court found itself interjecting the doctrine of reserved water rights into a context where permits for specific uses of water were granted according to the doctrine of prior appropriation—a "first come (to the water permit office), first served" approach to distributing water rights. Although *Winters* assigned the Indian tribes water priority dates equal to the dates of the establishment of their reservations—priority dates generally superior, legally, to those of the users who had received state permits based on prior appropriation—in practical terms, the tribes have often found that much of their reserved water has already been put to use by state permit holders. Against this backdrop, Charles N. Estes, Jr. reviews the major court decisions following *Winters* and the congressionally enacted McCarran amendment to show how the limited supply of water has led to these judicial and legislative attempts to quantify Indian water rights, to define the uses to which Indian water may be put, to determine the water rights of non-Indian purchasers of Indian land, and to decide who—the states or the federal government—has jurisdiction to appropriate water among users and what jurisdiction tribal governments have over Indian and non-Indian use of reservation water.

Traditionally, Indian nations have been immune from suit in state courts and Indian water rights have accordingly been determined in federal court. Both the McCarran amendment, enacted in 1952, and *Colorado River Water Conservation District v. United States*, decided in 1976, raised the question of whether in the process of adjudicating the water rights of a particular river system, states could assume jurisdiction over Indian water rights. In an article that concludes Part I, Barbara W. Fritzemeier discusses several cases that have refined the question of federal or state jurisdiction, paying special attention to the conflicting interpretations of the Ninth and Tenth Circuits regarding states that have constitutional disclaimers of jurisdiction over Indian tribes. Her article goes on to discuss *Colville Confederated Tribes v. Walton*, a further adjudication of the water rights of non-Indian successors in interest to Indian allotments, and the recommendation of Special Master Tuttle that the Supreme Court modify its 1964 decree in *Arizona v. California* to grant the five Indian tribes of the lower Colorado River additional water to irrigate lands both omitted from the original decree and recognized as part of the five reservations only since the decree.

In his opening remarks to Part II, Richard A. Trudell describes how the vision of Indian communities has grown from one of establishing entitlement to and quantification of water under the *Winters* doctrine to one that encompasses uses for water not envisioned by the "irrigable acreage" standard of *Arizona v. California* and one that includes the assertion of rights to water of a specific quality as well as quantity. As Trudell points out, Indian access to water is often dependent on the Secretary of the Interior's adminstration of federal water reclamation projects; Wendell Chino further describes the difficulties Indian tribes encounter when trying to obtain water from federal reclamation projects and discusses some of the conflicting interests that seem to make it difficult for the United States to act in the best interests of Indians in its role as trustee. Specifically, Chino cites the failure of the federal government to advocate the permanent homeland concept as the proper measure of the quantity of water available to Indians and takes issue with the federal government's apparent willingness to have Indian water rights decided in state courts.

No matter in what forum a water law suit takes place, the cost of going to court in both time and money can be staggering, particularly in this era of decreasing federal monies to support Indian tribes in such efforts. Therefore, in his moderator's preface to the discussion of "Water and the Indian Future," W. Richard West, Jr. suggests that cooperative agreements or legislative settlements may offer less costly and more efficient means of settling Indian claims to water. These two alternatives, however, do assume the possibility of compromise. After reviewing the workings of prior appropriation water law, Frank J. Trelease discusses the restrictive quantifications suggested by the recent *Colville Confederated Tribes v. Walton* case, where off-reservation claims would be tested against the primary and secondary purposes of reservations and each reservation asked to define the minimum quantity of water needed to fulfill its purpose, and notes these as the parameters of possible compromise between Indian and non-Indian users.

Quantification of Indian water rights is fraught with difficulties, particularly since future as well as present needs must be assessed. Robert S. Pelcyger notes, however, two recent water decisions, *Cappaert v. United States* and *Arizona v. California,* where the Supreme Court has allowed judgments of quantification to be enlarged based on proof of changing need, and suggests other legal doctrines under which Indians may be able to claim water in addition to their reserved rights. In any case, quantification depends on the technical research of soil and hydrologic experts and federal monies are necessary to provide tribes with this support. Claudeen Bates Arthur reviews the internal workings of the Department of the Interior with specific discussion of how increasingly limited federal monies influence Indian tribes involved in water litigation and urges the tribes to define their research needs with utmost precision so that they will get the most benefit from the limited federal dollars expended on their behalf. Russell Jim discusses how the fight to control the administration of water in Indian country influences the availability of federal construction dollars for Indian water projects and emphasizes the importance of insisting on a specific quality of water, explaining how this relates to maintenance of fisheries.

Fishing is only one of many non-agricultural uses that tribes have for water. After describing the frustrating experiences that the San Carlos Apache Tribe has had with litigation and negotiation for its water rights in Arizona, Ned Anderson highlights the limitations of the "practically irrigable acreage" standard of quantification, pointing out that some reservations not widely irrigable, nevertheless, have sources of wealth such as mineral lands, forests, fisheries, grazing lands, and dam and power sites that need water for development. With specific reference to power projects in his home state of Nebraska, Reuben A. Snake notes the ecologically disruptive effects of water overdevelopment and cautions Indian people not to be led along this path in their quest for economic growth. Placing the issue of water rights in the larger context of the survival of the human race, he urges the red man to assume the role of reeducating his fellow man to adjust the quantity of his water needs and to live in harmony with nature.

Addressing the topic "Balancing Competing Interests," Joseph A. Myers emphasizes that a proper balancing can occur only through mutual understanding. The path to follow toward this understanding is, however, not so clear as Myers notes that litigation has the disadvantage of being a "win/lose" proposition and legislation the disadvantage of being frequently the product of special interest groups. According to Gary D. Weatherford, competition for water occurs within the context of four larger themes of scarcity, sovereignty, stability, and survival. Weatherford describes the way in which competing forces for water can align in particular situations and makes the point that competition alone cannot insure that a wise balancing of interests will take place. In Arizona, scarcity of water is paramount, as John B. Narcho points out, and the struggle for water is a struggle for the underground acquifers. As Narcho describes the experiences the Papago Tribe has had in attempting to litigate, negotiate, and legislate their water rights, he notes that in this region of extreme scarcity water competition seems to align both the state of Arizona and the federal government with the non-Indian interests.

After reviewing the water situation of the Confederated Tribes of the Umatilla Reservation in Oregon, Douglas Nash suggests a fourfold approach to protecting water rights from the encroachments of economic feasibility that others would place upon them. His approach involves: preparing an information base about tribal water resources and needs, dealing with state regulatory agencies, dealing with competing non-Indian water users, and relating the interests of fisheries to water rights. Richard B. Collins points out that competing for water involves not just competing for the resource itself but competing on a nationwide basis for federal monies with which to construct water projects and notes that currently more water development money is going to the relatively "wet" southeastern United States than to the arid West. John A. Folk-Williams describes the highly competitive non-Indian decision-making process that Indians must attempt to influence on their behalf and discusses how the competition for water goes on on two separate levels—the level of competing for proprietary rights to the resource and the level of competing for governmental regulatory control of water.

In his remarks opening the discussion of "Managing the Resource," Alan R. Parker also notes the dual nature of Indian tribes—as owners of proprietary water rights and as governments seeking to manage this vital resource. He notes the tremendous pressure being put on tribes to "use or lose" their reserved water and suggests that leasing water rights temporarily to non-Indian users may provide a partial solution, giving the tribes a way out of the "use or lose" dilemma while offering a source of income that can be used to build Indian water projects. From the perspective of a state water manager, Ronald B. Robie discusses the responses to the assertion of Indian water rights including the extreme proposal of Senator Gorton (R.-Wash.) to terminate unexercised Indian water rights after a seven-and-a-half-year period. Robie suggests that physical solutions, such as lining canals to conserve water, may exist in areas where assertion of Indian water rights seems to imply extinguishment of junior, state-authorized claims.

David H. Getches addresses the jurisdictional aspect of water resource management, reviewing the problems tribes have encountered with the Department of the Interior and Congress in trying to extend jurisdiction to non-Indian users of reservation water and urges tribes to pursue all available avenues to gain this jurisdiction in order to become truly effective managers of their reservation water. He also discusses the problems of leasing Indian water rights—how at present congressional action is required to separate the conveyance of water rights from the conveyance of rights to the land itself. Lee Brown discusses the positive contributions of economic markets to water management, *e.g.*, the stimulation of material improvement, but also outlines the necessity for creating a mechanism that will stop the markets from operating when a goal other than material improvement is desired. He suggests that water leasing may offer one option in this situation where the right to water use can be withdrawn when the end to which it is being put becomes socially unacceptable. Frank Tenorio points out how Indian/non-Indian conflicts over water are based, in part, on differing perceptions of this resource—Indians perceiving water as a living spirit and non-Indians perceiving it largely as a commodity. Tenorio also highlights another obstacle to effective Indian water management—the fact that many cities adjoining reservations are depleting tribal underground supplies.

Water abundance is the experience of the Quinault Indian Nation in Washington. From this standpoint, Guy McMinds envisions a day when water management will involve interstate transport of water by pipeline and urges the tribes to consider developing an agency to coordinate intertribal exchanges of water. Water is also abundant in Alaska, where Native-owned corporations, created through the Alaska Native Claims Settlement Act, are facing the problems of managing the water needed for competing interests—fisheries and logging, to name a couple. Chris E. McNeil of the Sealaska Corporation and Nelson N. Angapak of the Calista Corporation discuss the early efforts of these corporations to meet these management challenges.

Managing legal resources is also key to effective management of water. Kenneth L. Smith discusses some of the problems involved in the Department of the Interior that make it sometimes difficult for the United States to perform in its trustee role without conflict of interest and talks about recommendations he is developing with the Solicitor's Office to make sure Indian representation is not weakened by the trustee's competing interests. However, even when all legal resources are mustered to pursue litigation, legislation, and negotiation, during the time required by these processes water may dry up leaving tribes with only a paper resource to manage. Therefore, Peter MacDonald challenges tribes to find ways to put water to use now, possibly through an intertribal confederation that would allow tribes to trade and lease water among themselves. Beyond pursuing legal avenues to water rights and water management, Joseph DeLaCruz sees the task of Indian people as one of educating non-Indians about the sovereign nature of Indian governments. Only when the Indian nations are perceived as having goverment-to-government relationships with the United States can Indian people work out their proper water management rights from a position of their rightfully acknowledged power.

In opening the discussion of "Strategies for Clarifying and Protecting Indian Water Rights," John E. Echohawk notes that the traditional method of litigation has been made problematic by the debate over federal vs. state forum. Negotiation, still largely untested, may be a way out of this dilemma. No matter which public forum Indians choose to pursue their rights, Charles F. Wilkinson suggests that their case can be presented most strongly from the point of view of water conservation and eliminating water wasted by users, especially in areas where water systems are already overcommitted. Through these approaches, Wilkinson suggests, sufficient water may be found to meet Indian needs while minimally disrupting the already established users. Describing how in her opinion the era of significant water development is over, Dr. Helen Ingram sees the leasing of Indian water rights as the most exciting avenue for progress available to the tribes.

To Henry Loble, Chairman of Montana's Reserved Water Rights Compact Commission, negotiation appears to be the most fruitful strategy because it is flexible and more efficient and because a compact resulting from a negotiation gives each party a real wet water right instead of a paper entitlement. Scott McElroy, however, still sees many benefits in pursuing litigation, particularly if parties can resolve certain issues like choice of forum and number of interested parties out of court, thereby eliminating the delays that resolution of these in court can cause. After reviewing various congressional efforts to cut appropriations for Indian programs, Suzan Shown Harjo makes detailed suggestions for negotiating ground rules that would put tribes on an equally assertive footing and reaffirms the necessity for Indians to take their concerns to the Departments of Interior and Justice and to demand funding for the soil and hydrological studies necessary to protect Indian water rights in any forum.

Legislative settlements have not worked well for the Gila River Indian Community as Rodney B. Lewis explains with specific reference to the Coolidge Dam. Given these experiences, Lewis suggests that perhaps the only way tribes can negotiate water rights from a position of strength is through pursuing litigation first. Speaking from the perspective of tribes engaged in litigating their rights—the Shoshone and Arapaho Tribes of the Wind River Reservation in Wyoming—Robert N. Harris, Sr. discusses plans to use the tribes' adjudicated water rights to the Big Horn River to challenge the adjudicated rights of other users in negotiations. According to Ronnie Lupe, whose White Mountain Apache Tribe in Arizona has filed a federal suit against the U.S. Attorney General and the Secretary of the Interior for submitting the Apache water rights to state court, negotiations should proceed with the trustee, not the states. These negotiations should pursue two objectives: (1) negotiation for protection of *Winters* rights and (2) determination of money damages due from the United States to the tribes for past violations of Indian water rights.

In the West the possession of water means economic and political power. Clearly, although significant case law is on the side of Indian tribes, prodigious efforts remain in securing actual rights to wet water. Choice of forum remains a thorny problem for litigants. Funding for technical studies needed to support water claims pursued in any forum are harder and harder to come by as are federal dollars for construction of Indian water projects. Meanwhile, wet water continues to be appropriated by state-authorized non-Indian users, intensifying the pressures on Indian nations to find ways to protect and use their reserved water as soon as possible, and legal obstacles remain to be confronted as tribal governments strive to effectively manage all water rights within their reservations. If Indian tribes are effectively foreclosed from exercising their reserved water rights, an extreme hardship will be cast upon the economic and political development of tribal self-government. Nothing less than the future of the tribes' permanent homelands is at stake.

PART I

INDIAN WATER IN CONTEXT

The following summaries of conflicts relating to Indian water rights in thirteen western states were prepared by John Folk-Williams, President, *Western Network*. These are brief excerpts from a book-length study of Indian water issues, entitled WHAT INDIAN WATER MEANS TO THE WEST, which will be available in August 1982. That study includes an overview of the sources of conflict relating to Indian water, the record of past decision-making and settlement processes, and discussion of proposals for new approaches to resolving such disputes. The core of the publication is a survey of specific conflicts in more than sixty western water basins, including detailed entries identifying the major parties, issues, and settlement processes in use for each case. A set of documents and reference materials round out the volume, giving a comprehensive review of the subject.

Western Network is a non-profit research and communications program examining problems of decision-making relating to the West's natural resources. Its program combines research, publication and conference events in an effort to stimulate dialogue among western constituencies in competition for resources about how to improve decisional processes.

SURVEY OF TRIBAL-STATE CONFLICTS OVER INDIAN WATER RIGHTS

ARIZONA

There are nineteen Indian reservations within Arizona, comprising 20 million acres of land, or 26.8 percent of the total area. Most of this state lies within the Colorado River basin, and its history of water disputes revolves around the complex interstate allocation and federal regulation of the Colorado River and its tributaries.

Arizona's share of the flow of the Colorado River is restricted by the Colorado River Compact, by a series of federal statutes, and by the decision of the United States Supreme Court in *Arizona v. California*, one of the major Indian water rights cases, which is still in final phases of litigation. The state share amounts to 2.8 million acre-feet, but a substantial part of this total is reserved for use by tribes along the main stem of the river, and these tribes are currently attempting to have that amount increased.

The state's plan for using its share of Colorado River water is to divert an annual average of 1.2 million acre-feet to the metropolitan areas of Phoenix and Tucson by means of the Central Arizona Project (CAP), a system of tunnels, pumping stations and aqueducts now under construction by the United States Bureau of Reclamation. Because this project is a federal one, the United States Secretary of the Interior has power over the allocation of its water for the purpose of satisfying Indian and federal reserved rights. There is current controversy over the amount that the Secretary will allocate for Indian tribes in the southern and central parts of the state and over the methods for sharing water shortages among Indian and non-Indian water users.

The Gila River, a tributary of the Colorado, which crosses the southern part of the state and joins the main stem near Yuma, is the major river system supplying the region which will receive CAP water. It is so heavily appropriated now that there is no regular flow reaching the Colorado River. The Salt River, which flows into the Gila west of Phoenix, is also fully appropriated, and both these streams are subject to ongoing Indian litigation over Winters Doctrine rights.

Tucson, the only major city in the United States completely dependent on the pumping of groundwater, is attempting to reach agreement with the Papago Tribe over Winters Doctrine rights to the groundwater resources. The city frankly acknowledges that resolution of Papago claims is the most important water issue facing the region, and negotiations involving all major users have been underway for some time. A legislative proposal embodying the results of this process passed the Congress but was vetoed by the President on June 1, 1982.

In the northern part of the state, the Little Colorado River, another tributary of the Colorado that flows into the main stem at the Grand Canyon, is the subject of litigation to determine Navajo and Hopi water rights.

Almost every reservation in the state is involved in significant litigation. Because Arizona combines the classic Winters Doctrine questions with the issues of Indian entitlements to federal reclamation project water as well as groundwater, the state has been the scene of a series of the most complex and hard fought conflicts over Indian water rights in the country.

CALIFORNIA

California has the largest Indian population of any state (the 1980 census estimated at least 201,000 Indian citizens) yet the state's Indian land base is quite small, consisting of dozens of tiny reservations and rancherias and a few larger Indian tracts in the northern part of the state. These have a total area of approximately 540,000 acres. A number of small reservations are clustered near the urbanized coastal region between San Diego and San Bernardino, and it is in that area that an important Indian water rights dispute has emerged. Aside from that case, California's major concern with Indian rights has focused on its eastern borders.

The historic source for much of southern California's urban and agricultural development has been the Colorado River, and the state has been involved in the *Arizona v. California* suit (described in the Arizona section) for the past thirty years. The Supreme Court's 1964 decree in that case reduced California's entitlement to Colorado River water by about 1 million acre-feet from the amounts that have been used in recent decades. Partly to offset that reduction, California has launched its massive State Water Project, which transfers water from the northern part of the state to the central and southern areas.

California water planners are concerned that increasing consumptive uses of the Colorado River water for energy development and for Indian economic projects will jeopardize the quality as well as the quantity available to southern California, possibly putting greater pressure on the State Water Project to find additional supplies for its water delivery contracts. This is a long-range problem that has not resulted in any specific conflict with Indian tribes, except in the context of *Arizona v. California*.

Lake Tahoe lies over a portion of the border between Nevada and California, and California's interest in the Truckee River system that flows from this mountain lake has brought the state into the complex litigation surrounding the rights of the Pyramid Lake Paiute Tribe (as described in the Nevada section below). The interstate compact of 1968, which allocates the waters of the Truckee, Carson and Walker River systems between Nevada and California, has never been ratified by Congress, and the extent of Indian rights to these streams remains a concern of California.

There has been a major fishing rights controversy on the Klamath River of northern California where the Yurok Indians and the state fishing authorities have sharply disagreed over Indian fishing rights and related regulatory issues concerning the salmon resource. As cases in the states of Washington and Oregon suggest, Indian fishing rights may imply an important right to protection of the fisheries environment, a protection that may place a significant constraint on state regulation and non-Indian economic use of the waters of the Klamath River.

Because California has become so dependent for its water allocation system on transbasin diversions, any substantial new claims by Indians on the feeder streams for these massive engineering works poses a possible threat to non-Indian agricultural and urban interests. Two reservations have a great deal to lose if certain elements of the State Water Project are built. The Round Valley Reservation on the Eel River and the Grindstone Rancheria in the Sacramento system might both be inundated if certain projects, in only the study phases now, are ever built.

The Paiute communities of the Owens Valley, whose original reservation lands and associated water rights were exchanged for new ones when Los Angeles was building its aqueduct system there in the 1920s, have a grievance over water that involves the L.A. Department of Water and Power. That agency agreed to provide 10,000 acre-feet to the Paiute communities as part of the exchange for their original water rights, but only a fraction of this amount has actually reached reservation lands. The Los Angeles water supply is heavily dependent on the transbasin diversion from the Owens Valley, and non-Indian landowners there have for years been protesting the city's drain on their water supplies. A potential Indian claim could add a major new dimension to this controversy. None of these situations, however, has yet become an active conflict.

The California Department of Water Resources has created an Ad Hoc Committee on Indian water rights, but there exists no mechanism for the negotiation of conflicting Indian and non-Indian claims.

COLORADO

Although the prior appropriation doctrine is often called the Colorado Doctrine because of that state's early commitment to its principles, the state did not enact comprehensive regulatory and administrative legislation on water allocation until the 1960s. The 1969 Water Right Determination and Administration Act created seven water divisions in the state, corresponding to major water drainages, each of which is administered by a water judge and an engineer. During the 1970s major cases emerged from water adjudications in three of these divisions that brought before the United States Supreme Court the question of whether or not federal and Indian reserved water rights could be adjudicated in the context of this state scheme for determining water rights.

The *Eagle County* and *Water Division No. 5* cases, both decided by the United States Supreme Court in 1971, established the principle that Congress in 1952, through passage of a law known as the McCarran Amendment, gave consent for the water rights of the United States to be adjudicated in comprehensive state court proceedings.

A later case originating in Water Division No. 7, which includes the southwestern portion of Colorado within the San Juan drainage basin, posed the question of whether or not the McCarran Amendment also allowed Indian reserved rights to be adjudicated in state proceedings.

In the case entitled *Colorado River Water Conservancy District v. United States,* also known as the *Akin* decision, the Supreme Court decided that the McCarran Amendment did extend to Indian water rights, since its basic principle was to include within a single adjudicatory proceeding all the water rights of a given basin. It established state forums as concurrent with federal ones for determining Indian rights but indicated that where concurrent jurisdiction led to simultaneous federal and state suits on the same Indian water rights issues "wise judicial administration" might cause dismissal of the federal suit under special circumstances.

The *Akin* decision did not *require* Indian suits to be handled by state courts, and a recent decision by the Ninth Circuit Court of Appeals in a series of Montana and Arizona cases suggests that *Akin* may be of limited applicability to other states.

The remand to state water court from the *Akin* decision will lead to quantification of the water rights of Colorado's only two Indian reservations, those of the Southern Ute and Ute Mountain tribes.

IDAHO

Idaho has five Indian reservations, but the state's relatively abundant water resources have thus far prevented the conflicts that have beset other western states. The Fort Hall Shoshone Bannock Reservation, bordering the Snake River, not only enjoys access to surface supplies but also overlies one of the most abundant groundwater sources in the country, the Snake River aquifer. The Kootenai, Nez Perce and Coeur D'Alene lands in the northern part of the state are in an area of sufficiently heavy precipitation to allow dryland farming. The Duck Valley Reservation which is bisected by the Nevada-Idaho border, has so far had good water resources from the Owyhee River and the Wildhorse Reservoir. (See also the entry below for Nevada on Duck Valley.)

Despite such relative abundance of water, dryland farming often depletes soils in this region, and many large operators have turned to irrigation as part of a program to rebuild soil fertility. The Coeur D'Alene Tribe hopes to establish an irrigation project of this type and is pressing the Department of the Interior for help in adjudicating water rights on one of their major streams.

Of great concern to the northern tribes, especially the Nez Perce, have been fishing rights. As discussed in California and Washington cases, treaty-protected fishing rights have been found to imply an important water right, the right to sufficient water flow and water quality to guarantee the preservation of the fisheries resources.

The State of Idaho published a detailed survey of the possible extent and the legal basis for Indian water rights in 1978. That document and state action with regard to Indians have shown a cautious approach based on respect for the judicially established rights of the Indians, a concern to examine the potential quantification of each reservation's entitlements based on these rights, and a reluctance at present to seek broad adjudication of Indian rights.

The Idaho legislature has recently created a joint committee to work with tribal leaders to resolve a wide range of disputed issues by non-litigative means. It is expected that water rights problems will be covered during the state-tribal discussion process, but a specific agenda for the committee has not yet been devised.

Idaho is also participating with the other three states of the Columbia River basin (Montana, Oregon and Washington) in a planning process mandated by the Pacific Northwest Electric Power Planning and Conservation Act of 1980. This act created the Northwest Power Planning Council, consisting of representatives from the four states, and required it to devise a Fish and Wildlife Program detailing specific methods for balancing the protection of fisheries and the production of electric power within the basin. The fisheries and water resources divisions of the four states have joined with several tribes and the Columbia River Inter-Tribal Fish Commission to make recommendations for maintenance of instream flows, protection of Indian fishing and water rights, and operations of dams for hydroelectric power production. The Northwest Power Planning Council is scheduled to publish its final plan by November 15, 1982. The Bonneville Power Administration and other federal agencies responsible for operating the dams and reservoirs of the basin will be required to implement the Fish and Wildlife Program.

While this is only a planning and advisory process and does not affect the disposition of water resources relating to immediate disputes, it could have an important effect on the long-term management of the waters of the Columbia basin. For the first time, fisheries protection has become a major management goal, and specific effects of this legal change relating to Indian rights will be discussed in future editions of this publication.

MONTANA

Montana has seven Indian reservations, located in widely separated regions of this vast state. In 1973 Montana passed a comprehensive water use act, which provided for systematic adjudication of water rights. In 1975 the United States and the Northern Cheyenne Tribe filed suits in federal court seeking adjudication in that forum of Indian and federal reserved rights for the Cheyenne and Crow reservations in the southwestern part of the state.

The Supreme Court's *Akin* decision of 1976, recognizing state jurisdiction over Indian water rights under certain circumstances, influenced Montana's 1979 revision of its water use act. New provisions created an independent court system for water rights adjudication and required that every water basin in the state be subject to these proceedings.

The Montana legislature also created the Reserved Water Rights Compact Commission, authorized to negotiate compacts with the federal government and with Indian tribes to resolve issues concerning water claims. These events formed the background for further filings in federal court by the United States concerning four more Indian water cases, covering the remaining reservations in the state.

The stage was thus set for a court test over the issue of whether state or federal courts would adjudicate Indian rights. The seven Indian water cases were dismissed from federal district court in 1979 for hearing under the state's new system of water adjudication, and an appeal to the Ninth Circuit was made. In February of 1982, the Ninth Circuit returned these cases to federal court. The state can be expected to appeal to the Supreme Court.

The filing of these water cases by the United States, especially the last four in 1979, aroused intense reaction from the many thousands of Montana ranchers, farmers, and small-town leaders who found themselves served with notice of their involvement in federal litigation. Senator Melcher of Montana held hearings of the United States Senate Select Committee on Indian Affairs to record non-Indian reaction to this litigation, as well as to document the strong Indian feeling about the necessity of defending tribal rights.

Besides these stream adjudication cases, there has been considerable controversy over two Indian cases involving ownership of land underlying bodies of water. Though these cases involve basic issues of jurisdiction and ownership rather than water rights, they will have an impact on the regulatory control over water claimed by Indians.

The case involving the ownership of the bed of the Big Horn River within the boundaries of the Crow Reservation was decided in March of 1981 by the Supreme Court in favor of the State of Montana, which was determined to be the owner instead of the tribe. A similar case is pending over ownership of the bed of Flathead Lake on the Flathead Reservation, and both will have an important impact on the issue of regulatory authority of the state over major water courses on Indian lands.

Despite the contentious nature of many of these disputes, four tribes have begun negotiations with the Montana Reserved Water Rights Compact Commission. The Northern Cheyenne, the Crow, Fort Peck and Fort Belknap governments have formally entered the negotiation process. The Commission is also considering whether to begin talks with the Turtle Mountain Tribe of North Dakota, whose members own individual allotments in the northern part of the state. Montana is the only state in the region with a uniform, state-wide negotiation process.

Montana is also participating with the other three states of the Columbia River basin (Idaho, Oregon and Washington) in a planning process mandated by the Pacific Northwest Electric Power Planning and Conservation Act of 1980. (See Idaho introduction for further background.) This process, carried out by the Northwest Power Planning Council, will result in publication of a Fish and Wildlife Program by November 15, 1982. The program, which will be binding on the Bonneville Power Administration and other federal agencies, will implement the act's provisions making fisheries protection a major purpose of basin management along with electric power production. This change in management goals could have important consequences for Indian rights (possibly affecting the Blackfeet and Flathead tribes in this state), and impacts resulting from actions of the Northwest Power Planning Council and the Bonneville Power Administration will be discussed in future editions of this publication.

NEVADA

Most of the state of Nevada lies within the Great Basin, a high desert area with self-contained water systems that have no outlet to the sea. It is a state with critical water shortages that require groundwater pumping in many regions. The state's fast growing metropolitan areas are Las Vegas and Reno, each of which has been involved in major water litigation.

The southern tip of Nevada, including the area of Las Vegas, lies within the watershed of the Colorado River, thus drawing Nevada into *Arizona v. California* to determine its share of the Lower Colorado waters. (See entries under Arizona and California for discussion of that case.)

The Reno area lies within the Truckee River system, one of the most disputed water regions in the country. The Truckee River flows from Lake Tahoe in the Sierra Nevada mountain range of eastern California into Pyramid Lake, which is surrounded by lands of the Pyramid Lake Paiute Reservation. Along the way, waters are diverted for agriculture near Reno, for urban and industrial use in the Reno-Sparks metropolitan area, as well as for irrigation of major reclamation projects, for wildlife protection, power production and several other purposes.

The Truckee system exemplifies more clearly than any water region the relationship of Indian claims to the full context of competing water usage.

Other cases in Nevada illustrate unique problems associated with groundwater depletion caused by potential development of the MX missile system and by the granting of desert land entries by the United States Bureau of Land Management. Such problems affect the small Indian colonies established in the 1930s that have land use and water rights on hundreds of thousands of acres at off-reservation sites. Many of these colonies are the homes of Western Shoshone bands, and a major unresolved land claim of these groups could also have significant implication for water rights.

In northeastern Nevada the Duck Valley reservation has been involved in a negotiation process to resolve a dispute about ownership and use of the Wildhorse Reservoir on Owyhee River.

Several other communities are studying the possibility of Winters Doctrine litigation to expand water rights for new uses.

NEW MEXICO

There are three major basins in New Mexico involved in Indian water rights litigation, and the Indian lands within these basins comprise ten percent of the total land area of the state.

The Rio Grande basin, covering the central portion of New Mexico from Colorado in the north to Texas in the south, is the site of eighteen Indian Pueblo reservations as well as parts of the Jicarilla Apache lands.

The Pecos River flowing through the eastern side of the state is a tributary of the Rio Grande (the two join in Texas) but has been the subject of a separate compact and is considered for these purposes as an independent watershed. The Mescalero Apache have a large reservation west of Roswell in the southern New Mexico portion of the Pecos basin.

The Colorado basin, divided by interstate compacts into upper and lower basins, occupies the western part of the state. The San Juan River drainage lies within the Upper Colorado basin and comprises the northwest corner of the state, an area of extensive Navajo lands with smaller tracts belonging to the Ute Mountain Ute and Jicarilla Apache Tribes. A portion of the lower Colorado basin includes the Zuni Pueblo and Ramah Navajo Reservation within the drainage area of the Zuni River, which joins the Little Colorado in Arizona.

The State of New Mexico is attempting to litigate most Indian water rights through general stream adjudication lawsuits. The major cases involve the San Juan River, several tributaries of the Rio Grande, and the Rio Hondo in the Pecos basin. This state, like Montana and Washington, believes it has the right to issue water permits for non-Indians appropriating unreserved water within Indian reservations, but as yet this issue has not been finally resolved in litigation.

Competition for water supplies between Indians and non-Indians is often linked with New Mexico's rapidly growing energy industries. The San Juan basin, a rich source of coal and uranium, has no permanent surface flow south of the San Juan River itself, and consequently energy development will put new pressure both on groundwater sources and on allocations from the river. The Navajo Nation has major claims to both the surface and underground sources, and tribal estimates of water needs potentially exceed the supplies of the San Juan River. The outcome of current litigation to determine Indian rights in this stream will have an important impact on control of water resources in this major western energy-producing region.

There are also potential conflicts over the pumping of underground water supplies, a few of which have already arisen in the southern parts of the San Juan basin. Just as the Papago Tribe of Arizona discovered the basis for a major lawsuit against Tucson in that city's depletion of aquifers underlying reservation lands, so the Navajos may find a similar cause of action due to off-reservation energy development. Whether or not such a conflict actually emerges will depend on the pace and specific location of new energy projects, but one of the cases cited below—involving depletion of domestic wells in the Navajo community of Crownpoint—could indicate a future trend.

New energy production and urban growth have also led to several disputes involving water quality, and the outcome of these will have an important effect on the ability of several tribes either to use water resources for economic purposes or to preserve areas important for religious reasons. The mining of coal and uranium, the milling of uranium ore, geothermal development and exploration for other minerals are causing significant impacts on local ground and surface water supplies on Indian lands or on federal lands to which Indians have maintained access. Several of these disputes are summarized to illustrate an important trend in Indian concern about water, even though traditional water rights are not involved.

NORTH AND SOUTH DAKOTA

Though outside the *Western Network's* usual range of geographical coverage, North and South Dakota contain large Indian reservations on the main stem of the Missouri River, and determination of associated Indian water rights will be important to the entire Missouri Basin.

The two state governments take different approaches to Indian water rights. North Dakota is attempting to begin a negotiation process while South Dakota has initiated a massive water adjudication in state court that involves the rights of all Indian tribes to waters of the Missouri River in the western part of the state.

Running diagonally from the northwestern to the southeastern parts of these states, the Missouri divides both North and South Dakota into fairly humid eastern regions, where most of the Indian lands are concentrated. *Western Network* is primarily concerned with the arid or "West River" country in both cases.

The Missouri River, registering an average annual flow at Sioux City of some 28.4 million acre-feet, is a vast water resource that is only beginning to be put to new uses. Its upper basin embraces much of South and North Dakota, as well as parts of Montana, Wyoming, and Colorado.

Agricultural use has accounted for about ninety percent of annual water depletions in South Dakota, and that percentage is expected to decline as major industrial applications of water increase through the present decade.

The state has six dams and reservoirs constructed by the federal government on the main stem of the Missouri, and their storage capacity is well in excess of existing demand. Nevertheless, the state expects accelerated depletions from several sources to begin to strain water supplies in the western part of the state in the next few decades. South Dakota is primarily interested in defining water rights of the Missouri in order to clarify the amounts available for out of state sales. The South Dakota state legislature recently approved the pumping of Missouri River water to Wyoming for use in a coal slurry pipeline.

The United States Army Corps of Engineers is interested in diverting substantial amounts of upper Missouri water to help alleviate the critical over-drafting of the Ogalalla aquifer that provides the major groundwater source for irrigated agriculture in the central and southern Great Plains.

Energy corporations have discussed the possibility of large-scale diversion projects to bring water from the Missouri in South Dakota to the western slope of Colorado, a water-short region expected to undergo intensive energy development by the end of this century.

Indian uses of water within the state on the Pine Ridge, Rosebud, Yankton, Lower Brule, Crow Creek, Cheyenne River and Standing Rock Reservations can also be expected to increase sharply as the tribes make more economic use of the approximately 5 million acres of land in their possession.

Because of these pressures on water resources, South Dakota indicates that it wishes to quantify rights at this time rather than wait for conflicts later on.

North Dakota contains part of the Standing Rock Reservation (which also extends into South Dakota) and the Fort Berthold Reservation along the Missouri and two other reservations in the eastern portion of the state (Turtle Mountain and Devil's Lake). The North Dakota Water Commission is attempting to initiate negotiations with tribes over water rights, and discussions preliminary to formal processes have been taking place over the past two years.

Fort Berthold and Standing Rock, like other tribes on the main stem of the Missouri, have expressed interest in selling water, as South Dakota has done, in order to generate revenue for future on-reservation water projects. Before contracting to sell water the tribes will very likely have to clarify the quantity of water under their jurisdiction and the role the federal government must play in approving such transactions.

OREGON

Like the state of Washington, Oregon is divided by the Cascade Mountains into a water abundant western coastal region and an arid eastern portion that comprises most of the state and shares climatic conditions with the Great Basin region. Understandably, the eastern region has experienced much more adjudication of its streams, and so dry are conditions there that in some cases water appropriations with priority dates of 1870 are the only ones assured of satisfaction from available sources. Irrigation began on the western side of the Cascade range at a much later date and conditions on many streams still allow for new appropriations.

Oregon's major Indian reservations are the Umatilla, within the Umatilla River basin, and the Warm Springs, within the Deschutes River basin. Both areas are part of the Columbia River drainage but are not presently in litigation with the state or non-Indian water users over water rights.

The governments of Warm Springs and Umatilla are concerned about management of the fisheries resources of the Columbia system, in particular of the traditional fisheries along the main stem of the river to which they claim treaty-protected access.

The Confederated Tribes of the Umatilla Reservation have been able to reach negotiated settlements on a few water issues with the state and with local irrigation districts but still face problems over maintenance of in-stream flow on the Umatilla. The Warm Springs Reservation has participated in many state water planning efforts and is perhaps the only tribe in the country with a water code approved by the United States Secretary of the Interior. Warm Springs has also begun construction of a hydroelectric dam in the Deschutes River. This will be the first such project under Indian control and exemplifies the willingness of tribes to engage in major water development even without full federal funding. (This project is financed by a federal loan, by tribal funds, and by private borrowing.)

Formerly the largest Indian reservation in Oregon, the Klamath Reservation of the southern part of the state, outside the boundaries of the Columbia River basin, was terminated by Congress in 1954. Yet the state's major Indian water rights conflict involves the rights to water that survived the elimination of the formal reservation. Indian lands were first transferred to a private trustee, then sold to non-Indians, the largest purchaser being the federal government itself, which used the land to add to the Winema National Forest and to create the Klamath National Wildlife Refuge. A complex lawsuit concerning conflicting rights to the Williamson River in the Klamath basin poses questions about the rights of individual Indian allottees as well as of the tribal government to water in a situation where they no longer own any lands.

The state established a water permit system in 1909, but the method used for establishing priority dates before 1909 is by adjudication in state court. The state brought suit to establish priorities on the Williamson River almost twenty years after the initial steps of termination of the Klamath Reservation. This is the last unadjudicated basin in eastern Oregon.

Oregon is also participating with the other three states of the Columbia River basin (Idaho, Montana and Washington) in a planning process mandated by the Pacific Northwest Electric Power Planning and Conservation Act of 1980. (See Idaho introduction for further background.) This process, carried out by the Northwest Power Planning Council, will result in publication of a Fish and Wildlife Program by November 15, 1982. The program, which will be binding on the Bonneville Power Administration and other federal agencies, will implement the act's provisions making fisheries protection a major purpose of basin management along with electric power production. This change in management goals could have important consequences for Indian rights, and impacts resulting from actions of the Northwest Power Planning Council and the Bonneville Power Administration will be discussed in future editions of this publication.

UTAH

The two largest tracts of Indian land in Utah are the Uintah and Ouray Reservation of the Ute Tribe and a portion of the Navajo Reservation. Both are located within the Upper Colorado River basin, the Ute land in the Green River basin in east central Utah, and the Navajo in the San Juan River basin in the southeastern corner of the state. Most of the rest of the state consists of closed basins associated with the Great Basin region. This western section of Utah contains only a few Indian communities with reservation lands; many other communities were terminated in the 1950s and are now seeking re-establishment of their federal status. Conflicts over water thus focus on the Ute and Navajo water rights.

Utah, like Arizona, has been working for years with the United States Bureau of Reclamation to secure completion of a major transbasin water diversion project, the Central Utah Reclamation Project, as a means of satisfying water demands of the state's principal urban region, Salt Lake City and the Jordan Valley area. The Central Utah Project would divert water from the Green River system in the Uinta basin to the Jordan Valley by means of a system of tunnels, aqueducts and storage reservoirs. This project will enable Utah to use its share of Colorado River water as provided in the Upper Colorado River Compact of 1948. The Compact assigns twenty-eight percent of the Upper Basin flow to Utah, but as is true in state shares of other compacts, that amount is subject to Indian claims.

The Uintah and Ouray Reservation occupies lands along the Duchesne, White Fork, Yellowstone, Lake Fork, Green and White Rivers and thus has a potential Winters Doctrine claim that conflicts directly with the diversion requirements of the Central Utah Project. Rather than litigate this claim, the Ute Tribe and the state have been attempting for the past twenty years to settle the issue by means of a negotiated agreement, and, although this effort has not yet come to a conclusion, it remains one of the most significant examples of the use of voluntary, non-judicial dispute settlement processes in the area of Indian water rights.

The potential conflict between the state and the Navajo Nation presently has more to do with jurisdiction over water resources management than with quantification of rights. The State is considering litigation as a means of preventing the Navajo government from implementing a water code which the state feels is incompatible with its planning and regulatory objectives.

Utah thus has responded to Indian claims on a case-by-case basis rather than by formalizing a single process for dealing with Indian water conflicts.

WASHINGTON

The State of Washington is divided by the Cascade Mountains into an arid eastern portion, which includes a large part of the Columbia River basin, and a western region with abundant rainfall and surface water resources. Most of the 2.5 million acres of Indian land in the state, some six percent of the total land area, is contained within the three large eastern Washington reservations of the Yakima, Colville and Spokane tribes. Each of these reservations possesses substantial fishing and water rights in the Columbia basin and has been involved in major Winters Doctrine litigation over the past decade.

More than two dozen small Indian communities reside within the Puget Sound and Coastal watershed regions. While their lands are quite small, sometimes even non-existent, all have important fishing rights in the salmon-producing streams of the region, and their water concerns have centered around protection of the fisheries on which their economies depend.

An important federal district court ruling of 1980 held that treaty-protected fishing rights implied a right to environmental protection. That implied right may have important effects on non-Indian planning for projects that utilize the waters of salmon-producing streams. The issue has already been raised over construction of the Northern Tier Pipeline and can be expected to occur in several other cases.

The issue poses an important conflict for Washington, since ninety percent of its electric energy is produced by hydroelectric power plants. The use of streams for small hydro projects has been encouraged by recent federal legislation, and almost every river in the western portion of the state is under study by the United States Army Corps of Engineers and other agencies for possible hydroelectric sites. Groups concerned about protection of fish and wildlife as well as the Indian governments are resisting this potentially widespread conversion of water resources from fisheries protection to production of electric energy.

The attitude of the State of Washington on the conflict between fisheries preservation and hydroelectric energy is complex. On the one hand, its statutes on water appropriation recognize fish and wildlife protection and maintenance of in-stream flows as beneficial uses of water and require the State Department of Ecology to consider environmental consequences of new water appropriations. That department may reject applications for new appropriations that interfere with minimum in-stream flows required for wildlife purposes and is now conducting widespread surveys to establish acceptable flow levels for fisheries protection. On the other hand, the state opposes the establishment of many Indian water and fishing rights which might have the same effect of protecting in-stream uses of water. Thus, even though the state and Indian governments share certain objectives regarding maintenance of in-stream flows for fisheries protection, they are far apart on the nature of Indian treaty rights and the regulatory role that tribal governments should play in managing water and fisheries resources. The state has been involved in extensive litigation with most of the Indian governments of Washington over these issues, and negotiations have been attempted in only a few situations.

Washington is also participating with the other three states of the Columbia River basin (Idaho, Montana and Oregon) in a planning process mandated by the Pacific Northwest Electric Power Planning and Conservation Act of 1980. (See Idaho introduction for further background.) This process, carried out by the Northwest Power Planning Council, will result in publication of a Fish and Wildlife Program by November 15, 1982. The program, which will be binding on the Bonneville Power Administration and other federal agencies, will implement the act's provisions making fisheries protection a major purpose of basin management along with electric power production. This change in management goals could have important consequences for Indian rights, and impacts resulting from actions of the Northwest Power Planning Council and the Bonneville Power Administration will be discussed in future editions of this publication.

WYOMING

The Wyoming State Engineer's Office has divided the state into seven water districts, corresponding to hydrologic basins, and the state's single Indian reservation lies wholly within one of these, District 3, the Bighorn River basin. The Wind River Reservation is home for the Shoshone and the Arapaho and consists of more than 1.8 million acres of land, most of which is owned by the tribes. The Wind River, a major tributary of the Bighorn, crosses the reservation, and the state and the tribes are now involved in litigation to establish the rights of all water claimants within the Bighorn basin, which comprises some twenty-one percent of the land area of the state.

After the *Arizona v. California* decision of 1963, the Shoshone and Arapaho tribes of the Wind River Reservation asserted "first paramount and immemorial rights to all water, surface and underground, natural or as augmented by weather modification, desalination or any other scientific means, so long as those waters occur or arise on or pass through or border the reservation." After the Supreme Court decisions recognizing state court jurisdiction over Indian rights in the context of comprehensive stream adjudications, Wyoming enacted legislation authorizing the attorney general to initiate such suits, and a case was filed to adjudicate Bighorn River rights in 1977.

The relations between the state and the two tribes have thus been consistently adversarial, and the complex Bighorn litigation is now well underway in state court before a Special Master. It is Wyoming's only Indian case and when completed, should resolve the reserved rights question. The suit, however, promises to be extremely expensive to all concerned. The state has already allocated several million dollars for its prosecution, and the tribal and federal investment is also substantial.

JOHN A. FOLK-WILLIAMS
President, Western Network
Santa Fe, New Mexico

INDIAN WATER RIGHTS
An Introduction

The basic principles of Indian water rights were formulated by the United States Supreme Court in 1908 in the now-famous case of *Winters v. United States.*[1] Since that case a body of law has developed that lends critical protections to Indian water resources.

The United States brought the *Winters* case to stop non-Indian settlers from diverting waters needed downstream to irrigate land on the Fort Belknap Indian Reservation. The non-Indians had begun their water uses before completion of the Indian project, and under Montana's prior appropriation water laws they would have been entitled to a priority in the use of the water. But the Court declared that the Indians had a superior water right to irrigate their reservation lands. This right was preserved when the reservation was established. The Court held that the reservation was entitled to priority over the water usage initiated by the non-Indians under state and territorial law.

The recognition in *Winters* of the "reserved rights" doctrine was confirmed in *Arizona v. California,*[2] where the Supreme Court held that the five Indian tribes located on the lower Colorado River were entitled to reserved water rights sufficient to irrigate all the "practicably irrigable" land on their reservations. These two judicial decisions are the foundation on which Indian tribes today claim water rights of immense value, rights that play a key role in influencing the further development of the West.

Water Law Concepts
Riparian Rights

The system for allocating water, used in the eastern states and a few western states, is the common law concept of riparian rights. In its purest original form the riparian system entitled each landowner abutting a stream to insist on maintenance of the stream flow in its natural condition. The modern view allows each riparian landowner to make reasonable use of the stream consistent with the equal rights of all the other riparian owners upstream and downstream from him.

Riparian rights differ fundamentally from rights in the appropriative system. To establish riparian rights it is not necessary to put water to beneficial use; nor are riparian rights lost by nonuse. They exist simply as an incident of ownership of land bordering a stream, and the water used under the system must remain on riparian land. Riparian rights are not confined to a definite quantity of water based on actual use, but rather are limited only by the necessity of sharing the supply with the other riparian owners along the stream. Finally, riparian rights are not arranged in any order of priority based on dates of initial use. Rather, shortages are shared pro rata among the riparian owners.[3]

---

[1] 207 U.S. 564 (1908).

[2] 373 U.S. 546, 594-601 (1963), decree 376 U.S. 340 (1964).

[3] On the riparian system, *see* Clark, Waters and Water Rights, Vol. 1, Chap. 2, and Vol. 7, Chap. 31 (1967); *and* Hutchins, Water Rights Laws in the Nineteen Western States, Vol. 2, Chap. 10 (1971).

Doctrine of Prior Appropriation

In contrast to the riparian system, the principle that governs the allocation of water rights in the arid western states is the doctrine of prior apropriation. Prior appropriation is a system of first come, first served. Rights to the use of water are acquired by putting water to a continuing beneficial use. The principle of "first in time, first in right" then governs the distribution of water among users in times of shortage. Each water user is assigned a priority based on the date the water was put to beneficial use or, in most states, when application for a permit to do so was made.[4] When there is not enough water for all, the earlier or senior appropriators continue to receive their full measure of water. The later or junior appropriators bear the burden of the shortage.

An appropriative right is always stated in terms of a right to make use of a definite quantity of water with a definite priority. This right continues to exist for as long as it is actually exercised. The right may be lost by forfeiture or abandonment if the use ceases without excuse (such as insufficient water supply) for a period of time usually fixed by state statute. If the water appropriator begins his use again, he will be assigned a new priority date based on the date he begins his new use. Similarly, a water use may not be expanded to exceed the quantity of the initial right, except by establishing a new, supplemental right with a new, more recent priority.[5]

The development of the doctrine of prior appropriation was a feature of this country's westward expansion. The principle of allowing all riparian landowners to share commonly in the abundant supply of water in the East was soon recognized as impractical in the arid West. The first cases challenging the applicability of the riparian doctrine arose from the California gold fields, where a single miner's operation might require transportation of the water to a mine many miles away from the stream, miles from the riparian land. The California Supreme Court found the riparian system to be inapplicable to these conditions and recognized instead the validity of the legal system that had grown up by custom in the miners' camps, where the principle of sharing the supply had been rejected in favor of a first come, first served approach.[6] The courts of other western states were quick to follow in adopting the appropriation scheme, and in a series of congressional acts the federal government made it clear that these local customs and laws would define the water rights acquired by private patentees of the public lands.[7]

---

[4] *See* Clark, Waters and Water Rights, Vol. 6, Chap. 27, Administrative Practice and Procedure under Permit Systems (1967).

[5] For a detailed treatment of the system of prior appropriations *see* Clark, Waters and Water Rights, Vol. 1, Chap. 2, and Vol. 5, Chap. 22 (1967); *and* Hutchins, Water Rights Laws in the Nineteen Western States, Vol. 1, Chaps. 6–9 (1971).

[6] *Irwin v. Phillips*, 5 Cal. 190 (1855). The California courts initially side-stepped the question of whether riparian rights automatically vested in landowners when California adopted the common law by noting that neither plaintiff nor defendant owned the public land that they were mining, and thus, that neither had riparian rights based on land ownership. Later, in *Lux v. Haggin*, 69 Cal. 255, 10 P. 674, 721 (1886), the California Supreme Court did find that riparian owners were entitled to riparian rights in some circumstances, creating a hybrid appropriative/riparian water rights system that has bedeviled California water law ever since. *See* Clark, Waters and Water Rights, Vol. 5, Chap. 24 (1967). Most western states simply rejected the riparian doctrine, *in toto*. Hutchins, Water Rights Laws in the Nineteen Western States, Vol. 2, (1971).

[7] Act of July 26, 1866, 14 Stat. 253, 30 U.S.C. §51; Act of July 9, 1870, 16 Stat. 218, 43 U.S.C. §661; Desert Land Act of March 3, 1877, 19 Stat. 377, 43 U.S.C. §§321–323. Under the Property Power of the Constitution, Congress presumably could have defined the water rights acquired by patentees of the federally owned public domain, but was held not to have done so in the important case of *California-Oregon Power*

To the original system of acquiring water rights by beneficial use most of the western states have now added comprehensive administrative control.[8] Normally a permit to appropriate water is required. The permit can be granted only upon a finding by the administrator, often called the state engineer, that existing rights will not be impaired. In most western states, administrative control extends to ground water uses as well as diversions from surface streams.[9]

Determination of Indian Water Rights
The Winters Doctrine

In general the doctrine of prior appropriation created a legal system that was well suited to the development of the water-short West. By granting secure rights to those who first arrived with the capital and knowledge needed to put water to use, the system encouraged investment in water-based enterprises. It soon became apparent, however, that the priority system could not adequately or fairly provide for the needs of Indian tribes. Prior appropriation relied on competition to allocate the limited water supply, and most tribes were simply not on a competitive footing with their non-Indian neighbors. Often they were inexperienced in farming and dependent on Congress for the funds needed to construct extensive irrigation works. The available water was often appropriated by settlers on the lands surrounding the reservations before the Indians were ready to put it to use.

This was the background of *Winters v. United States,*[10] the first case to raise the question of Indian water rights before the United States Supreme Court. The United States brought this suit on behalf of the Gros Ventre and Assiniboine Tribes of the Fort Belknap Reservation in Montana to prevent diversions of water by settlers upstream from the reservation on the Milk River, which formed the reservation's northern boundary. The reservation had been created by an agreement between the tribes and the United States, which was ratified by Congress on May 1, 1888. By the terms of the agreement the tribes surrendered their interest in a much larger tract of land, set aside for their use by an act of Congress in 1874,[11] in exchange for certain payments and a continued recognition of their right to occupy the diminished reservation. The agreement did not mention the subject of water rights, but it did declare that the purpose of creating the reservation was to encourage the Indians to abandon their previous nomadic ways and pursue agriculture as a "pastoral and civilized people."

Shortly after the agreement was approved, the lands ceded by the Indians were opened to settlement under the public land laws. Lands were patented upstream from the reservation on the Milk River and the settlers began diverting large quantities of the river flow. After the non-Indians had been irrigating for several years, the government completed a large irrigation project for the Indians downstream and found that insuffi-

Co. v. Beaver Portland Cement Co., 295 U.S. 142, 79 L.Ed. 1356, 55 S.Ct. 725 (1935). The Court there rejected the argument that a federal patent implicitly carried with it riparian water rights and held that under the acts cited, Congress left the definition of private water rights up to each state.

[8] *See* Clark, Waters and Water Rights, Vol. 6 Chap. 27, Administrative Practice and Procedure under Permit Systems (1967); Hutchins, Water Rights in the Nineteen Western States, Vol. 2, Chap. 16 (1971).

[9] *See* Clark, Waters and Water Rights, Chap. 25, Western Ground Water Law (1967); Hutchins, Water Rights Laws in the Nineteen Western States, Vol. 2, Chaps. 19, 20 (1971).

[10] 207 U.S. 564 (1908), *affirming* 143 F. 740 (9th Cir. 1906).

[11] Act of April 15, 1874, ch. 96, 18 Stat. 28.

cient flow was left in the river. The government sued in the federal circuit court for Montana to enjoin the upstream diversions.

The non-Indians responded that they had properly appropriated these waters under the laws of the territory and State of Montana, and that under those laws they were entitled to protection against subsequent appropriators, including the reservation Indians. The Montana circuit court rejected the argument of the non-Indians and granted the government's requested injunction. The court reasoned that, although the agreement said nothing about water rights, its obvious purpose was "to encourage farming among the Indians." Water for irrigation would be indispensible to that objective and the court observed that "the parties to the agreement evidently appreciated this necessity, and purposely fixed the boundary line of the reservation at a point in the middle of the main channel of Milk River. . . ." The court concluded that "the intention was to reserve sufficient of the waters to insure to the Indians the means wherewith to irrigate their farms." The court therefore held that

> when the Indians made the treaty granting rights to the United States they reserved the right to the use of the waters of Milk River, at least to an extent reasonably necessary to irrigate their lands. The right so reserved continues to exist against the United States and its grantees as well as against the State and its grantees.
>
> From this it follows that if any patents issued by the Land Department for lands held by defendants [the non-Indian irrigators] are subject to the treaty, defendants can acquire no rights to the exclusion of the reasonable needs of the Indians.[12]

The trial court's decision was affirmed by the Ninth Circuit Court of Appeals.[13]

The Supreme Court upheld the injunction limiting the non-Indians' upstream diversions. It concurred that the May 1888 agreement, resulting in the creation of the Fort Belknap Reservation, was critical to the decision:

> In the construction of this agreement there are certain elements to be considered that are prominent and significant. The reservation was a part of a very much larger tract which the Indians had the right to occupy and use and which was adequate for the habits and wants of a nomadic and uncivilized people. It was the policy of the government, it was the desire of the Indians, to change those habits and to become a pastoral and civilized people. If they should become such the original tract was too extensive, but a smaller tract would be inadequate without a change of conditions. The lands were arid and, without irrigation, were practically valueless. And yet, it is contended, the means of irrigation were deliberately given up by the Indians and deliberately accepted by the government.[14]

The Court noted the argument of the non-Indians that, since their lands were arid and would need irrigation, the cession of these lands by the Indians must have included a cession of the waters "without which they would be valueless." There is therefore a "conflict of implications," but "that which makes for retention of the waters [by the Indians] is of greater force than that which makes for their cession." After all, the Court reasoned:

---

[12] Unpublished opinion of the Federal District Court for the District of Montana.

[13] 143 F. 740 (9th Cir. 1906).

[14] *Winters v. United States,* 207 U.S. 564, 575–576 (1908).

> The Indians had command of the lands and the waters—command of all their beneficial use, whether kept for hunting, 'and grazing roving herds of stock,' or turned to agriculture and the arts of civilization. Did they give up all this? Did they reduce the area of their occupation and give up the waters which made it valuable or adequate?[15]

The non-Indians' interpretation of the agreement simply could not be accepted, particularly in view of the established rule that "ambiguities occurring [in agreements with Indian tribes] will be resolved from the standpoint of the Indians." The Court affirmed the lower courts' holdings that water for the Indians' lands had been reserved by implication of the agreement settling the reservation boundaries in 1888. The waters so reserved were "exempt . . . from appropriation under the state laws" and hence the Indians' rights were superior to those acquired by the non-Indians.[16]

Insofar as Indian reservations are concerned, the *Winters* opinion rejects the western state law rule that water rights can only be established by actual water use. Under the rules of prior appropriation, the non-Indians in *Winters* would have prevailed. Since they were the first to put the water to use, their rights would have been senior to those the government sought for the Indians and would have been entitled to protection.[17] The *Winters* decision recognized the inappropriateness of this doctrine to the situation of the western Indian tribes. Permitting the non-Indians to obtain superior rights to most of the available water before the Indians had a chance to even begin the development of their reservations would have completely frustrated the mutual intent of both the government and the tribes. The intent was that the reservations be a place where the tribes could make their permanent home. From this consideration of the fundamental purpose for which reservations were established, the Court in *Winters* declared an implied reservation of sufficient water to carry out that purpose.

Reserved Rights Reinforced—*Arizona v. California*

In apportioning the waters of the Colorado River among the southwestern states in 1963, the Supreme Court examined the water rights of the five lower Colorado River Indian reservations.[18] The Court reaffirmed the reserved water rights doctrine articulated in *Winters* and made it clear that the doctrine extended to Indian reservations established unilaterally by executive order as well as to those established by agreement confirmed by Congress, as the reservation involved in the *Winters* case had been.[19] In addition, the Court extended the reserved rights doctrine to "other federal establishments," including national forests and national wildlife refuges. It further declared that at the time these federal reservations were created "the United States intended to reserve water

[15] *Id.* at 564.

[16] *Id.* at 564.

[17] There has been some confusion about this point, because in their pleadings both the government and the non-Indians stated that they had been the first to put the water to use. The Supreme Court's "Statement of the Case" reveals that the case was decided in the tribal court on the pleadings alone. 207 U.S. at at 565. The defendant's allegations were, therefore, assumed *arguendo* to be true. Thus, the case was decided on the assumed fact that the non-Indians' use had been established prior to the Indian irrigation project (although this finding is of no legal consequence). In any event, this fact is rather clearly established by affidavits in the circuit court record.

[18] *Arizona v. California*, 373 U.S. 546 (1963).

[19] 373 U.S. 546, 598 (1963).

sufficient for the future requirements'' of reservations, in addition to water that was reserved for immediate requirements.[20] With respect to Indian reservations, this holding had been persuasively recommended by the Special Master appointed by the Court to try the case:

> I have concluded that enough water was reserved to satisfy the future expanding agricultural and related water needs of each Indian reservation. Invariably the United States intended that the Indian tribes settled on a reservation would remain there for generations, and the possibility that other Indians would be settled on the reservation would not be excluded. Certainly the possibility of expanding populations, expanding agricultural development, and hence expanding water needs must have been apparent at the time each reservation was created. It is unreasonable to attribute to the United States an intention or an expectation that the Indians would remain stagnant or die out when they were settled on a reservation. Since the Indians could remain on these reservations and develop their society and economy only if water from the Colorado River was available to meet their future needs, I have found that the United States, when it reserved water, reserved it for all of such needs.[21]

The remaining uncertainty about the total quantity of water that had been reserved was removed by the Court's holdng that the quantity was measured by the needs of the lands within the reservation that were susceptible of irrigation, the ''practicably irrigable acreage.'' Arizona had argued that the quantity of water reserved should be measured by the Indians' ''reasonably forseeable needs,'' which the Supreme Court said in fact meant ''by the number of Indians.'' In rejecting the State's contention, the Court said:

> How many Indians there will be and what their future needs will be can only be guessed. We have concluded, as did the Master, that the only feasible and fair way by which reserved water for the reservations can be measured is irrigable acreage.[22]

Arizona v. California thus established that Indian reservations, whether created by treaty, agreement approved by Congress, or executive order, are entitled to reserved

---

[20] 373 U.S. 546, 601 (1963). In *Cappaert v. United States* the Supreme Court held that when Devil's Hole National Monument in Nevada had been reserved by Presidential Proclamation in 1952, sufficient water had been reserved to maintain a habitat for the unique Desert Pupfish found in the Devil's Hole. The Court summarized the scope of the reserved rights principle, stating: ''This Court has long held that when the Federal government withdraws its lands from the public domain and reserves it for a federal purpose, the government, by implication, reserves appurtenant water then unappropriated to the extent needed to accomplish the purpose of the reservation. In so doing the United States acquires a reserved right in unappropriated water which vests on the date of the reservation and is superior to the rights of future appropriators. Reservation of water rights is empowered by the Commerce Clause, Art. I, §8, which permits federal regulation of navigable streams, and the Property Clause, Art. IV, §3, which permits federal regulation of federal lands. The doctrine applies to Indian reservations and other federal enclaves, encompassing water rights in navigable and non-navigable streams.'' 426 U.S. 128, 138 (1976).

[21] Master's Report, pp. 260–261, *Arizona v. California,* 373 U.S. 546 (1963). Although this conclusion seems inherent in the *Winters* reasoning, the Court in that case was not called upon to expressly declare that water had been reserved for all the tribes' future needs. The Court simply affirmed an order of the Montana Circuit Court requiring the upstream non-Indians to release ''5,000 inches'' of water to the reservation, the amount needed for the irrigation project that had been constructed and was the subject of the controversy. However, the Ninth Circuit, in *Conrad Inv. Co. v. United States,* 161 F. 829 (1908), had granted the Indian tribe an open-ended decree that could be modified to reflect its growing needs.

[22] 373 U.S. 546, 600, 601 (1963).

water rights sufficient to irrigate all of their practicably irrigable acreage, with a priority dating from the creation of the reservation. These rights are based on the purposes for which the reservations were created and are not subject to state laws on forfeiture or abandonment for nonuse.

Origin of Indian Reserved Water Rights

In recent years some discussion has developed concerning the precise origin of the reserved water rights of Indian tribes whose reservations lie within their original homelands. Do the water rights emerge from the Indians' aboriginal title to the land? Or were they instead guaranteed by the United States at the time Indian reservations were established in exchange for lands ceded to the government by the tribes? Or do the reserved rights represent an act of largess bestowed upon the tribes by the United States?[23]

Aside from the academic and symbolic interest in clarifying the theoretical underpinnings of the reserved rights doctrine, the chief significance of the inquiry seems to lie in the conflicting priority dates suggested by the theories. If the government unilaterally reserved the water rights, the proper priority date of Indian rights can be no earlier than the date of each reservation's creation. If these rights have an aboriginal source, their priority may be prehistoric or immemorial.[24]

The Supreme Court's opinion in *Winters* lends support to both theories. Most of the opinion speaks unmistakeably in terms of a simple property transaction in which the Indians ceded much of their original domain, but retained, along with the lands reserved, a right to use enough water to make their remaining lands productive. As the Court noted, prior to negotiations with the government "the Indians had command of the lands and the waters—command of all their beneficial use, whether kept for hunting and grazing roving herds of stock, or turned to agriculture and the arts of civilization." And as the Court rhetorically asks, "Did they [the Indians] give up all this? Did they reduce the area of their occupation and give up the waters which made it valuable or adequate?" Because it would have destroyed the purpose of the agreement between the tribes and the government, the Court refused to find that "the means of irrigation were deliberately given up by the Indians and deliberately accepted by the government."[25]

This language characterizes the agreement between the United States and the Indians as one in which the Indians retained certain rights and granted others to the government. This reservation of rights was binding on non-Indian individuals because they were merely grantees of the government. As such, they obtained no greater rights than those that were granted by the Indians to the United States. Any argument that this arrangement was void because it was inconsistent with state or territorial law, which recognized no such reserved water rights, was invalid because of federal supremacy under the Constitution, and Congress' plenary power to enter into agreements with the Indian tribes, regardless of inconsistent state laws. This analysis is supported by a previous opinion of

---

[23] Cohen, Original Indian Title, 32 Min. L. Rev. (1947); Note, Indian Title: Rights of American Natives in Land They Have Once Occupied Since Time Immemorial, 75 Colum. L. Rev. 655 (1975); Veeder, Indian Prior and Paramount Rights to the Use of Water, 16 Rocky Mt. Min. L. Inst. 631 (1971); Bloom, Indian Paramount Rights to Water Use, 16 Rocky Mt. Min. L. Inst. 669 (1971).

[24] Since most Indian reservations were established prior to non-Indian settlement in their watersheds, a priority date of reservation establishment will often be superior to all other priorities in any event. In *United States v. Adair,* 478 F. Supp. 336, 6 Indian L. Rptr F-150 (D. Ore., Sept. 27, 1979), the court held that the Klamath Indian Tribe had water rights with an immemorial priority for hunting and fishing and additional water rights for irrigation, dating from the the creation of the tribe's reservation in 1864.

[25] 207 U.S. at 576 (1908).

the Supreme Court, cited in *Winters.*[26] By the terms of a treaty in 1855, Indian tribes in what is now the State of Washington ceded a large area, but in addition to small reservations retained "the right of taking fish at all usual and accustomed places [outside the reservations], in common with the citizens of the territory."[27] Non-Indians who had acquired patents to lands along the Columbia River sought to exclude the Indians from the lands, even though such lands were among the fishing places reserved by the treaty. The Court declared that the Indians still had valid rights to enter non-Indian lands and fish. The Court explained that:

> The right to resort to the fishing places in controversy was a part of larger rights possessed by the Indians, upon the exercise of which there was not a shadow of impediment, and which were not much less necessary to the existence of the Indians than the atmosphere they breathed. New conditions came into existence to which those rights had to be accommodated. Only a limitation of them, however, was necessary and intended, not a taking away. In other words, *the treaty was not a grant of rights to the Indians, but a grant of rights from them—a reservation of those not granted.*[28]

The rights retained by the Indians were binding on the non-Indians as grantees of the government. This arrangement, the Court noted, was surely "within the [Constitutional] competency of the Nation." The *Winters* opinion also contains language supporting the view that *Winters* rights derive only from action by the United States. Near the conclusion of the decision the Court notes the power of the government to reserve waters and states that the waters of the Milk River were reserved by the government for the use of the Indians of the Fort Belknap Reservation.[29]

It may be, however, that this inconsistency in the *Winters* opinion is more apparent than real. Perhaps the Court's reference at one point to rights retained by the Indians and its reference at another point to rights reserved for the Indians' benefit by the government was a simple recognition that there were two parties to the agreement. And both parties clearly intended that rights to sufficient water were to be set aside, exempt from appropriation, ultimately to make the reservation productive. In addressing the government's reservation of water, the Court may have only been referring to the government's intent to accept a limited surrender of rights from the tribe. Reserved from that surrender by mutual intent were specified lands and the water needed to sustain them. It could be maintained that the power of the government to which the Court refers is simply the federal power to conclude a valid and lasting agreement with the Indian tribes, regardless of inconsistent state laws.[30]

This analysis may apply even when Indian rights are reserved by a unilateral act of the United States, as was the case with the reservations involved in *Arizona v. California.* It is true that the Court there refers solely to the intention of the United States to reserve the water. There was no corresponding Indian intent because there was no bar-

---

[26] *United States v. Winans,* 198 U.S. 371 (1905).

[27] *Id.* at 378.

[28] *Id.* at 381 (emphasis added).

[29] 207 U.S. at 577 (1908).

[30] The Court's citation of *United States v. Winans* in this context seems to support this interpretation. Both the *Winans* case and *United States v. Rio Grande Dam and Irrigation Co.,* 174 U.S. 690 (1899), also cited by the Court, can be read for the simple proposition that when the federal government acts within its proper constitutional sphere, its power is supreme, whether the subject be Indians or water.

gain. Yet, even when the government acts unilaterally to establish a reservation, if it carves the reservation out of a tribe's ancestral lands, the Supreme Court has declared that tribal aboriginal rights are simply carried over to the lands reserved, albeit usually diminished in extent.[31] Again, a reservation of rights by the government, whether to lands or to waters, does not mean that the rights have their origin in governmental action. Reservation of these rights may mean simply government confirmation of a portion of the tribe's aboriginal property rights. This is usually accompanied by extinguishment of any remaining interests.[32]

Intent to Reserve Water Rights

In *Winters,* the Supreme Court ruled that water rights had been reserved by implication in the land cession agreement between the tribes and the United States in 1888. The purpose of the agreement was to permit the tribes to remain on the lands reserved as a "pastoral and civilized people." Given the arid climate of the region, this purpose would have been defeated if the right to sufficient water had not been guaranteed.

In *Arizona v. California* the Supreme Court rejected Arizona's contention that a specific intention to reserve water rights had to be shown in order to establish reserved water rights. Citing *Winters,* the Court emphasized that the Colorado River reservations would simply not be "liveable" without the right to sufficient water. Since that fact was fully known when the reservations were established, the Court confirmed the *Winters* conclusion that "the government, when it created the Indian Reservation[s], intended to deal fairly with the Indians by reserving for them the waters without which their lands would have been useless."[33] It is evident that the "intention" to which the Court referred was the government's intention to provide the Indians with a liveable homeland, not a specific, express intention to reserve a given quantity of water.

The Court confirmed this analysis in *Cappaert v. United States,* in which it stated that:

> In determining whether there is a federally reserved water right implicit in a federal reservation of public land, the issue is whether the government intended to reserve unappropriated and thus available water. Intent is inferred if the previously unappropriated waters are necessary to accomplish the purposes for which the reservation was created.[34]

So the guarantee of reserved water rights for an Indian reservation may be established by demonstrating that water rights are necessary to satisfy the purposes for which the reservation was established.

Purposes for Which Water Rights May Be Reserved

The Indian water rights cases that have been fully adjudicated have focused on the necessity of ensuring the availability of water for irrigation of irrigable reservation lands. But it is apparent that many Indian reservations were established for purposes other than irrigable agriculture. In *Winters,* the record reveals that stock grazing was expected to

[31] *See United States v. Santa Fe Pacific R. Co.,* 314 U.S. 339 (1941).

[32] It is true that the Supreme Court specified the priorities of the Colorado River reservations as the dates of their establishment in *Arizona v. California,* but no earlier priority was urged in the case.

[33] 373 U.S. at 600.

[34] 426 U.S. 138, 139 (1976).

be the principle use of reservation lands. Other reservations were established with treaty guarantees that Indians would have access to fishing resources.[35] If water is needed to fulfill the purposes of the reservation, it seems reasonably clear that courts will find that sufficient water rights were reserved to meet the need. Otherwise, the purposes for which the reservation was established would be defeated.

A more difficult issue arises with respect to the use of water for purposes not specifically foreseen at the time the reservations were established. This could include water for mineral development and recreational or industrial uses. Two questions may arise with respect to such uses.

- May a portion of a tribe's water rights, if determined with reference to the reservation's irrigable land, nonetheless be used for nonagricultural purposes?
- Will the total measure of a tribe's water rights include water for purposes reasonably anticipated when its reservation was established, as well as for additional purposes that may have been conceived more recently?

As to the first question, once a tribe's right to water is decreed there seems to be no reason not to permit its exercise for any purpose, so long as the total water consumption is not increased. At least the Special Master in *Arizona v. California* so concluded. He noted that "the reservations of water were made for the purpose of enabling the Indians to develop a viable agricultural economy" and that "other uses, such as those for industry... were not contemplated at the time the reservations were created.... [T]his does not necessarily mean, however, that water reserved for Indian reservations may not be used for purposes other than agricultural and related uses." On the contrary, the Special Master added that:

> The water rights established for the benefit of the five Indian reservations and enforced in the recommended decree are similar in many respects to the ordinary water rights recognized under the law of many western states: They are of fixed magnitude and priority and are appurtenant to defined lands. They may be utilized regardless of the character of the particular user. Thus Congress has provided for the leasing of certain reservation lands to non-Indians [25 U.S.C. §415,], and these lessees may exercise the water rights appurtenant to the leased lands. *Skeem v. United States,* 273 F. 93 (9th Cir. 1921). The measurement used in defining the magnitude of the water rights is the amount of water necessary for agricultural and related purposes because this was the initial purpose of the reservations, but the decree establishes a property right which the United States may utilize or dispose of for the benefit of the Indians as the relevant law may allow. See *United States v. Powers,* 305 U.S. 527 (1939).[36]

In an unpublished memorandum opinion, the Solicitor of the Department of the Interior adopted the Master's reasoning in declaring that a portion of the reserved water rights of the Colorado River Indian Reservation could validly be used by the non-Indian lessees of a part of the reservation in connection with a housing and resort development:

> We know of no reason for holding that the Indians' water rights must be used only for agriculture any more than for holding that their lands themselves must be so used. The water right itself is but a special type of real property which is a part and parcel of the reservation.

---

[35] *See, e.g., Pyramid Lake Paiute Tribe v. Morton,* 354 F.Supp. 252 (D.D.C. 1973).

[36] Master's Report, pp. 265-266, *Arizona v. California,* 373 U.S. 546 (1963).

> Approximately 100 years have passed since the Colorado River Reservation was first established. During this time, there have been marked changes all over the country in the types of uses to which land and related resources are put. Indian land and water may bring larger returns or other benefits to their owners if used for commercial or industrial purposes than if cultivated for crops. Where circumstances warrant the use of Indian lands for recreational, commercial, or industrial purposes rather than for agriculture, we believe that the reserved water rights remain available for these other purposes.[37]

The answer to the second question previously posed is probably more subject to argument. In determining the extent of a tribe's reserved water rights, may a court award not only water rights to satisfy the "initial purposes" of the reservation, but also additional water to meet any further needs that may have developed since the reservation was established?

The fact that it was not possible to foresee all potential water uses when Indian reservations were established should not preclude the courts from awarding water rights sufficient to include such uses. To date, the judicial and administrative decisions that water rights were reserved for tribal use have not been based on any findings of specific intent in agreements or statutes. Rather, the guarantee of water rights was founded on satisfying the purposes for which Indian reservations were established. Determinations of the scope of Indian rights should also depend on an analysis of those purposes, instead of evidence of the specific water uses the parties had in mind at the time the reservation was created.

While there is no doubt that encouraging Indian agriculture was a major purpose for which most western reservations were established, the courts have also specifically noted that reservations were intended to be places where the Indians could "maintain . . . their way of life, which included hunting and fishing."[38] The Court of Appeals for the Ninth Circuit, for instance, recognized this:

> We find it inconceivable that the United States intended to withhold from the Indians the right to sustain themselves from any source of food which might be available on their reservation.[39]

It is fair to say that the basic purpose for which Indian reservations were established was to provide the tribes with permanent, liveable homes. As the Supreme Court stated with respect to the Annette Island Reservation in Alaska, "[the] purpose of creating the reservation was to encourage, assist and protect the Indians in their effort to train themselves to habits of industry, become self-sustaining, and advance to the ways of civilized life."[40] This view of reservation purposes suggests that water rights should be seen as having been reserved to satisfy any reasonable use of tribal resources, not just agriculture.

---

37 Memorandum to the Secretary of the Interior, February 1, 1964. It might also be noted that changes in the purpose or place of use are normally permitted under state law appropriation systems as long as other water users' rights are not impaired. It is usually necessary to obtain administrative approval for changes. For a more exhaustive treatment of this issue, *see* Ranquist, The Effect of Changes in Place and Nature of Use of Indian Rights to Water Reserved under the 'Winters Doctrine,' 5 Nat. Resources Law 34 (1972).

38 *Menominee Tribe v. United States,* 391 U.S. 404, 406 (1968).

39 *United States v. Finch,* 548 F. 2d 822, 832 (1976), *reversed on other grounds,* ______ U.S. ______ (1977). Finch held the use of a fishery to be among the purposes for establishing the Crow Reservation in Montana, even though the Crow Indians were not a fishing people.

40 *Alaska Pacific Fisheries v. United States,* 248 U.S. 78, 89 (1918).

This analysis of the law is supported by a series of cases holding that Indian tribes are entitled to make use freely of all the resources on their reservations, whether they were known or latent when the reservations were established. For instance, in *United States v. Shoshone Tribe,*[41] the Supreme Court declared that the tribe was entitled to the value of minerals and timber included in their reservation, which was partially "taken" when another tribe was settled on the reservation. The right to these resources, the Court held, was inherent in the tribe's original right of occupancy in the land, and these rights were taken away when the reservation was established. A federal district court has specifically held that the value of lands condemned within the Crow Reservation in Montana include the value of potential water power.[42]

The fact that the courts have recognized inherent Indian rights to all reservation resources lends strong support to the suggestion that the development of all such resources was among the purposes for which reservations were established, regardless of whether all potential resources were originally identified. The *Winters* opinion, after all, expressly acknowledged that the tribes' rights to water for their reservation was "kept for hunting and grazing roving herds of stock, or turned to agriculture and the arts of civilization." Even in the nineteenth century it was reasonably foreseeable that mastering the "arts of civilization" might require uses of water for purposes not then specifically identified. Recognizing reserved rights for all such uses seems consistent with the Supreme Court's approach to Indian water rights.[43]

Quantity of Water Reserved

Present federal law dictates that most Indian reservations are entitled, at a minimum, to sufficient water to irrigate their "practicably irrigable acreage." The precise meaning of that phrase has yet to be determined. While the term "practicable" suggests that some considerations of project feasibility may be relevant to determining tribal water rights, the broad purposes for which Indian reservations were established suggest that strict

---

[41] 304 U.S. 111 (1939). The Court of Claims has also held that original Indian title included rights to all the resources of the lands occupied, whether or not used by or known to the Indians at the time reservations were established. *Otoe and Missouria Tribe v. United States,* 931 F. Supp. 265, 290–291 (1955). *And see* Op. Atty. Gen. 171 (1924) for a strong opinion by then Attorney General Harlan Fiske Stone to the same effect, quoted in Felix Cohen, Federal Indian Law, pp. 650–655 (1958).

[42] *United States v. 5,677.94 Acres of Land,* 162 F. Supp. 108, 114 (Mont. 1958). It is true that the Court in *Arizona v. California* decreed that water rights for the Indians measured only with reference to the reservations' "practicably irrigable land." The question of whether Indian tribes may also be entitled to additional water for other purposes was not determined. The United States asked only for "enough water to satisfy future agricultural and related uses."

[43] In the case of *United States v. New Mexico,* 438 U.S. 696 (1978), the Supreme Court ruled that the national forests had been reserved for only two purposes: "To conserve the water flows [from mountain watersheds in the forests] and to furnish a continuous supply of timber for the people." The forests were not reserved, the Court declared, for "aesthetic, environmental, recreational, or wildlife-preservation purposes." The Court stated that water had only been reserved for these two "primary" purposes and that any water intended for "secondary uses" permissible on forest land had to be acquired under state law. No case has applied this primary/secondary distinction to the determination of Indian water rights and the distinction does not seem appropriate. *United States v. New Mexico* rested in large part on the Court's observation that Congress had largely deferred to state law in connection with water uses on federal lands. Federal reserved rights were intrepreted as a narrow exception to this policy and one to be applied as narrowly as possible. The Court also noted that in fully-appropriated watersheds, additional water uses by the United States for its property would have a gallon-for-gallon impact on established private water uses. Neither of these considerations seems applicable to the Indian situation. Congress has

commercial feasibility of potential projects ought not to impose a limit on the scope of Indian rights. Any project that would promote Indian self-development in a reasonably efficient manner ought to be qualified for reserved water rights.

Likewise, water rights for nonagricultural uses should be recognized where the uses are reasonably efficient means of encouraging Indian economic and social development. In some cases, this may involve a guarantee of sufficient water to maintain minimum stream flows or minimum lake levels for Indian fisheries. or commercial recreation uses.[44]

Water Sources Subject to Indian Rights

An important issue that is yet to be resolved is the determination of those water sources to which Indian reserved rights may extend. Indian water rights under the *Winters* doctrine resemble riparian rights in that they exist independent of actual water use, and it has been presumed that *Winters* rights extend only to streams to which a reservation is riparian. In *Winters,* for example, the Milk River formed the reservation's northern boundary. In *Arizona v. California,* however, one small reservation did not actually abut the stream from which the water rights were awarded.[47] Future determinations of water sources to which Indian reserved water rights may extend will necessarily have to consider the understanding of tribes and the United States when the reservation was created and the rights that were reserved. If it was reasonably clear that the water from a nearby stream would be needed for use on the reservation, the fact that the stream does not physically cross tribal lands should not bar the tribe's claim to the water.

Indian reserved rights to ground water on the reservation is the subject of continuing litigation in the arid western states.[48] While the Supreme Court has not ruled on the issue, the 1976 decision in *Cappaert v. United States* suggests that the Court may construe Indian entitlement to ground water use as within the scope of tribal reserved rights.[49] In *Cappaert,* the Court upheld a lower court order imposing strict limitations on ground water pumping by a private landowner adjacent to the Devil's Hole National Monument in Nevada. The pumping was lowering the level of water needed for survival of the endangered pupfish found only in the Devil's Hole. Noting the hydrological fact that "groundwater and surface water are physically interrelated as integral parts of the hydrological cycle," the Court declared that Cappaert's pumping must be restricted to maintain a water level sufficient to accomplish the purpose for establishing the federal reservation. That meant that there must be enough water in the pool for the pupfish to live and spawn. The Court further noted that:

---

never even remotely suggested that Indian water rights should be obtained under state law. On the contrary, "the policy of leaving the Indians free from state control is deeply rooted in our nation's history." *Rice v. Olson,* 324 U.S. 786 (1945). The equitable considerations also seem entirely different. Requiring the forest service to obtain additional water rights under state law may only require the government to condemn such water and pay for it. Failing to award Indian tribes water rights sufficient to develop their reservations leaves them little alternative but to continue to lag behind the rest of the nation's economic growth.

[44] *See Pyramid Lake Paiute Tribe v. Morton,* 354 F. Supp. 252 (D.D.C. 1973).

[45] Final Report to the President and to the Congress of the United States by the National Water Commission, Water Policies for the Future, Chap. 14, p. 473 (1973).

[46] *Id.,* Accepted premises No. 6, p. 477.

[47] *Arizona v. California,* 373 U.S. 546 (1963), Master's Report, pp. 88, 268.

[48] *See, e.g., United States v. City of Tucson,* Civil No. 75-39 JAW; *Gila River Indian Community v. United States,* Civil No. 77-11 WEC (D. Ariz., Jan. 4, 1977).

[49] 426 U.S. 128 (1976).

> Since the implied reservation of water doctrine is based on the necessity of water for the purpose of the federal reservation, we hold that the United States can protect its water from subsequent diversion, whether the diversion is of surface or groundwater.[50]

If the reserved rights of Indian tribes do extend to ground water supplies, then it appears that tribes that are dependent on such supplies, either for their immediate needs or for the long-range development of their reservations, may be able to limit excessive uses of ground water by the owners of adjacent non-Indian land who are contributing to a decline in the water table beneath tribal lands. Lowering the level of ground water makes its use by the tribe more expensive. Even its potential use in the future may be more costly because, depending on geologic and climatic conditions, it may take years for the aquifer to recharge. Indians will have to drill deeper wells at a higher cost with a yield of less water.[51] In addition, pumping of ground water off the reservation may dry up streams flowing on the reservation, thereby interfering with Indian surface rights. Unless the private right is senior to the reservation priority, it would appear that the non-Indian use should be subject to limitations designed to conserve the supply.

Water Rights on Allotted Lands

Pursuant to the General Allotment Act of 1887[52] and numerous special allotment measures, a great deal of irrigable land on many Indian reservations has been allotted to individual Indians. While some of this land is still held by the United States in trust for individual Indians or for Indian tribes, a great number of former Indian allotments have been conveyed to non-Indians. The nature of the water rights that may be exercised

---

[50] *Id.* at 143.

[51] This was the situation confronting the Ak Chin Indian Community of Arizona, which depends for its existence almost entirely on its farming and agricultural development of tribal lands. Rather than pursuing prolonged litigation to resolve the community's right to ground water, the Ak Chin Community approached the state, surrounding non-Indian landowners and the Congress to seek a legislative solution to the problem. The Congress found that, "the Ak Chin Community is a small Indian community located due south of Phoenix, Arizona, which exists on agriculture and which, to date, has been highly successful both agriculturally and financially. In fact they could be considered a model of Indian independence and self-sufficiency. Their farming is entirely dependent upon pumping of ground water. They are already pumping at depths of up to 600 feet. They currently have no natural sources of surface water. For many years now the lands surrounding the reservation have been heavily farmed by non-Indian farmers who have also relied on pumping of ground water for irrigation. The non-Indian lands form a far larger area than the Ak Chin lands and have been more intensely farmed. Consequently the aquifer underlying the reservation has been constantly overdrawn and according to estimates from reliable sources the Indian's sole source of water could disappear within 5 to 8 years. The intensive ground pumping has also dried up surface water sources that once existed in the area and upon which the Ak Chin once expected to rely." Hearing before the U.S. Senate Select Committee on Indian Affairs on S. 1582, Relating to the Settlement Between the United States and the Ak Chin Indian Community of Certain Water Rights Claims of Such Community Against the United States, July 25, 1977, p. 2. On July 28, 1978, Congress enacted Public Law 95-328, 92 Stat. 409, in response to the problem confronting the Ak Chin Community, in which the tribe relinquished all claims against the United States for failing to act consistently with its trust responsibility to protect and deliver the water resources of the community in exchange for the construction of a well field and water delivery system from nearby federal lands to meet the emergency needs of the community and to meet the community's needs for a permanent supply of water, in a fixed amount to be available upon a certain date. This legislative resolution of conflicting claims to ground water use may indicate that the source of water to which Indian reserved rights may extend need not be confined to surface water or riparian waters.

[52] 24 Stat. 388, 25 U.S.C. §381, *et seq.*

in connection with these allotments has been a subject of controversy for many years.

In *United States v. Hibner*, a federal district court in Idaho ruled that Indian allottees on the Fort Hall Reservation were entitled to sufficient water to irrigate "that portion of their lands which the evidence discloses is susceptible to irrigation, . . . with a priority of February 16, 1869" [the date of the treaty establishing the reservation].[53] The court held that a non-Indian purchaser "of such land and water rights acquires, as under other sales, the title and rights held by the Indians; . . . there should be awarded to such purchaser the same character of water right with equal priority as those of the Indians." In other words, the non-Indians were entitled to share the reservation's 1869 priority.

On the other hand, the *Hibner* court refused to recognize that non-Indians had any indefinite right to bring new land on the allotments under cultivation and still relate back to the reservation priority date for the new development. The court stated that "the white man, as soon as he becomes the owner of the Indian lands, is subject to those general rules of law governing the appropriation and use of the public waters of the state." Thus, non-Indian purchasers were entitled "to a water right for the actual acreage that was under irrigation at the time title passed from the Indians, and such increased acreage as [they] might with reasonable diligence place under irrigation" with the original early priority. But purchasers could not wait "an indefinite period to reclaim the balance of [their] land" without forfeiture of water rights for the land left unreclaimed.[54]

The issue reached the Supreme Court in *United States v. Powers* but was not definitively resolved. The *Powers* case was initiated by the United States to stop all diversions of water by non-Indian purchasers of Indian allotments on the Crow reservation in Montana. The diversions were upstream from an irrigation project built and operated by the government for the Crow Tribe. The allotments were among those made to Crow tribal members pursuant to the Treaty of May 7, 1868, establishing the reservation, and a later special allotment act. The issuance of fee patents was authorized by an act of Congress in 1906. Each patent conveyed the land "together with all the rights, privileges, immunities and appurtenances, of whatsoever nature thereunto belonging,"[55] but no express provision for water rights was included. During the drought of 1931 to 1934, there was not enough water left in the stream after the diversions by the non-Indians to supply the reservation irrigation project downstream.

The non-Indian buyers of allotments argued that they had derived the right to an equal share of the available water from their Indian predecessors. The United States contended that it had dedicated the water to the irrigation project before the upstream allotments were made. This followed because Congress had given the Secretary of the Interior control of reservation waters and irrigation projects initiated under his authority prior to allotting tribal lands, and the responsibility of dedicating and reserving sufficient water for full utilization of these projects. Rights acquired by the allottees were then subject to this reservation.

The Court rejected the government's argument and declared that under the Treaty of 1868 waters within the reservation were reserved for the equal benefit of tribal members (citing *Winters*). When allotments of land were duly made for exclusive use and thereafter conveyed in fee, the right to use some portion of tribal waters essential for

---

[53] 27 F. 2d 909 (D. Idaho 1928).

[54] *Id.* at 912.

[55] 305 U.S. 527 (1939).

cultivation passed to the owners. The Court went on to note, however, that it "did not consider the extent or precise nature of [the non-Indians] rights in the waters."[56] Thus, while it was clear that Indian allottees would be entitled to a just and equal share of the reservation waters, the Court did not specify whether the non-Indian purchasers acceded to precisely the same rights.

In *United States v. Ahtanum Irrigation District,* the Ninth Circuit relied on *Powers* in ruling that "white transferees of . . . fee patented Indian allotments were, equally with individual [Indian] allottees . . . entitled to distribution of the waters diverted for [an] Indian irrigation system . . . to the same extent as if their lands were still in possession of the original allottees."[57]

Adjudication of Indian Water Rights

Most western states have special statutory procedures for the determination of all water rights on a stream or ground water basin (or manageable portions thereof). The forum is usually a single administrative or judicial proceeding titled a "general adjudication" and it is normally commenced by state administrative officials. All water users on a particular stream or ground water basin are required to come before the court or administrative body to present their water rights claims for determination. The result of an adjudication is the tabulation for administrative purposes of all water rights by location, nature of use, quantity, and priority.

Until the 1950s neither federal nor Indian water rights were subject to these proceedings. The only adjudications of such water rights had been in federal courts. In 1952, however, Congress adopted the "McCarran amendment," providing that:

> (a) Consent is given to join the United States as a defendant in any suit (1) for the adjudication of rights to the use of water of a river system or other source, or (2) for the administration of such rights, where it appears that the United States is the owner of or is in the process of acquiring water rights by appropriation under state law, by purchase, by exchange, or otherwise, and the United States is a necessary party to such suit. The United States, when a party to any such suit, shall (1) be deemed to have waived any right to plead that the state laws are inapplicable or that the United States is not amenable thereto by reason of its sovereignty, and (2) shall be subject to the judgments, orders, and decrees of the court having jurisdiction, and may obtain review thereof, in the same manner and to the same extent as a private individual under like circumstances . . . .[58]

In *United States v. District Court in and for the County of Eagle* and the companion case of *United States v. District Court in and for Water Division No. 5,*[59] the Supreme Court ruled that the McCarran amendment was intended to include federal reserved rights among the water rights that the United States had consented to have adjudicated in a general state proceeding encompassing a whole "river system." These two cases did not concern Indian water rights, but rather federal reserved water rights for several national forests.

---

56 *Id.* at 532.

57 236 F.2d 321 (9th Cir. 1956).

58 Act of July 10, 1952, ch. 651, §208 (a–c), 66 Stat. 560, 43 U.S.C. 666.

59 401 U.S. 520 (1971); 401 U.S. 527 (1971).

For a few years, it remained unclear whether Indian reserved water rights would also be subject to adjudication in a general state court proceeding involving a river system.

The question was answered affirmatively in *Colorado River Water Conservation District v. United States.*[60] The case had been initiated by the United States in federal district court to adjudicate federal water rights and the water rights of the two Ute reservations in southwestern Colorado. Shortly after the suit was filed, the United States was served with notice to appear and defend those water claims in an on-going water rights proceeding in state court. The federal district court abstained in favor of the state court proceeding, and its decision was affirmed by the Supreme Court.

In the *Colorado River* opinion, the Supreme Court rejected the argument of the Colorado River water users that state courts had been given *exclusive* jurisdiction over federal and Indian water rights by the McCarran amendment. Federal jurisdiction was not impaired by the amendment, and federal and state courts have potential concurrent jurisdiction over water adjudications. The Court declared that since no difficult issues of state law were presented by the United States' complaint, the case was not technically proper for abstention. However, the Court found that there may be another ground to sustain federal court dismissal in favor of the state proceeding: Where concurrent jurisdiction results in two courts proceeding simultaneously with the same subject matter, "wise judicial administration" may call for dismissal of the federal case. The Court held that the McCarran amendment's policy of avoiding "piecemeal" water adjudications on the same stream called for unified proceedings for which the on-going state proceeding was best equipped. The Court rejected the government's argument that the McCarran amendment should be read to give only federal and not state courts jurisdiction to hear cases involving Indian water rights.

While the *Colorado River* decision makes it possible to require the adjudication of Indian rights in state courts, its application may turn out to be rather limited. Unified water adjudications may be handled as efficiently in federal as in state courts. Where Indian rights are not being added to a state court adjudication in which extensive proceedings have already occurred (as was the case in Colorado), there may be no reason for preferring state over federal proceedings. It is also not clear, since McCarran speaks in terms of adjudication "suits," whether the United States can be joined in state *administrative* proceedings (which are the statutory scheme in many western states). Finally, there may still be a question of whether state courts can exercise jurisdiction over Indian water rights in states whose own constitutions contain express disclaimers of jurisdiction over Indian property (Colorado's does not).[61] In any event, the *Colorado River* decision emphasized that the substantive rights of Indians to reserved water, including volume and scope, would not be affected by the fact that their rights were to be determined by a state court, since Indian water rights present federal questions that could be reviewed by the United States Supreme Court after final judgment by the state supreme court.[62]

---

60 424 U.S. 800 (1976). These factors were: On-going proceedings in state court; distance between the affected divisions that would be required to adjudicate; the extensiveness of state water rights involved in the proceeding; and the adequacy of the state proceedings in this case for resolving the federal claims.

61 The Tenth Circuit, however, has ruled that the disclaimer clause in New Mexico's constitution does not bar state jurisdiction over Indian water rights. *Jicarilla Apache Tribe v. United States,* 601 F.2d 1116 (10th Cir. 1979), *cert. denied,* ________ U.S. ________ (1979).

62 424 U.S. at 813.

Protecting the Quality of Indian Water Resources

One important question yet to be answered is whether the *Winters* case reserved the rights of Indians, in addition to entitling them to a certain quantity of water, also entitled them to water of some minimum quality. Water pollution results not only from the discharge of industrial or municipal wastes, but also from the practice that is typical in western states of intensively using and reusing the water of a stream as it flows to the sea. As the water slowly evaporates, each use tends to increase the level of dissolved minerals in the water that flows to the next user downstream. Eventually, the water may become too saline for further agricultural use.[63] If the quality of water available to an Indian tribe is substantially impaired by practices such as these, does the tribe have any legal recourse?

The basis of the reserved rights case has been the recognition by the courts that the arid lands of Indian reservations could not be developed without an adequate supply of water for irrigation. This consideration seems to require that water of usable quality as well as sufficient quantity be reserved for the Indians' use. Tribal water rights would then include the right to prevent practices that substantially impair the quality of water available to meet a tribe's needs. This right would take precedence over any water uses initiated subsequent to the creation of the reservation, and such junior users would have to modify or terminate practices inconsistent with the Indians' right to a usable water supply sufficient to irrigate its irrigable acreage. Similar considerations should govern protection of tribal water supplies needed for other purposes, such as maintaining a fishery.[64]

This position seems consistent with the approach to water quality problems generally taken by the states in which prior appropriation prevails. As noted in a leading water rights treatise: "An appropriative right to the use of water from a water course or lake extends to the quality of that water as well as to its quantity. A subsequent appropriator may not pollute the water supply of a prior appropriator so as to destroy or substantially impair the latter's superior rights."[65]

Conclusion

The importance to Indians throughout the arid West of identifying and protecting rights to water can hardly be overemphasized. While the *Winters* doctrine provides a sound basis for that protection, unanswered questions and difficult practical problems remain. The solutions to those problems become increasingly more elusive as greater demands are placed on often inadequate water resources, particularly in the Southwest. Quantification of Indian water rights, controversy over state and federal jurisdiction to control the use of water, and the validity and reach of tribal water codes are just a few of the other legal issues pending in Indian water rights law. Their resolution will further define Indian reserved rights to water and sorely test the enforceability of those rights.

CHARLES N. ESTES, JR.
Attorney
Albuquerque, New Mexico

[63] *See* Gindler and Holburt, Water Salinity Problems: Approaches to Legal and Engineering Solutions, 9 Nat. Resources J. 329 (1969).

[64] *See Pyramid Lake Pauite Tribe of Indians v. Morton*, 354 F.Supp. 252 (D.D.C. 1973).

[65] 3 Clark, Waters and Water Rights, "Water Pollution and Quality Controls."

RECENT DECISIONS AFFECTING INDIAN WATER RIGHTS

In the past year several major decisions, representing new developments in Indian water law, have been handed down in federal courts. These recent opinions interpret the jurisdictional issues raised by the McCarran amendment [1] and *Colorado River Water Conservation District v. United States* [2]; determine the rights of non-Indian successors in interest to Indian allotments in water reserved for Indian tribes; and recommend that additional Colorado River water be allocated to five Indian reservations to irrigate lands added to the reservations since the 1964 decree in *Arizona v. California*, [3] as well as for lands omitted from that decree.

Adjudication of Indian Water Rights

In January 1982, the District Court for the District of South Dakota issued its decision in *South Dakota ex rel. Meierhenry v. Rippling Water Ranch*. [4] The action was a general adjudication of rights to water in the Missouri River system in an area comprising roughly the western two-thirds of the State of South Dakota. South Dakota initiated suit in state court, joining the United States in its own capacity as trustee for Indian tribes pursuant to the McCarran amendment. The United States removed to the federal district court and the state moved to remand, arguing that the McCarran amendment and *Colorado River* implicitly prohibit removal of an adjudication of this kind to federal court. The McCarran amendment is silent on the issue of removal, and the court concurred with the decision in *In re Green River Drainage Area* [5] that in enacting the McCarran amendment Congress did not intend to foreclose federal jurisdiction over water adjudications when the United States is a party.

South Dakota's second argument, that the Supreme Court's decision in *Colorado River* prohibits removal, was rejected on the ground that *Colorado River* is narrowly limited to its facts. In that case, the Court held that, although state and federal courts have concurrent jurisdiction over general water adjudications under the McCarran amendment, the doctrine of "wise judicial administration" requires the federal district court to decline jurisdiction in favor of state court proceedings. Factors considered by the Court as supporting dismissal of the federal actions include the desirability of avoiding piecemeal litigation, the advanced stage of state proceedings, *forum non conveniens* considerations, the inability of the United States adequately to protect Indian water rights as trustee without conflict of interest, and the extent of the state water rights at stake. Applying these factors to the facts in *Rippling Water Ranch*, the district court found "nothing in its reading of *Colorado River* which would require a remand to state court." [6] Although inter-

---

[1] 43 U.S.C. §666 (1952).

[2] 424 U.S. 800 (1976).

[3] 373 U.S. 546 (1963), *decree entered*, 373 U.S. 340 (1964).

[4] 531 F. Supp. 449 (1982).

[5] 147 F. Supp 127 (D. Utah 1956).

[6] 531 F. Supp. at 453.

ests in water created under state law were extensive, federal and Indian claims were also large. The other facts that mandated retention of state jurisdiction in *Colorado River* were not in issue in *Rippling Water Ranch*.

In *amicus* briefs, the tribes had presented strong arguments for retaining federal jurisdiction because of the presence of extensive Indian water rights, asserting that Indian interests can be adequately protected only in federal court. Relying on the language in *Colorado River*, the court held that Indian rights may be fully defended in a state forum.

The court in *Rippling Water Ranch* held that the federal action must be dismissed on the technical ground that all defendants had not joined in the United States' removal petition, as required by federal law.[7] The court refused to consider these nonfederal, non-Indian parties to be "nominal, formal and unnecessary parties" without significance for removal purposes. The court also rejected arguments brought by the tribes and the United States that non-Indian defendants who have perfected water rights under state law be realigned as plaintiffs. The court noted that the controversy is between all the parties, and that the interests of each are adverse to those of *everyone* else. "All defendants have something to lose by this lawsuit, and nothing appears why some should be designated as plaintiffs, while others maintain the status of defendants, simply because some derive their rights from state law, and others derive their rights from federal law."[8]

The McCarran amendment was also an issue in the Ninth Circuit's opinion in *Northern Cheyenne Indian Tribe v. Adsit*,[9] where the court considered whether the McCarran amendment overrides express disclaimers of jurisdiction in adjudications involving Indian water rights. The Northern Cheyenne Tribe first filed suit in the federal district court in January 1975 to determine rights to water from the Tongue River and Rosebud Creek. In March 1975 the United States brought suit for the same purpose in its own behalf and as trustee for the Northern Cheyenne Tribe and other tribes. In July 1975 the Montana Department of Natural Resources and Conservation initiated an action in state court to determine the same rights according to state law. In August 1975 the United States brought suit, again in the federal district court, to determine the water rights of the Crow Tribe. The district court consolidated these actions and stayed proceedings pending the Supreme Court's decision in *Colorado River*. Finally, in 1979, the district court dismissed the consolidated actions in favor of the state proceeding as an exercise of "wise judicial administration," interpreting the Supreme Court's holding in *Colorado River* to mean that the McCarran amendment overrides tribal immunity to suit in state courts when the United States asserts Indian water rights in its role as trustee.

Two issues were raised on appeal: (1) whether the McCarran amendment grants jurisdiction over Indian tribes in a general water adjudication where, unlike Colorado, the state constitution and enabling act contain express disclaimers of jurisdiction over Indian lands, and (2) whether the absence in Montana of the specific factors requiring dismissal of the federal action in *Colorado River* requires the federal court to retain jurisdiction.

With regard to the first question raised, the Ninth Circuit held that subject matter jurisdiction over Indian water rights is missing in a state that has not validly repealed its constitutional disclaimer to jurisdiction over Indian lands under Public Law 280.[10]

---

[7] The court cites to several cases that have held that a "removal petition must ordinarily be signed by all of the defendants." *Id.* at 455.

[8] *Id.* at 456.

[9] 668 F. 2d 1080 (1982).

[10] A procedure was established by Public Law 83-280 whereby the states can automatically assume jurisdiction over Indian tribes within their borders by legislative action if the state has no constitutional disclaimer,

> The McCarran amendment overrides sovereign immunity of the United States in comprehensive water adjudications and the immunity of an Indian tribe represented by the government in such a proceeding. It cannot be read to amend a state constitution disclaiming subject matter jurisdiction over such matters.[11]

It remains to be determined whether Montana's water consolidation plan, enacted in 1979, constitutes a valid legislative repeal of the state's constitutional disclaimer and, secondly, whether such a repeal requires tribal consent before becoming effective.[12] Remanding the case to the district court for these determinations, the Ninth Circuit held that absent a valid repeal of the disclaimer, the McCarran amendment cannot override the sovereign immunity of Indian tribes in a suit involving Indian water rights.

As to the second question, the Ninth Circuit held that even if Montana has validly repealed its constitutional disclaimer, the federal court has a "virtually unflagging obligation" to retain jurisdiction and may only relinquish it under "exceptional circumstances." The specific circumstances that required dismissal of the federal action in *Colorado River*[13] were not present in *Northern Cheyenne Tribe.*

> The circumstances of the Montana litigation are sufficiently distinct from the factors warranting exceptional treatment in *Akin (Colorado River).* The conflicts of interest present, the embryonic stage of state and federal proceedings, and the procedural status of the Montana case favor retention of federal jurisdiction.[14]

The court examined the factors in *Colorado River* that were considered exceptional enough to warrant dismissal on the federal level, and like the court in *Rippling Water Ranch,* found *Colorado River* to be a narrow holding limited to the facts of that case and inapplicable under the facts of *Northern Cheyenne Tribe.* The Ninth Circuit specifically commented that if *Colorado River* were to be further extended, it would permanently frustrate all efforts of Indian tribes to litigate their water rights in federal court. "Each time a tribe is sued in federal court, the state need only join the United States as a party to obtain dismissal of the federal action."[15]

In a similar action, *San Carlos Apache Tribe v. Arizona,*[16] four Indian tribes in Arizona brought suits to adjudicate their rights to water in several water systems within the state. The Ninth Circuit was asked to consider precisely the same issues as those presented in *Northern Cheyenne Tribe.* The Arizona Enabling Act and Constitution contain disclaimers to jurisdiction over Indian lands that are identical to those in the Montana Enabling Act and Constitution. Accordingly, the court adopted in full its analysis of the disclaimer

---

and can amend the state constitution if the state enabling act contains a disclaimer to jurisdiction over Indian lands. A 1968 amendment to Public Law 280 requires tribal consent before the state can extend civil or criminal jurisdiction to Indian country.

[11] 668 F. 2d at 1085 (1982).

[12] The 1968 amendment to Public Law 280 may require such consent before a state statute can be enforced against Indian tribes.

[13] The factors present in *Colorado River* that required dismissal of the federal action in favor of an ongoing state proceeding are enumerated *infra.*

[14] 668 F. 2d at 1090.

[15] *Id.*

[16] 668 F. 2d 1093 (1982).

issue in *Northern Cheyenne Tribe,* and remanded the case for a determination as to whether Arizona has validly repealed its disclaimer pursuant to Public Law 280.

In a third case, *Navajo Nation v. United States,*[17] the Navajo Nation sought a declaration of its rights to water from the Little Colorado River. The federal district court assumed jurisdiction over the claim, but stayed the federal action pending the outcome of a state proceeding concerning the Little Colorado River. The Ninth Circuit reversed the lower court order and stated: "that Arizona has disclaimed jurisdiction over the Indians' water rights compels us to reverse the district court's holding that the state court has jurisdiction over the Indian claim."[18]

The holdings of the Ninth Circuit in *Northern Cheyenne, San Carlos Apache,* and *Navajo Nation* conflict with the Tenth Circuit's decision in *Jicarilla Apache Tribe v. United States.*[19] In that case, considering precisely the same issue, the Tenth Circuit refused to recognize a distinction between those states with constitutional disclaimers and those without. The Tenth Circuit interpreted New Mexico's disclaimer to "prohibit the state from asserting a proprietary interest in Indian lands, but does not constitute a disclaimer of state control which does not interfere with reservation self-government or impair a right granted or reserved by federal law."[20] According to the Tenth Circuit, Congress has regulatory authority over Indian lands that it delegated to the states when it passed the McCarran amendment. Final resolution of the disclaimer/nondisclaimer issue will have to await adjudication in the Supreme Court.

Water Rights on Allotted Lands

In *Colville Confederated Tribes v. Walton*[21] the court considered the water rights of a non-Indian successor in interest to Indian allotments. The Colville Confederated Tribes had sought to enjoin Walton, a non-Indian purchaser of three Indian allotments, from using surface and ground water in the No Name Creek Basin. The tribes asserted a right to water that they were not currently using to maintain sufficient flow in the creek, which is a spawning ground for Lahonton cutthroat trout, and thereby to support a tribally managed fishery in Omak Lake. The tribes have traditionally depended on the Columbia River salmon, a resource that has been destroyed by dam construction on the Columbia, and the fishery established in Omak Lake is intended to replace the lost salmon runs. The district court had found that the tribes were entitled to the water needed to propagate trout, but did not allot water for this purpose because the federal government supplies fingerlings free of charge. The court had held that Walton was entitled to water not currently used by Indians and that the State of Washington had the authority to regulate water in the No Name Creek basin that had not been reserved for Indian use. In a decision that was later withdrawn, the Ninth Circuit essentially agreed with the lower court holding.

In its revised decision in the *Walton* case, the Ninth Circuit found that the Colville Tribes' traditional fishery had been destroyed, and that the Omak Lake fishery was intended to substitute for this loss. Preservation of the fishery was determined to be one of the purposes for which the reservation was created. "Under the circumstances, we

---

17 668 F. 2d 1100 (1982).

18 668 F. 2d at 1102.

19 601 F. 2d 1116 (10th Cir. 1979), *cert. denied,* ______ U.S. ______ (1979).

20 *Id.* at 1135.

21 647 F. 2d 42 (1981).

find an implied reservation of water from No Name Creek for the development and maintenance of replacement fishing grounds."[22] This conclusion is based on documents concerning the creation of the reservation and the history of the tribes residing there, as well as on case law establishing an implied reservation of water to fulfill the purposes for which the federal government has reserved land.[23] The tribes' reserved right to water therefore includes water required to maintain the fishery, including the spawning ground in No Name Creek.

The court interpreted the General Allotment Act[24] provision that allotted land be held in trust for twenty-five years, thereafter to be conveyed to the allottee in fee free of all encumbrances, to mean that the fee included the appurtenant right to share in reserved waters, and saw no basis for limiting the transferability of that right.[25] An Indian allottee has a ratable share in water reserved for the reservation, prorated according to the irrigable acreage he owns, and a non-Indian successor in interest cannot acquire more extensive rights "to reserved water than were held by the Indian seller."[26] The non-Indian purchaser's right is further limited to the amount of water appropriated by the Indian successor in interest, plus such amounts as he "appropriates with reasonable diligence" after title has passed. The priority date of water rights acquired by either method by a non-Indian successor in interest to an Indian allotment is the date the reservation was established. Unlike the Indian allottee, the non-Indian purchaser may lose his right to reserve water through nonuse.

Walton's claimed water rights under state water permits are disavowed by the court, which holds "that state regulation of water in the No Name Creek was preempted by the creation of the Colville Reservation."[27] Further, the court held that since tribal or federal control of this water basin would have no effect off the reservation, the state's interest in regulating water use within the system is minimal, and that the state has no authority to issue water permits for appropriations from No Name Creek. The court's holding may be limited to situations in which the water system is nonnavigable and all surface and ground water within the system, as well as all the lands for which water rights are sought, are completely within the boundaries of the reservation.

Reserved Water: Quantification

On February 22, 1982, Special Master Tuttle issued his recommendation to the Supreme Court for modification of the 1964 decree in *Arizona v. California*.[28] In 1977 and 1978 the five Indian tribes of the lower Colorado River filed motions to intervene and the United States moved to modify the 1964 decree to provide water for additional irrigable acreage on the five reservations. The claims are for two different types of lands: (1) acreage recognized in 1964 as part of the reservations but erroneously excluded from the original decree (omitted lands), and (2) acreage only recently recog-

---

[22] *Id.* at 48.

[23] The court cites to the following cases: *United States v. New Mexico*, 438 U.S. 696 (1978); *Cappaert v. United States*, 426 U.S. 128 (1976); *United States v. Winters*, 207 U.S. 564 (1908); and *Arizona v. California*, 373 U.S. 546 (1963).

[24] 25 U.S.C. §331 (1887).

[25] 647 F. 2d at 50.

[26] *Id.* at 51.

[27] *Id.* at 52.

[28] Master's Report (1982), *Arizona v. California*, 373 U.S. 546 (1963), *decree entered*, 376 U.S. 340 (1964).

nized as part of the reservation within "newly final boundaries" (boundary lands).

The Special Master first considered the propriety of intervention by the tribes. Over the protest of the states whose intersts are directly affected by water allocated for Indian use, the Special Master would grant the tribes leave to intervene, because their financial interests are directly at stake and "because the asserted claims of the government's conflict of interest [in earlier litigation] created the possibility that the government's representation of the tribes' interest 'may be' inadequate. [Citation omitted.]"[29] The claims of the tribes are ancillary to an action already within Supreme Court jurisdiction. Consequently, the Special Master did not consider the state's eleventh amendment immunity to suit as a bar to tribal intervention. This conclusion is supported by the fact that the Supreme Court retained exclusive jurisdiction over this action. It is therefore the only forum in which tribes can defend their interests.

Considering first the water rights claims for omitted lands, the Special Master rejected arguments brought by Arizona, Nevada, and the Metropolitan Water District[30] that these claims were barred by res judicata and collateral estoppel. Article IX of the original decree provided:

> Any of the parties may apply at the foot of this decree for its amendment or for future relief. The Court retains jurisdiction of this suit for purposes of any order, direction, or modification of the decree, or any supplementary decree, that may at any time be deemed proper in relation to the subject matter in controversy.[31]

The Special Master also rejected the contention of the states and the district that they detrimentally relied on the 1964 decree when they proceeded with the construction of water projects intended to handle a given amount of water that will now be reduced by additional water being allocated for Indian use. The Special Master found absolute reliance on a modifiable decree to be misplaced, and was not convinced that either the states or the district altered their plans significantly in reliance on the 1964 decree. Furthermore, the Special Master found that the United States, representing the tribes as trustee in the earlier litigation, inexplicably failed in its duty to present the tribes' maximum claim, a circumstance that needs to be corrected. The Special Master therefore recommends that the Court reach the merits of the tribes' claims for water to irrigate omitted lands on the ground that "fairness to the tribes prevents the state parties' absolute reliance on a modifiable decree from foreclosing the omitted lands claim."[32]

With regard to boundary lands, the 1964 decree expressly provided for modification of the water allocation for the Colorado River and Fort Mohave reservations pending the outcome of boundary disputes. The 1979 decree in *Arizona v. California,*[33] which listed presently perfected rights to Colorado River water, further provided that the water rights enumerated were subject to further modification "in the event that the boundaries

---

[29] Master's Report 26–27 (1982), *Arizona v. California,* 373 U.S. 546 (1963).

[30] The Metropolitan Water District is the supplier of municipal water to Los Angeles and to agricultural concerns in California's Central Valley.

[31] Cited in Master's Report 32 (1982).

[32] Special Master's Report 55 (1982).

[33] *Arizona v. California,* 373 U.S. 546 (1963), *supplemental decree entered,* 439 U.S. 419 (1979). Cited in Master's Report 55 (1982).

of the respective reservations are *finally determined.*"[34] (Emphasis added.) The Special Master found that surveys by the Department of the Interior determining certain lands to be within the boundaries of the reservations constitute "final determinations" within the meaning of the 1964 and 1979 decrees. All but the Chemehuevi Indian Reservation now assert water claims for irrigable acreage within lands "finally determined" to be part of the reservations since 1964.

If accepted by the Supreme Court, Special Master Tuttle's recommendations will provide additional water to irrigate acreage on lands omitted from the 1964 decree and lands determined to be part of the reservations since 1964. In general, the Special Master accepted the soil analysis and crop projections advanced by the tribes and the federal government over arguments and evidence to the contrary advanced by the state parties. The priority dates for these additional water rights are to be "identical to the dates when the land to which the rights are appurtenant became part of the reservation."[35] The priority dates for "boundary lands" are subject to the 1979 decree, which states that in the event of a shortage all Indian rights are to be satisfied first, subject only to presently perfected non-Indian water rights with earlier priority dates.

Following the example of the former Special Master, Special Master Tuttle rejected theories advanced by the state parties that water quantification for the reservations should be limited to the present population and needs of the reservations, and that irrigable acreage should be measured according to the technology available when the land was first reserved for the Indians. The Special Master's recommendations would give the tribes adequate water to meet the "present and future" needs of the reservations by providing sufficient water to irrigate all practicably irrigable acreage within reservation boundaries. "Practicably irrigable," as that term was used by the former Special Master, is interpreted to mean "economically feasible" using presently available technology. Economic feasibility is determined simply by "a finding that annual benefits exceed costs . . ."[36] A hearing date for consideration of the Special Master's findings has not yet been set.

BARBARA W. FRITZEMEIER
Staff Attorney/Editor
American Indian Lawyer
Training Program, Inc.

[34] *Id.*, cited in Master's Report 56 (1982).

[35] Special Master's Report 116 (1982).

[36] *Id.* at 100.

PART II

SYMPOSIUM ON INDIAN WATER POLICY

SYMPOSIUM PROGRAM

MONDAY, November 9, 1981

Morning Session

Opening Remarks: **Richard Trudell**
Symposium Chairman

Keynote Address: **Wendell Chino**
President, Mescalero Apache Tribe

Slide-Tape Presentation: **"Water: The River of Life"**
Sue Bennett and John Running

Panel Presentation and Discussion

"WATER AND THE INDIAN FUTURE"

Moderator: **W. Richard West, Jr.**
Fried, Frank, Harris, Shriver & Kampelman

Panelists:

Frank J. Trelease
Professor of Law
McGeorge School of Law
University of the Pacific

Robert S. Pelcyger
Staff Attorney
Native American Rights Fund

Claudeen Bates Arthur
Field Solicitor
Office of the Solicitor
Department of the Interior

Russell Jim
Council Member
Yakima Indian Nation

Ned Anderson
Chairman
San Carlos Apache Tribe

Address: **Reuben A. Snake**
Vice Chairman, Winnebago Tribe

Afternoon Session

Panel Presentation and Discussion

"BALANCING COMPETING INTERESTS"

Moderator: **Joseph A. Myers**
Associate Director
American Indian Lawyer Training Program, Inc.

Panelists:

Gary D. Weatherford
Research Analyst
Center for Natural Resource Studies
John Muir Institute

John B. Narcho
Council Member
Papago Tribe

Douglas Nash
Special Counsel on Water Rights
Umatilla Indian Reservation

Richard B. Collins
Visiting Professor
School of Law
University of Colorado

John A. Folk-Williams
President
The Western Network

Addresses:

Kenneth L. Smith
Assistant Secretary for Indian Affairs
Department of the Interior

Peter MacDonald
Chairman, Navajo Nation

TUESDAY, November 10, 1981

Morning Session

Panel Presentation and Discussion

"MANAGING THE RESOURCE"

Moderator: **Alan R. Parker**
Counsel, Karl A. Funke & Associates, Inc.

Panelists: **Ronald B. Robie**
Director
Department of Water Resources
State of California

David H. Getches
Associate Professor
School of Law
University of Colorado

Lee Brown
Associate Professor
Department of Economics
University of New Mexico

Frank Tenorio
Secretary-Treasurer
All Indian Pueblo Council

Guy McMinds
Director
Department of Quinault Natural
Resources & Economic Development

Chris E. McNeil, Jr.
Corporate Secretary
Sealaska Corporation

Nelson N. Angapak
Chairman of the Board
Calista Corporation

Address: **Joseph DeLaCruz,**
President, Quinault Indian Nation

Afternoon Session

Panel Presentation and Discussion

"STRATEGIES FOR CLARIFYING AND PROTECTING INDIAN WATER RIGHTS"

Moderator: **John E. Echohawk**
Executive Director
Native American Rights Fund

Panelists: **Charles F. Wilkinson**
Visiting Professor
School of Law
University of Minnesota

Dr. Helen Ingram
Professor
Department of Political Science
University of Arizona

Henry Loble
Chairman, Reserved Water Rights
Compact Commission
State of Montana

Scott McElroy
Attorney
Department of Justice
Land & Natural Resources Division

Suzan Shown Harjo
Legislative Liaison
Native American Rights Fund

Rodney B. Lewis
Tribal Attorney
Gila River Indian Community

Robert N. Harris, Sr.
Chairman
Shoshone Business Council
Wind River Indian Reservation

Ronnie Lupe
Chairman
White Mountain Apache Tribe

OPENING REMARKS

In the 1960s and 1970s, Indian communities across this country made great strides toward achieving the goals of Indian self-determination and economic self-sufficiency. Many tribes have been successful in the development and managment of their resources. However, as demands for natural resources increase in this country, Indian tribes are confronted with increasing opposition to tribal control and management of these resources from some state governments and federal agencies who are unwilling to include tribes in the formation of national policies that will dictate how all resources are to be developed.

Now, at the beginning of the 1980s, probably the most critical issue facing Indian decision-makers is the development of a tribal water policy as they consider new uses for the resource, protection of traditional uses and assertion of regulatory authority over precious reservation supplies. Indian communities no longer look upon water issues as limited to establishing entitlement to the resource and quantification under the *Winters Doctrine*, though these remain of fundamental importance. Rather, tribal planning now embraces many specific activities and uses that depend upon water of protected quality, as well as quantity, and that require new expertise in governmental regulation.

Fishing rights are also viewed as water rights since protection of fisheries depends so directly on their environment. Recent litigation has recognized this connection by finding that traditional *Winters* rights have been reserved for fisheries and that the fishing rights themselves imply a degree of environmental protection if they are to have any meaning. Contamination of reservation supplies by energy development and urban effluent has also become a major concern, as has interference by non-Indian development with off-reservation waters required for religious or subsistence activities.

Several Indian governments, especially in the more arid areas of the West, find that their practical access to water depends upon powers exercised by the Secretary of the Interior in the administration of federal reclamation projects. The allocation of project water to ten tribes in southern Arizona has sparked controversy for the past decade, and six Pueblo communities along the Rio Grande have recently clashed with a conservancy district that has the responsibility for delivering their water. Increasingly, the powers of the Secretary of the Interior over stored water will be crucial to the satisfaction of Indian rights, whether or not those rights have been definitively established through litigation.

Some Indian communities have chosen to forego litigation as a principal tool for securing access to water. The Ak Chin Indian Community won passage of a congressional enactment in 1978 which substitutes the protection of a contract with the federal government for traditional remedies through *Winters Doctrine* litigation. The United States now has a contractual obligation to find and deliver 85,000 acre/feet of water each year to the reservation in return for a waiver by Ak Chin of other water claims. Other tribes are experimenting with negotiated settlement processes either as a supplement or an alternative to litigation.

Increasingly, Indian leaders are recognizing that water management and water rights are issues of universal importance and not limited to those regions with arid conditions. In the water-rich areas of the Pacific Northwest, the conflict over impounding vast quantities of water for the production of electricity instead of letting the water sustain important fisheries demonstrates that even in areas with abundant water resources the nature of competing uses can quickly claim the entire available supply. In the Missouri River region, there are interstate disputes over the apportionment of water between the upper basin states for energy development and the lower basin states for instream flows to protect river freight traffic. These disputes may limit amounts of water available to Indian reservations in South Dakota, despite a current surplus of water in that state.

In short, Indian leaders now must set policy for both new uses of water and new strategies to protect their supplies. Whether to litigate or negotiate; whether to assert jurisdiction over non-Indian use of Indian water; whether to develop new uses for water, such as hydroelectric production; how to deal with private corporations seeking the use of Indian water rights; what demands to make for water stored in federal reclamation projects—these are only a few of the policy questions facing Indian leaders.

Helping tribal decision-makers to understand this new range of problems and to consider their choices in shaping water policy is a major theme of this symposium on *Indian Water Policy in a Changing Environment*. The presentations that follow are intended to give an honest picture of the full context of non-Indian competition as well as state and federal policies that either hinder or promote Indian use and regulation of water resources. We have invited a diverse group of speakers who have different perspectives on tribal entitlement to water and tribal jurisdiction and regulatory authority over Indian water rights. It is important that Indian leaders fully understand what they are up against in the 1980s. We hope that hearing different perspectives on Indian water policy and management will help tribal governments respond to and resolve the problems of water resource planning and management.

RICHARD TRUDELL
Symposium Chairman
Executive Director, American Indian Lawyer Training Program, Inc.

Keynote Address

MR. WENDELL CHINO

President, Mescalero Apache Tribe,
Mescalero, New Mexico

MR. CHINO: I am grateful for the opportunity to be here this morning to address you on Indian homelands and water rights. I am honored to speak to such an impressive group—my peers, your attorneys, and your leaders—on the issue of our homelands and the waters to which we are entitled. To ensure sufficient water to our reservations is the most important task facing tribal leaders today. Only by procuring and protecting that water can our homelands become self-sufficient. I wish I could report to you that we could count on the support of the federal trustee in accomplishing this goal and this objective. You and I both know the opposite is true. The federal government is perhaps the greatest danger to our Indian water rights. The federal government continues to bow to non-Indian political pressures.

Wednesday of this week is Armistice Day in this country, when we honor and pay tribute to men and women who went forth in war to protect freedom, justice, equality. Indian people enlisted and went abroad to fight the common enemy, many never to return. They paid the supreme price for all of those things that we as Americans hold so dear. Yet I find it so ironic that these same people, who returned to their native homelands, today must continue to battle for some of the things that they thought would be theirs to enjoy for years and years to come. I find it difficult that we as Indian people still have to clamor and fight and battle for justice.

In the nineteenth century, direct force was used to take our Indian lands. The danger today is more subtle. Under the cloak of legal strategy and executive department policy decisions, a real threat is stalking all Indian leaders. These decisions regarding legal strategy and policy are designed to dry up the water from what little land has been left to us. We must be alert. We must protect our own rights. The consequences of losing our water would be as serious as those following the loss of our lands in the nineteenth century. By changes in governmental policies and legal theories the rules of the game are often changed. When the issues favor the Indians, who changes the rules? The non-Indians, for their benefit.

How have our rights been jeopardized? Look at the landmark case of *Arizona v. California*. The United States Supreme Court held that sufficient water was reserved to those Indians to irrigate all the practicably irrigable acres located within the reservations. The standard of measurement was to ensure sufficient water for the future as well as the present needs of our Indian reservations. Economics played an insignificant role in the determination of a practicably irrigable acre. Sufficient water was reserved to utilize all available tribal resources. In this way, the ultimate need of a permanent homeland could best be achieved.

Only when the practicably irrigable acres standard is compatible with the permanent homeland theory is there a reasonable answer for Indians. Immense problems arise when proper consideration is not given to the permanent homeland concept.

It seems to me that the permanent homeland theory is not necessarily based on legal theory. I think it is founded on the United States Constitution, for the commerce clause states that Congress shall have the power to deal with the several states, with foreign nations, and with whom? Indian tribes. This does not mean that Congress was given the ultimate power to wipe out the Indians from this continent. The framers of the Constitution only granted to the United States Congress power to make laws that would be compatible with Indians' permanent homelands on this continent, not power by subtle design to attempt to take away from us all of that we have.

Since the *Arizona v. California* decision, the attorneys for our trustee, the United States government, have voluntarily made Indian water rights more difficult to prove. The federal government has agreed by its actions to assume a unique burden of proof. Only Indian water rights must show both engineering and economic feasibility in order to count the irrigable acres. What was won in the *Arizona v. California* case the federal government gave away by adopting this self-imposed standard, to the disadvantage of our Indian people. In other words, the federal government will not assert an Indian water claim unless it has a benefit-cost ratio of 1:0 or better.

Superficially, this appears reasonable. However, it must be placed in proper perspective. Consider the enormity of this burden of proof the federal government has assumed. For the Indian to be awarded water, the benefit-cost ratio of a proposed project must be 1:0 plus. Yet study after study of projects completed under the Federal Reclamation Act clearly show that non-Indian irrigation projects have seldom been able to pay the capital costs involved.

Mr. Charles W. Howe, an economist at the University of Colorado, studied federal water projects. He concluded, and I quote, "The lesson of history has been consistent: Irrigators [non-Indian, that is] typically cannot repay construction costs, even on an interest-free basis." To assist non-Indian irrigators, therefore, the Reclamation Project Act of 1939 replaced the old repayment test with an "ability to pay" standard. Remember how I told you rules change? If an Indian gets into trouble, they don't change the laws. If a white man gets into trouble, they see that the laws are changed to benefit him.

How much do non-Indians actually pay for reclamation? The National Water Commission in its 1973 report said that non-Indian irrigation water users actually repay only about 10 to 15 percent of the costs, including interest. This is true despite the criticism that some of the allocations of construction costs to irrigation projects have been unjustifiably low. It is assumed that revenues from power production will pay for those construction costs that irrigation projects are unable to pay. Indian tribes had little choice in the location of their reservations. And few tribes, if any, can tie their location of irrigation projects to power production. The burden of showing that an Indian irrigaton project meets strict economic feasibility is therefore even heavier. Thus, Indian tribes must sustain a heavier burden merely to claim water than non-Indians do in order to receive a finished project. If the federal experts fail in their burden, your tribe and mine will not receive the water to which they are entitled. Is this the result intended by our federal trustees? We must guard against these subtle moves. The design is not in your best interest or in mine.

There is another problem with the government's approach. From 1939 to 1973, a very liberal approach to calculating the benefits of federal projects was used. National objectives concerned national economic development, environmental preservation, regional economic development, and the well-being of people. For twenty non-Indian projects during this period, benefits exceeded costs only when such secondary benefits were included. In fact, secondary benefits accounted for 50 percent of the total agricultural benefits.

In 1973, the inclusion of the value of secondary benefits was basically eliminated by the adoption of new Water Resource Council guidelines. These standards are nowhere made applicable to the litigation of Indian water claims. It is a purely arbitrary decision by the federal government to burden Indian water rights cases with these strict standards. Only four of the twenty selected non-Indian projects built prior to 1973 would pass muster under the new, more rigid standards. We must not permit our water claims to be diminished because they are litigated now, rather than prior to 1973. Shifting standards are inherently inconsistent with the permanent homeland concept.

This is why you and I, as Indian people, are still looking for justice. The federal government gave its solemn promise to create a permanent homeland for our tribes. It cannot thereafter place an economic condition on its promise. Like I said, federal Indian treaties are not predicated on budget cuts. It is fundamental that federal reservations are entitled to sufficient water to fulfill the purpose for which they were intended. Economics is not a factor. No one has ever argued that if a national forest or national monument is established, it gets only as much water as it can economically justify. Even under state law, water rights can be obtained without regard to economic feasibility. Like a national forest or a national monument, a permanent homeland for Indian people cannot be valued economically. Why then have we been singled out to meet this burden? Simply because the Secretary of the Interior goes around the country speaking of states' rights? What are Indian rights? What about treaty rights? What about the Constitutional rights of Indian people?

The federal government's approach is made even more burdensome by its refusal to claim benefits of the Leavitt Act. You all know that the Leavitt Act permits tribes to defer repayment of capital costs. Capital costs deferred by the Leavitt Act may be viewed as essentially the Indian projects' counterpart to the subsidizing of non-Indian irrigation projects by power production revenues. In addition, making a permanent homeland secure is a public benefit and costs allocated for that purpose ought to be considered nonreimbursable. This would treat Indian water rights in a manner consistent with those of non-Indians. I am glad that Indians, through their resources and the development of those resources, are helping to carry and pay the freight for their homelands.

The federal government's failure to make the permanent homeland concept the central focus of its approach jeopardizes claims other than those based on irrigation. If we ask whether when a reservation was founded it was intended that water be reserved for tourism, the answer will inevitably be "No." If, however, the permanent homeland concept is the focus, there is no impediment to allowing such a claim. Whatever assists in attaining a permanent homeland should be allowed. I'm here to tell you that policies and legal theories may change. But we as Indian people don't intend to go away. This hemisphere will continue to be part of our permanent homelands. And we intend to defend them!

Some courts apparently do not understand the distinction between the means to achieve a permanent homeland and the end of a permanent homeland itself. In its recent opinion in *Colville Confederated Tribes v. Walton*, the Ninth Circuit Court of Appeals felt compelled to apply the *United States v. New Mexico* test to certain tribal water claims. In the *New Mexico* case, the Supreme Court held that a secondary purpose of a federal reservation would not support a federal reserved water right. This test is irrelevant to a consideration of whether a secondary measure of water rights is available to achieve the primary end of a permanent homeland. The distinction between means and ends must be clear at all times. The federal government's approach fails to do this. Small wonder, then, that the courts are unclear. This is because our trustee compromises and subtly submits to political pressures, rather than to recognize treaties and the law, and to uphold justice.

Another area in which the federal government is jeopardizing Indian water rights is in the choice of forum. As you and I know, state courts have traditionally been antagonistic to Indian interests. There is no question about it. Everywhere in this country this animosity is magnified in the area of water rights. The scarcity of water in the West and the fact that state judges are elected mainly by non-Indians means that Indian tribes are at a serious disadvantage in state courts. The Mescalero Apache water rights case is being tried in a state judicial district that does not encompass the Mescalero reservation and its voters. It is not difficult to see the problem faced in such a situation and how that judge is going to decide on the case. He's not likely to make so much a judicial decision as a political one. And that is often the case when Indian rights are involved. Yet the current federal attitude is that a state court is the appropriate forum to try Indian water cases.

This past week I, along with other tribal leaders and attorneys, met with the Assistant Attorney General for the Lands and Natural Resources Division of the Department of Justice. Her attitude was that there was no reason to assume state courts were not competent to handle such cases. This policy seems calculated to ensure that Indian water rights will fall far short of their entitlements. I'm saying to you, the competency of the state courts is not the issue: Justice is the issue.

Tribal leaders from the Jemez Pueblo asked the Assistant Attorney General why their water case was not filed in federal court. Her response was that the Interior Department, through Solicitor Coldiron, has made a policy decision not to file the case. The Justice Department, we were told, tries cases; it does not make policy. And yet the obvious result of failure to file in federal court is to give the state the time and the opportunity to file in state court. Thus, the federal policy of inaction—sometimes deliberate, I believe—ensures that tribal rights will be litigated in courts antagonistic to Indian claims. The federal approach raises the question, "With friends like this, who needs enemies?"

Fortunately, the pueblos involved with the Jemez have decided to push forward on their own to protect their rights. This may need to be done by more and more tribes in the future. This is an expensive proposition. Yet this might be the moment that challenges each one of us as Indian leaders and Indian people to join our forces to defend the water, the river of life. Pressure must be put on the federal government to provide funds for this purpose. However, success in this area is unlikely, given the present climate. Even in more favorable times in the past, the federal government has refused to fund tribal efforts, except in cases of the most obvious conflicts of interest. Indian tribes may have to take the matter into their own hands. In this, Mescalero is ready to join you.

WATER AND THE INDIAN FUTURE

Moderator's Preface

That water is linked inextricably with the Indian future states a fact that should be obvious to anyone at all familiar with Indian country. In the largely arid western part of the United States, water is, as the Supreme Court emphasized more than half a century ago in the historic *Winters* case, the very lifeblood of Indians. For purposes of subsistence farming and ranching, as well as for hunting and fishing, water is absolutely essential. Beyond those quantities that are necessary to sustain their very way of life, Indian tribes obviously require even greater quantities of water if reservations are truly to flower economically—as clearly appears to have been intended under the law as interpreted on repeated occasions by the courts of this land.

The courts uniformly have held in decisions—most of which have their origin in the principles established by the Supreme Court in the *Winters* case—that Indian tribes are entitled to reserved water rights dating in priority at least from the establishment of their reservations. Completely apart from reserved rights, tribes also may have other legal bases for claiming water for the benefit of their reservations.

While water is necessary as a practical matter to the preservation and further development of Indian communities, the scarcity of water in the western United States is not a problem that Indians alone must face. Significant non-Indian interests—the states, local governments, private landowners, or indeed, the federal government—have competing claims to water. Over the next several years Indians and non-Indians alike will have to reach an accommodation or resolution of their water differences.

The possibilities for achieving this resolution are several, and each has a number of advantages and disadvantages. In the past Indian tribes and non-Indian interests frequently have resorted to litigation to clarify and quantify water rights. From the Indian standpoint, however, a number of disadvantages exist in using this approach. First, it is costly, which is an especially critical consideration at a time when federal resources that previously have aided and underwritten Indian efforts are in rapid decline. Furthermore, the time required to quantify Indian water rights through litigation may well stretch over many years.

Other approaches, including cooperative agreements or a legislative settlement, are relatively untested for Indian tribes. While they permit a more rapid resolution of conflicting interests, Indian tribes often are concerned about the compromise which is an almost inherent component of cooperative agreements or legislative settlements.

The panel "Water and the Indian Future" is intended to address a number of these issues. First, the historical and legal basis for Indian water rights will be explored. Second, through various panelists, those non-Indian interests competing for water will be identified. Finally, an effort will be made, based on specific tribal experiences, to define and assess the various approaches that might be utilized in defining Indian water rights, along with their comparative advantages and disadvantages.

W. RICHARD WEST, JR.
Attorney At Law, Fried, Frank,
Harris, Shriver & Kampelman
Washington, D.C.

MR. FRANK J. TRELEASE

Professor of Law, McGeorge School of Law
Sacramento, California

MR. TRELEASE: We see we have controversy attached to Indian water rights, and complex issues, conflicts over water, different arenas of water conflicts. But we end up speaking in terms of fundamental cooperation, trying to find equitable solutions. I think that is the progression that just has to be made in this area.

One reason why I am here is that if you are going to carry on a successful lawsuit, you must know not only the strength of your own case, but also the strength of the opponent's case.

I will start with the law of prior appropriation, which is what water law is all about. Water law doesn't deal with water; it deals with people. It regulates what people can do with water and what they must not do.

What do you want to do with water? What does the government—and that could be the United States, the state, or the tribe—want you to do with it? If there is something that the government wants you to do with your water, then the government will have water laws that will help you do it.

Western water law does a pretty good job of this. Prior appropriation law is a good law for projects, at least. Take the engineer. What does the engineer for an irrigation project want? He wants 3 acre-feet of water for 60,000 acres over a period of three months flowing at a rate of 1000 cubic feet per second. The plant manager of a steam power plant wants 20 million gallons a day, every day, in a continuous, ongoing flow. The City Water Department manager's needs are a little more flexible, but overall they are much the same, although he will have peak demands during hot weather and dwindling demands during the snows. But for all of these people, water is in the wrong place at the wrong time. You will always need a dam to store it, a ditch to take it to the place of use, a tunnel to bring it from another valley where the supply exceeds the demand.

An appropriation under western water law is something like a farm. It will have a fixed quantity for acreage, cubic feet per second for flows, acre-feet for stored quantities. The priority is the fence you can build around it. Priority distinguishes your property; it establishes the dividing line.

If you want to understand water law, think land. Western prior appropriation gives a water user a property right that is secure and firm. The person or the company that has it will try to make the most he can with what he has. The notion is that if all of the water owners are trying to achieve the maximum for themselves, looking out for Number 1, they will eventually achieve the maximum benefit for the state or the nation.

I may have water and someone else may have a need for water that may be better than mine. My water right is not only firm and secure, but it is flexible. I can sell it. It can move, under the influences of market forces, to a better and more productive use. Now, if I sell it under certain circumstances, I can do harm to other water users, to my neighbors. If I have land, say a lot in a city, and sell it to a factory, I might harm my neighbors who had a residential area there. So, like zoning laws, water laws have mechanisms to prevent harm from transfers.

Suppose the government wants my water back? The government was the original source of my water rights, but it was the source of my land rights, too. If the government needs my land for a school site or for a highway, they will buy it back. They will condemn it and pay me compensation for it. The same is true with water.

The government may, if it is wise and has foresight, make sure that some land never passes into private ownership. The very first real set-aside happened not very far from here, in the Yosemite Valley. There are no homesteads there.

In addition to these sorts of property rights, however, state water law has an administrative side. The first is the registration that provides titles and records that we call adjudications. States also have control over the initiation of water rights. They want to make sure that projects are good projects, not some pioneer jackleg sort of thing, but well engineered. Projects must be in the public interest. They must be the best. We must make sure that they advance the welfare of the people. By controlling initiation, we can put conditions on appropriations that will keep harm from occurring.

However, for some people, the water is in the right place. Some people want to keep it right where it is. Under modern conditions, we need to have environmental protection. There is demand for in-stream flows. The fishermen want flow of the streams sufficient to provide a fishery habitat, a healthy habitat with enough food for trout, and a passageway, a spawning ground for salmon and steelhead. The wilderness backpacker does not want a minimum flow, he wants an actual flow. It is shared somewhat by the Lakeside Property owner.

Now, the law of prior appropriation started out as irrigation law. In general, however, it has been adaptable to these more modern demands. We have had to make some considerable changes to allow for in-stream flows, recognizing beneficial uses for recreational purposes, recognizing environmental values. So law is an evolving, changing situation.

Water laws are moving now, I think, into a planning stage where we are planning development and non-development as well. We are planning both recreation projects and preservation. Western water law is very largely a law of protection of existing uses. What is the Indian water law, the reserved water right? It is much the same. The difference is the time frame, the time reference.

Most of the water that is claimed by Indian tribes is unused, unused at least in the sense that it is now not serving irrigation ditches, power plants, or industries. But what you eventually plan for it is much like what is planned for it under prior appropriation law.

I might say that this is not just a western American invention. This is the law that you will find in most of the dry parts of the world. Someone studied the laws of fifty-seven countries and concluded that priority is really the rule of law in the majority of those nations.

You have both the in-stream flow needs and reserves for future use. Reserves—who reserved? We can ponder two paragraphs in the *Winters* case: one follows the other. One of them says that the United States reserved the water rights. The next one says the Indians reserved the water rights There could be a big difference there. But you want agricultural developments, mineral developments, domestic and municipal supplies, preservation, and of course, fishing rights.

Community and tribal maintenance keeps your families, your tribes together, keeps your cultures, your lifestyles together. And then you have desires for Indian water codes that will regulate uses of water much the same way as the state appropriation codes. But to continue the analogy to land, the Indian water right is a kind of vacant lot. It is fallow land. But you find a squatter on it. The question is, how good is your title and how strong is your fence? Can you reestablish the fence?

Now, many of the property rights of the off-reservation users may be built on a flawed foundation, like a dam over a fault. Because if the Indian water right is put to use, the water may no longer be available for the off-reservation user. This, of course, frightens the off-reservation farmer, and he is fighting back. Many of the claims to Indian water rights, many statements about Indian water law, are the hopes of litigants and the arguments of lawyers—they are not fixed and certain rights and they are not adjudicated law. There are many uncertainties and unanswered questions.

In the *Colville Confederated Tribes v. Walton* case, the Ninth Circuit Court of Appeals said that the case of the *United States v. New Mexico* is applicable to Indian water rights. Now, that means that off-reservation uses may be subjected to this test of what is the primary purpose of the reservation? What is the supplemental, secondary purpose of the reservation? What is the minimum quantity that is essential to keep the purpose of the reservation from being entirely defeated? Thoughts like these are a very, very considerable cutdown from the broad statement of *Arizona v. California*. What is intent? Research is being done on just what was intended, what was said, what was written back in the days when reservations were being formed, treaties negotiated, and reservations being set aside. Well, my thesis is simply that there may be room for compromise. There are places where 100 percent use of 100 percent of Indian claims could dry up off-reservation farms and could cut into supplies for cities and could stop a copper mine and smelter. Will it happen? Could it happen without federal funds? Is Congress really likely to appropriate funds for projects like this? If the Indian water right is to be capitalized by being sold or leased to large agribusiness corporations or huge energy companies which then try to take large amounts of water from off-reservation farmers, the sympathies may be reserved. Is that a viable thing?

I worry a lot about non-Indian reservation rights. You know, it has been twenty-six years since we found out that not only do the Indians have reserved rights, but the federal government has reserved rights, as well. These rights were regarded as a terrible threat to western water law. But guess how much water the federal government has acquired through the enforcement of reserved water rights? Not one drop. Not a single drop of water.

And I worry a little bit about the possibilities of this happening to the Indians. Now, we have these uncertainties, these legal battles. We have economic and political competition. But the art of compromise usually means that you never settle a lawsuit on the basis of your best claim, the best that might happen to you. You always settle a lawsuit on the basis of the worst that might happen to you. There is not only the art of compromise, but there are also rewards in cooperation. I think the Indians who are perhaps closest to getting water in the ditch and corn in the field, not water rights on paper, are those in central Utah, the Yakima Project, and some other places where there is a joining of forces, a planning. The off-reservation water user is having a hard time with his projects. To the extent we can pull together, we may all be better off.

MR. ROBERT S. PELCYGER

Staff Attorney, Native American Rights Fund
Boulder, Colorado

MR. PELCYGER: Looking at the Indian water rights from a tribal perspective, I think there are two principles or overriding themes that permeate the subject. The first is that of seeing the water right as an instrument, a crucial instrument, to obtaining the goal for which all Indian reservations were established, that of a permanent tribal homeland.

The second major theme is another fundamental policy of all of Indian law that transcends the one field of Indian water rights—the policy of leaving Indians free of state control and state jurisdiction. That policy has particular and very important ramifications when applied to Indian water rights.

Contrary to popular belief, the law of Indian water rights did not begin in 1908 with the Supreme Court's decision in *Winters v. United States.* Its roots go back much farther than that. Its roots go back at least as far as 1832 when the Supreme Court decided *Worchester v. Georgia,* and even further back than that, to the United States Constitution itself, Article I, Section 8, Clause 3, the commerce clause, which defines a very particular kind of relationship in the federal system for Indians and Indian tribes.

Essentially, that role is for Indian tribes to be cut away from the states, to be separate and apart from the states. The language in the Constitution was inserted as a historical matter to overcome the ambiguities and uncertainties that had beset Indian policy under the rather confusing language in the Articles of Confederation. The idea of the Indian provision in the commerce clause was to make it clear that exclusive jurisdiction over Indians resided, perhaps not permanently and irrevocably, but at least in the first instance, with the Congress, with the federal government—and not with the states.

This fundamental predicate has very, very significant implications for Indian water rights. Because what it means is that Indian water rights are not governed by state law any more than Indians are subject to state taxes or Indian property is subject to state land use controls. The reason why the historic policy of leaving Indians free of state jurisdiction and state control is so important is emphasized in two recent Supreme Court decisions, construing deep-rooted federal policy, that basically leave water policy and water law up to the states. This makes for a rather consistent general policy for the federal government and the United States Congress to defer to state water laws.

The perspective that is represented by the *Winters* doctrine is a result of the federal courts' and particularly the United States Supreme Court's misreading of history. A misreading, because they failed to perceive that this area of western water law was a matter that Congress had entrusted to the states rather than to the federal government. In contrast, long before Congress began deferring to the states with regard to matters of western water law, the United States in the Constitution itself had become firmly set on a course of preserving exclusive jurisdiction over Indian matters, over all Indian matters, leaving no room for the states to govern Indian property or the rights of Indians.

So historic policy, has by and large survived intact, and remains intact at least from a legislative standpoint. Congress has not, with the single exception perhaps of the McCarran amendment, subjected Indian water rights to state control and state jurisdiction. Under the Constitution's commerce clause, that means that those matters are left for federal law exclusively.

Looked at against that backdrop, when the *Winters* case came to the Supreme Court, the question presented to the court was not so much whether state law or federal law would apply, but rather what the content of the federal law was. It was taken as a given, based on *Worchester v. Georgia* and the entire line of precedents that flows from *Worchester v. Georgia,* that state law does not apply to Indian water rights.

Essentially, the Supreme Court's decision in the *Winters* case, and followed up on in *Arizona v. California,* is that the content of the federal law of Indian water rights is shaped fundamentally by the purpose for which Indian reservations were established. Water is the lifeblood of the West, and the purpose of the Indian reservations—that is, the establishment of permanent homelands—cannot become a reality without a reservation of water.

This means that the two critical elements of the water right are the amount of the water that is reserved and the priority that attaches to that amount of water. The critical aspects of the Indian water right are, first, that the amount of water that is reserved, unlike other water rights in the West, has nothing to do with the amount of water that is put to use at any point in time, that is actually put to beneficial use. Rather, it depends on the amount of water that is necessary to fulfill the purposes of the reservation. This definition should include future purposes as well as present purposes—that is, at the time the adjudication takes place—and certainly not the amount of water that was put to use at the time the reservation was created.

The second aspect of the water right is the priority. Here again, the priority does not depend upon the time that the water is put to use, but rather goes back to the date on which the reservation was established. Since most reservations were established relatively early in the West's history, the priority of most Indian water rights is superior to those of most non-Indian rights.

While the broad outline of the *Winters* doctrine is clear, and has been since 1908, the specific contours of Indian water rights as a matter of law are at this time extremely uncertain. It is important, in trying to determine policies for the management of the resource, to bear in mind the legal uncertainties that beset the reserved water rights doctrine in the courts.

Before getting to that, though, I think it is important to keep one thing in mind: Most of the time when we talk about Indian water rights, we talk about federally reserved rights. That is the doctrine that is unique to Indian tribes in this country. But I urge you not to forget other potential sources of Indian rights that Indians may have or may share in common with others. There are, for example, Indian tribes that have claims to water rights that may be better than *Winters* doctrine rights under Spanish and Mexican law. Particularly, those rights of the pueblos in New Mexico, whose titles antedate the annexation of portions of the country to the United States, may trace back to Spanish and Mexican law.

Similarly, some Indian reservations may have been created out of lands that were formerly in private ownership. And while those lands were in private ownership, rights may have attached to them under state prior appropriation laws, and Indians may have claims as successors in interest to the prior owners.

Other reservations, particularly in western states that still recognize the riparian doctrine, may claim rights under state riparian law. And Indian tribes also claim rights on the basis of their aboriginal use and occupancy of lands, at least in those areas where current reservations are carved out of aboriginal territory. Thus, in particular cases and controversies, there may be other sources of water rights in addition to federally reserved rights under the *Winters* doctrine.

Focusing on the decisions of the United States Supreme Court, and not on lower court decisions, I have found in the ten or twelve years or so in which I have been litigating in this area that matters previously taken for granted have turned up in the Supreme Court, and the answers the Supreme Court has given in recent years were certainly not the answers that I would have predicted. The uncertainty and confusion, I think, that surround this whole area is best illustrated by two decisions of the Supreme Court, neither of them dealing expressly with Indian water rights, but dealing with other kinds of federally reserved rights, and they came only two years apart: the decisions in the pupfish case, *Cappaert v. United States,* and in the national forest case, *United States v. New Mexico.* Here we had the same nine justices of the Supreme Court, as I say, two years apart, writing opinions on the same or similar subjects that couldn't be more different from each other in terms of spirit and tone. The *Cappaert* decision was basically a resounding reaffirmation of the reserved water rights doctrine as applied to Devil's Hole National Monument, while the *United States v. New Mexico* decision was a severe cutback in reserved water rights law.

Indian people, of course, know about the unpredictability of the Supreme Court these days, as witnessed by the recent decision in the case of the *United States v. Montana,* which again severely restricted the scope of prior law governing both ownership of riverbeds and the tribes' sovereign authority over the lands, even non-Indian lands, within their reservations. So the first uncertainty is the uncertainty of our judicial system, particularly our present judicial system with the present Supreme Court.

There is, first of all, uncertainty concerning the measure of Indian water rights. The one criterion that the Supreme Court has applied has been "practicably irrigable acreage." However, even that measurable yardstick provides very little guidance, because how is it determined what acreage is practicably irrigable? The specific question is: What kinds of economic criteria, if any, inform the determination of practicably irrigable acreage? And to the extent that economic criteria are involved, to what extent are Indian water rights, or at least the quantity of Indian reserved water rights, simply a function of the economic times in which the suit happens to be litigated?

Other claims for water rights for other purposes are pending. These include claims to water for hunting and fishing to carry out the purposes of the reservation, for recreation purposes, for mineral development as well as mineral extraction, and for industrial development. All of these matters are ones that the Supreme Court has yet to speak on. In just the last two or three years, the lower courts have upheld water rights for hunting and fishing purposes.

The priority of the water right is also a question of some uncertainty. The principal uncertainty is whether the water right has a priority from time immemorial, an aboriginal priority, or whether it dates from the time of the reservation's formal establishment by treaty or statute or executive order. In many cases, the difference between an aboriginal water right and a water right dating from the establishment of the reservation will not be a significant, practical one, because the reservation's water right will be, in essence, first on the stream in either event. But in other cases it may make a significant difference.

Another uncertainty relates to the scope of the water right, and particularly which waters are encompassed within the water right. Certainly, any water right, to be effective and meaningful, has to extend to waters outside the boundaries of the reservation, just like any landowner's water right has to be enforced off his property. Other potential users have to be prevented from taking the water to which he claims a prior and paramount right. So the water rights extend off the reservation, but there are questions. For example, to what extent can a reservation claim a right to surface water to which it is not riparian?

One significant and often overlooked fact is that one of the reservations' adjudicated water rights in *Arizona v. California* was close by the Colorado River, but was not riparian to the river, suggesting that a source of water does not actually have to cross or bound a reservation in order for reserved water rights to attach to it.

A more significant question relates to the nature and existence of Indian water rights to ground water that underlies the reservation. This is an extremely difficult issue, particularly difficult when it is considered that the same ground water basin that underlies an Indian reservation in many instances also extends off the reservation and underlies lands of non-Indians. In this situation, you have jurisdiction exercised by at least two sovereign entities over the same source of water.

An additional question, which comes in under the rubric of the *Winters* doctrine, relates to water quality. To what extent do Indian water rights encompass not only waters of sufficient quantity to preserve the purpose of the reservation, but also of sufficient quality? This becomes an issue with regard to virtually all uses of water, particularly irrigation uses. When salinity levels increase, they can no longer be effectively utilized for certain crops, or at least the yields obtained by crops diminish as the quality of the water deteriorates. Water quality is also an extremely important issue in relation to water for fishery purposes.

In the recent decision of the district court in Phase II of *United States v. Washington*, the court, in holding that the treaty guaranteed and protected the fishing rights of the tribes in western Washington, which encompasses a right to environmental protection of the resource, relied on the *Winters* line of decisions for that part of its decision.

Other matters concern the finality of decrees. Once an Indian water right is quantified and established, to what extent can that decree later be reopened when it turns out, for example, that the amount of water that was predicted for future use is not sufficient to fulfill all the purposes of the reservation? Other issues relate to compacts; for example, what is the status of Indian water rights when the federal government or Congress approves a compact allocating sources of water from an interstate stream between the states in a manner that, if applied to Indians, would restrict the amount of water that could be used within, say, the Arizona portion of the Navajo Indian Reservation? That issue hasn't been addressed.

So far, all of the issues that I have talked about relate to tribes' rights as proprietors—the property right itself, the right to use the water. But in addition to that there is also the tribes' rights as sovereigns—not as proprietary owners of water, but having rights as sovereigns to regulate and control the use of water. And in this area, the uncertainties are even greater than they are in the proprietary area.

The major competitor, of course, for the tribes' sovereign control here, as elsewhere, is the state. The question is: Who allocates water within the boundaries of the reservation? What law governs? Is it tribal law? Is it state law? Is the water resource within the reservation subject to unitary control and management? Or is there a bifurcated authority, with Indian tribes' jurisdiction attaching to water uses by Indians on trust lands and state law attaching to water uses by non-Indians on non-trust lands, on fee lands?

A subsidiary issue has been one on which the courts have not spoken very clearly yet, and that is whether the McCarran amendment, in addition to subjecting Indian water rights to adjudication in state courts, might also subject Indian water rights to administration by state agencies.

This is the extremely uncertain legal climate that forms part of the necessary backdrop to policy and management issues.

FROM THE FLOOR: I believe it is necesssary for somebody to define what quantification is. I think there may be many people, not only Indians but other people, who do not realize what you are talking about when you speak about quantification.

MR. PELCYGER: Well, quantification, as applied to Indian water rights, principally means determining the amount of water that is required to fulfill the purpose or purposes of the reservation. Instead of simply a broad statement that Indian tribes have a water right for sufficient water to carry out the purposes of the reservation, quantification entails determining the amounts of that water. It involves determining, for example, how much acreage is irrigable and how much water it would take to irrigate that acreage. Quantification also means determining how many people not only live on the reservation today, but also how many people might be living on the reservation in the year 2050 and how much water would be necessary to support them. It includes determining how much water is required to maintain or preserve, or in some instances to restore, traditional hunting and fishing grounds where tribes have hunting and fishing rights or other means of traditional subsistence. And quantification can entail the determination of how much water may be required to extract and develop coal, uranium, copper, or other minerals on the reservation. It is basically putting a number next to the uses to which the reservation's water would be put.

The danger or problem with that is that, because of the nature of Indian water rights, the water rights are quantified not with reference to present or past uses, but to future uses. And in determining how much acreage is going to be irrigable in the year 2050, or how much copper or coal there is and how much water is going to be necessary to extract and develop them, quantification entails risk. We are dealing with future projections; that is always a hazard.

One of the unanswered questions in the area of Indian water rights is the extent to which a quantification by a court can be subsequently modified.

I would just briefly add two things. First of all, there is some precedent for change. The case of *Cappaert v. United States,* dealing not with Indians but with the amount of water required for the survival of the pupfish in Devil's Hole National Monument in Nevada, was tried and went to the Supreme Court. The original district court's injunction limiting the amount of pumping by non-Indians adjacent to the monument was affirmed by the Supreme Court. After the case went to the Supreme Court, the government went back to a district court and claimed that additional biological evidence had been uncovered while the case was winding its way tortuously through the courts, and asked the court to modify the injunction to provide more water for the pupfish based on this new biological information. And the court did modify its previous injunction to provide more water for the pupfish.

The second example is one that many of you are familiar with. The United States and the five Indian tribes that were adjudicated water rights in *Arizona v. California* are now back before the Supreme Court seeking water rights over and above those which were originally quantified in 1963, on two different theories. One theory is that some boundary adjustments or boundary determinations were made and that additional water rights are required to sustain the practicably irrigable additional lands that were not considered to be within the reservation at the time of the original adjudication. The other, and perhaps more significant, claim is that the original adjudication of practicably irrigable acreage omitted certain lands that were then and are now clearly practicably irrigable, and that the decree should be modified to provide additional water rights for those lands.

That matter should be heard before the Supreme Court before the end of the current term so we should soon have an answer on how flexible decrees of that nature might be.

Fortunately, in the Supreme Court's final decree in *Arizona v. California* there is a specific provision, common to decrees in the West, that provides for subsequent modifications. The United States and the tribes are invoking that article of the original decree in seeking additional water for those purposes.

MS. CLAUDEEN BATES ARTHUR

Field Solicitor, Office of the Solicitor,
U.S. Department of the Interior
Window Rock, Arizona

MS. ARTHUR: I have been asked to speak about the general role of the United States in Indian water litigation, Indian water matters.

The United States is generally joined in water litigation both as the United States, which includes the Interior Department and the Department of Agriculture, and includes many things besides Indian water claims. The issues in all of these cases concern the determination of the quantity and the priority dates of water rights held by the United States government for itself in national forests, national parks, wildlife refuges, military reserves, and other federal lands. And in connection with these, most times the water rights are held in trust by the United States for Indian reservations. So an initial and major problem that the United States faces in dealing with water issues is simply coordinating and resolving how to deal with all of these various and many times conflicting interests that the United States holds. That includes coordination with the Bureau of Indian Affairs, the Justice Department, the Solicitor's Offices for both the Department of the Interior, and for the Department of Agriculture, and pulling together the resources of the United States to present to a court the United States' point of view, when many times the United States' point of view is different for different departments, different for different agencies.

If there is a general stream adjudication on a particular stream, you might have a field office in Window Rock, Arizona, involved for the Navajos. You might have a field office in Phoenix involved for the Hopi. You might have a Bureau of Indian Affairs office in Window Rock and a Bureau of Indian Affairs office in Phoenix involved. You have national forest lands that have a different solicitor in the Department of Agriculture. And that is a major problem for Indian tribes in dealing with the United States, because the United States is not solely looking out for the interests of Indian tribes in water litigation. They also are sued in their own behalf for all of these other interests.

In order to deal specifically with Indian issues when all of these various interests come up, the federal government is put in the position of saying, "Can we best serve the Indian tribes by representing them ourselves?" In a limited number of cases, the United States has decided that it can best serve Indian interests by providing them with the financial backing to present their own cases. But a major problem in the present climate is that the United States is cutting back on federal monies and federal programs, and it is generally presumed to be costly and sometimes wasteful to litigate and pay for two different sets of expenses—expenses of the tribe to represent itself and expenses of the federal government if it has a different point of view in the litigation. I believe that it is important for tribes to realize that, although they would like to think that their water cases and their water claims are not based on appropriations from Congress, the reality of the situation is that unless tribes have resources of their own, they are going to have to depend on federal appropriations that, as we know, are becoming less and less available. And that is a reality, a hard reality.

If tribes are going to have federal dollars for their water litigation over which they have control, they must also recognize not only the limited dollars, but also a limitation in the structure and setup of federal programs. The United States Interior Department does not have separate appropriations for defending water litigation or any litigation on behalf of tribes. And, therefore, we use program money. The soil scientist, the range technologist, the hydrologist, the engineers that the Bureau of Indian Affairs hires for program activities, for range management, for irrigation projects—those folks are required many times to stop their program activities to provide evidence and to collect evidence for a water litigation case. And many times we find that the Bureau of Indian Affairs personnel simply do not have the expertise necessary to do the data collecting and the evidence gathering. Then what is required, on many occasions, and the federal government has done this throughout, is the hiring of additional people on contract who have the expertise that is recognized in their field.

A major problem that I see developing, and that I think is important for tribes to recognize, is that if they have a right under Public Law 93-638 to contract program activities, to carry on programs, then where in the federal budget system will there be money to carry on litigation? The programs are not set up for litigation support, but those are the people that we use.

Then another problem I see generally, and overall with other people I speak with who are dealing with federal litigation in water areas, is that when the federal government or the tribes hire consultants on a contract basis, the writing of those contracts in a manner to develop exactly what it is you want has not been finely tuned. And many times, both the tribes and the federal government find themselves with very expensive, voluminous documents and reports that do not provide the evidence that they want to support the litigation. I think that is a matter of a learning process. I think it is important for the tribes to realize that as federal dollars get fewer and fewer, the contracts they have with their consultants must be written more tightly, so that they get exactly what it is they want and don't have to go back and do a second round.

Talking about program activities that are needed to support litigation, I thought maybe it might be of interest to go through the process that those of us involved in these sorts of cases use to develop the data and the evidence. What is it we are getting at? What is it that we want to get? How many people does that take? What kinds of things will they be doing for us?

The basic bottom line is land and soils information. We generally begin with what is called an appraisal level to do irrigable lands classifications. That takes soil scientists going out there and walking over and looking at every acre of land and digging little holes and putting bits of soil in little bags and writing dates and times and places and sending that information off to a lab that runs chemical tests. That takes a lot of people. That takes a laboratory. That takes soil people. That takes mapping people. When they are doing that sort of thing, those people are not running your land management programs. They are out there putting soil in little bags and running the tests on the soil, rather than running tests on the milk products that might be coming in to the schools.

The other large area is to match up water availability with the soil. That requires a surface water supply investigation to determine the location of the water that runs on the surface of the land. In recent times, that has also required ground water supply investigation, and a determination of the relationship of two ground water supplies to each other. A large area that I have found very few people know anything at all about is the hydrologic relationship between surface and ground water.

If you are taking water and pumping 30 miles down, how does that affect your stream flow in the river 30 miles away? And do you want to have a project pumping water 30 miles down where there is no surface water, if that, in fact, affects your stream flow? Very few experts have information in this area. Just in the last few months, the United States has gone to the United States Geological Survey to assist on water cases. Those of you who know anything about the federal government know that the USGS has prided itself on being very neutral and in past years has not been of assistance to the federal government in its water cases. We hope for that to change. This again is the result of a need to use the resources that we have rather than hire outside consultants, because of the monetary situation.

Once we look at the soils, once we look at the hydrology and say that these soils are good, that there is water to put on this land, then we are in the position of looking at the engineering feasibility of these lands. In doing that, we have focused on agricultural uses, looking at agricultural practices, existing irrigation, and the history of irrigation on reservations. We hire engineers to do preliminary design work for irrigation and drainage systems. In recent times, the drainage of lands has become an important factor that we haven't looked at as extensively as before. We also then look at dam and reservoir sites and hire engineers for that particular purpose.

To date, the position of the United States has been that Indian tribes are entitled to nonagricultural water claims. Those claims are being studied, and we intend to go forward with them, at least unless we hear otherwise.

Finally, an issue that tribes are very concerned about is the economic consideration. The United States does take a position that economics are a consideration for presenting water projects. However, I do not believe that it is the position of the United States that economics are the only consideration.

Once this is all put together, we hire historians to do a history of the tribe to determine the reason for setting aside the reservation, in order to identify the purposes of the reservation, whether they are actually stated or implied. Then we work into all of this data and information a legal determination of the reservation purposes, the priority date, and the theories of the case.

I believe I was asked to comment on what I think is important for tribes to realize. From a federal perspective, what I can say to tribal people is that this sort of litigation takes a great deal of money. Yet, the financial resources available to the United States and to tribes are simply going to be fewer and fewer. So it becomes important to ask: What do the tribes really want? And if they really want this water, are they willing to put their own resources on the line? Because the federal resources are becoming meager. What is it that you want? And what are you willing to put on the line for the water?

MR. RUSSELL JIM

President, Affiliated Tribes of Northwest Indians
Council Member, Yakima Indian Nation
Toppenish, Washington

MR. RUSSELL JIM: Good morning, ladies and gentlemen. My name is Russell Jim. By virtue of being the President of the Affiliated Tribes of Northwest Indians and the Area Vice President of the National Congress of American Indians, I was asked to be here, to perhaps not reaffirm and reiterate much of history, which you have already heard and seen, but to give you a layman's point of view and, from a cultural perspective, to tell you what the water means to us.

There were 12 million indigenous people that were here when the first transients landed on their destination, which was no fault of their own, except that they were here. Coupled with the manifest destiny, these transients have been prevailing upon not only this country back then but now, specifically in and around the issue of water. The key to this whole thing, I believe, is the administration and control of the water, for example, the attempts by the National Water Resources Council to nationalize Indian water. It deals also with the economics and benefit-cost ratios of water.

All these things are tied together in relation to the control and administration of water, a very important resource that nothing can live without. The water, I believe, is a mineral. We have mineral rights. All of us have mineral rights. But I think, more importantly, we have a right to life. Most importantly, I have a right to my way of life, a cultural way, that the Creator has seen fit to put me on this earth to live in this manner.

I know many of you perhaps don't want to hear the philosophies that have always prevailed in Indian country. But Indians are always great philosophers. We now live in this world backed by the laws created on this earth. The laws have prevailed upon us. The *Winters* doctrine, 1908. But if not the *Winters* doctrine, then what? We would have been dependent upon something else other than the *Winters* doctrine if it wasn't the *Winters* doctrine, per se.

It relates also to the issue of water and fish. Fifty percent of the fish have now been given to the Indians in the Northwest and 50 percent to the State of Washington. But as was eloquently put by a member of our Fish Committee, Mr. Boldt gave away 50 percent of our fish.

A lot of misunderstandings have prevailed in this country, and these have been put upon the indigenous people that are in the way. Perhaps one day they will go away. I do not plan to go away. I do not plan to be remembered only in history. I abhor the picture of the "End of the Trail" Indian. I think that should be stricken from history books.

To be as brief as possible, there are problems facing this whole country not only as to the quantity but the quality of water. This water I tasted here is not the best water in the world. But it is hard also for people who live right here in this area that drink this water to understand the concept of clear cut and blacktop, and that there is clear, cool, good tasting water in many parts of the country left, and that must be preserved.

When I say the key to this whole thing is administration and control, I believe that it is the intent not only of the federal government but of the state government to gain control of administration of that water. I know of projects in Indian country that have a very good benefit-cost ratio, but because they do not have—and when I say "they" I mean the Corps of Engineers, Bureau of Reclamation, Tennessee Valley Authority, Department of Housing and Urban Development, the federal government, the National Resources Water Council—administration and control of all Indian water, those Indian projects will never be built. When they gain control of administration of the Indian country water, those projects will be built tomorrow. So I would like to have had the water policy being brought by the Assistant Secretary for Indian Affairs, Mr. Smith, a couple of days ago so that we wouldn't have to re-kneejerk it here. But I guess that's the way things work.

I am very impressed with the turnout of this crowd and appreciate very much the opportunity to address this crowd. I hope I can have some answers for any questions you would direct toward me. I hope that what comes out of this conference is a fierceness. The fierceness of attorneys, the fierceness of the Indian people to protect that water, to protect their way of life. When I feel low, I always remember the story a friend told me. He says, "Hey, these are transients. They devised a way to come across the Great Water. One day they will devise a way to travel through other worlds. But you will still be here. You have been here since time immemorial. You will be here for thousands and thousands of years to come. But, in the meantime, until they devise this sophisticated means of travel, as your ancestors have taught you, be a gracious host." Develop that space shuttle!

Excuse my facetiousness. That seems to be the point sometimes you get to. You get very discouraged. You can get very down.

In my country, the almighty apple prevails. There is constant economic development and expansion. The almighty apple hangs across the river from us, across the way, contributes to the economy of the entire community.

The fish below the one diversion dam go belly-up because of no water. That only contributes to the economy, only to the culture of a people. Again, we are back to this thing, manifest destiny.

MR. NED ANDERSON

Chairman, San Carlos Apache Tribe
San Carlos, Arizona

MR. ANDERSON: We are talking about water and the Indian future today, a very timely subject. It has been said time after time that without water Indian tribes have no future in the positive sense. They face cultural and political extinction.

Non-Indian private lands in Arizona are about 12 percent of the total land base of the state. That land is largely developed, owing to the Bureau of Reclamation and huge federal subsidies. In Arizona, Indian tribes own over one-third of the state, including headwaters and watersheds of all the major sources of water. Indian lands in Arizona are largely undeveloped. As a result, we have a 50 percent to 65 percent unemployment rate on Indian reservations.

As we move toward self-sufficiency, we pose a threat to those who presently have the wealth. The Salt River Project, our primary foe, has an ad on the TV that says, "In Arizona, water is more precious than gold, oil, or diamonds." Well, in Arizona, when it comes to water, they practice the Golden Rule: "The guy with the gold rules."

Thus, they intend to keep it. Neither the state nor the Salt River Project approaches Indian water rights morally or in good faith. They would rather see no water being used to any reasonable extent on Indian reservations. I would like to give you three examples. I think it will give you an indication as to the type of people that we deal with insofar as our water rights fights are concerned.

My reservation is composed of approximately 2 million acres of land. There are 8,000 tribal members, the San Carlos Apaches, of which I am Tribal Chairman. We are located in east-central Arizona, approximately 120 miles from Phoenix and 120 miles from Tucson. Gila River traverses this reservation on the southern portion of the reservation. The river is temporarily stopped at Coolidge Dam, a dam located within the reservation. It eventually heads toward Phoenix.

The Black River borders the reservation on the north side, a river that is shared by the White Mountain Apache Tribe and the San Carlos Apache Tribe.

So far as Gila River is concerned, our foes contend that the San Carlos Apache Tribe is entitled to no more than 6,000 acre-feet of water for 1,000 irrigable acres. How will 8,000 people survive on a mere portion of water they say we are entitled to?

As far as Salt River is concerned, they are saying that the Kent decree precludes us from any entitlement at all. To them, the Kent decree says that, because we were not represented when it was being heard (nor did we represent ourselves because we didn't know about that), the Kent decree dealt with water rights below the Granite Reef Dam. The closest that we are to Granite Reef is 130 miles, but above the dam. We believe that the Gila River decree is fraudulent because the United States government, our so-called trustee, stipulated away our water rights.

According to our foes, the Kent decree places a legal obstacle before us known as *res judicata*. In other words, the case is closed; you were not there either by yourselves or by representation.

We say that for *res judicata* to apply all the parties had to have been before the court. And that was not the case.

We also claim, among other things, that the State Territorial Court, the court handing down the decree, had no subject matter jurisdiction—in this case, the water rights.

I believe it was Dean Trelease who suggested that there may still be room for compromise. Well, I hope it works for you, because it didn't for us in Arizona.

In 1978, we began negotiating with the various parties, including the State of Arizona and the Salt River Project. Before we even started discussing the merits of the situation, we agreed on certain parameters. One of those was that before a party would file process the other party should know about that first. They did not stick with that agreement. They mailed the process on a Friday, and we, the Indian tribes, received the process on Monday, unexpectedly. We asked them, "What about the agreement?"

"Well, a mistake was made, but we won't do it next time."

We had no choice but to respond, for if we hadn't, we would have been in default. The State of Arizona and other parties were using a code that had not been changed in at least sixty years. It was the water code. Given this, in our response we pointed out the flaws and we indicated, among other things, that the whole thing was unconstitutional.

Around about this same time, the Arizona Academy scheduled a town meeting on Indian water and Arizona's future at Rio Rico, about 70 miles south of Tucson. Tucson is roughly two hours' drive from Phoenix. Many of these Arizona Academy members were also members of the Arizona legislature. The day when the Indian water rights was going to be discussed these same members also scheduled a hearing regarding the amendments that they wanted to make to this water code—because of the flaws that we pointed out—in Phoenix.

We asked that they reschedule the Phoenix meeting because we had to be over at this town hall. On the same day, they also scheduled a hearing on San Pedro River, which is on the southern tip of our reservation, over at Douglas, many miles away.

This water is claimed by us, the San Carlos Apaches, and the Gila River Tribe. There was no way we could be at the hearing in Phoenix or at the hearing in Douglas. So we opted for the town hall hearing. They went ahead and had those other hearings.

Based on the flaws we pointed out, the Arizona state legislature ramrodded the amendments to the code through in record time—nine days from the time it was introduced to the time the Governor of the State of Arizona signed the amendments.

Among other things, we claimed that isolating Indian people was in the nature of a classic bill of attainder, targeted at confiscating the property of a specific people and singling them out for a legislative harassment.

Earlier you heard mention made of the Central Arizona Project. You know where that aqueduct is going to go and where it will end: supposedly Tucson by way of Phoenix. I believe it was in 1976 when Secretary of Interior Kleppe apportioned water from the Central Arizona Project to various parties. Some of the tribes were left out of the apportionment. We, the San Carlos Apache Tribe, were left out as far as the apportionment went, as well as some of the other tribes. We were left out despite the fact that the history of the Central Arizona Project legislation specifically mentioned us. When Andrus was Secretary of the Interior, he believed in equitable apportionment. Andrus used the tribal homeland concept to allocate water to several tribes, including the San Carlos Apache Tribe. We were given 12,700 acre-feet.

It is not ours yet, though. As soon as Andrus' reapportionment was announced, Governor Bruce Babbitt of the State of Arizona filed a lawsuit, the very same day. Not too long ago we had a meeting sponsored by the Inter-Tribal Council of Arizona, of which I am also president. We met with Governor Babbitt on that day. The first question we had for him was, "When are you going to drop the lawsuit regarding CAP?" He said he had already taken the steps that would eventually end the lawsuit.

The very same day, we met with Secretary Watt. We also posed the same question to him. He said, when it came to whether the contracts that were signed regarding CAP with the ten tribes were valid, and I quote him, "I am a law and order man." I understand it is now within his hands to drop the lawsuit, thereby validating the contracts. We shall see.

I guess you can see from what I have said so far that we have not necessarily dealt with saints as far as our water rights are concerned. And is it any wonder that some of us who are law trained are now disenchanted with the practice of law? No matter what we were promised, they are changing the rules. We face ever-increasing opposition to water use. There are continuous obstacles to our economic development. It begins with quantification. The Salt River Project and State of Arizona want to use the date of the formation of reservations for a priority date. They completely disregard the fact that we have lived on our homelands for thousands and thousands of years. That was the time we walked backwards into this continent.

They say that if we have water rights they are only *Winters* rights and not aboriginal rights or protected by Spanish or Mexican law. That is convenient but incorrect. The *Winters* case, you will remember, recognized that the reservation and water in aboriginal lands were not grants from the United States, but rather tribes were reserving to themselves all except that which was granted to the United States.

They next moved to a measure of quantification. They said that the only measure is practicably irrigable acreage. That was defined in *Arizona v. California*, because the reservations involved in that case were nearly all irrigable. It was fine there for present and apparently future needs. However, on many reservations the land is not widely irrigable. They have some irrigable lands, some mineral lands, some forests, some fisheries, some grazing lands, some dams and power sites.

The measure insisted upon by the Salt River Project and the State is "practicably irrigable acreage." We contend that that was not intended in *Winters* or *Arizona v. California*. *Winters* anticipated water to develop the arts of civilization. So you can see they want to use limiting standards for measuring irrigability. Their aim is to exclude much, if not all, of Indian lands.

We face problems when it comes to actual use. The tribes of Arizona intend to develop water on a concept that assures that our reservations are permanent tribal homelands in the modern sense of that term. In other words, we want to develop vertically integrated economies so as to provide a reasonable livelihood for our people. The primary impediment to that development is money—development capital. We do not want to use the real estate as collateral for loans. We lost 100 million acres in thirty-eight years that way under the General Allotment Act. We have been told by the State of Arizona and Salt River Project that we cannot change our use of water. If we get 6 acre-feet to irrigate 1 acre, we cannot irrigate 2 acres with 3 acre-feet using improved technology. We do not believe that is what *Winters* or *Arizona v. California* intended. In fact, *Arizona v. California* said, and I quote, "Once the quantity is determined, the water can be used for any purpose." If this is not the case, the future portion of the term "water for present and future use" becomes meaningless.

I believe we, the Indian people, have something that we can resort to despite what we face, not only with water rights but also with other things. If you will look at our history you will see that there have been no major holocausts on any of the Indian reservations. You hear about people being wiped out by the thousands because of earthquakes, flooding, and the like. You do not see that on Indian reservations. Why? Because we have a belief that there is a Supreme Being who has seen us through thus far and He will continue to see us through. There is native religion as well as modern religion. Remember that. Even though our foe may be wealthy and a giant, we still have the Supreme Being on our side.

Luncheon Address

MR. REUBEN SNAKE

Vice Chairman, Winnebago Tribe
Winnebago, Nebraska

MR. SNAKE: Ladies and gentlemen, I want to greet you all with good feelings at this time. I want to thank my friend Richard [Trudell] for inviting me over here to share a few of my thoughts with you and to take some small part in this conference.

The way my relatives and I back home try to do things is that we try to think about the traditional things. We Indian people, we have a way of life, we have a culture, and we have values that are taught to us. One of my grandfathers was talking to me about this creation, and what he was telling me is that there are two things that the Indian people really respect in relation to this creation. They know that these things are very sacred. He said they came from the same place, these two gifts that we have. He said one of them is fire and the other is water. On this creation that we walk, my grandfather was saying we cannot live without these two things. We cannot live without the fire and the water.

He told me that from time to time you should take a little time out, stop in your everyday life, and think about these things here and try to say something to the Great Spirit in thanksgiving for these gifts that keep us going. Without the fire from the sun, we wouldn't last too long here. Without this water every day, we wouldn't last very long either.

When you come in here and sit down, don't pick up that water glass and drink it right now. Get up some morning before sunrise and say something about this creation. Then try to go from sunrise to sunset without taking a drink of water. Then you might gain a little respect for this creation. These are the kinds of things Indian people think about.

As another one of my elders was telling me, he said, "Nephew, you go down and talk to a lot of people. You try to express your concern for this life that we have." And he said, "And I'm going to tell you," he said, "what's happening right about now in this land of ours." He was saying that one time, toward the spring of the year, the ice in the river was breaking up and the ice was moving downstream. There was an eagle flying over the land. The winter had been very hard and difficult. All of the living creatures were having a hard time surviving. This eagle was that way. This eagle had gone for a long time without nourishment, without anything to eat. So he was looking for something to eat. Lo and behold, as he flew over the river and the ice was moving down the river, he saw a dead rabbit lying on a cake of ice that was moving down the river.

So then this eagle flew down and landed on that cake of ice and began to feed on this dead rabbit. As the cake of ice was moving down the river, the water was lapping over this cake of ice and it was flowing over the eagle's talons as he was sitting on the ice, feeding on this rabbit.

The eagle didn't pay attention to that, because he was hungry and was gorging himself. All of a sudden, way up in the distance, this eagle could hear a sound. Still, he didn't pay attention. He just keep feeding. Pretty soon, the sound got louder and louder. All of a sudden, the eagle raised his head and he looked downstream and saw the white water, the rapids. There was a waterfall there. He knew he was in danger. He tried to lift himself off of that ice, but he had frozen to it. He went over into the rapids and over the waterfall. That was his end.

This is what my uncle told me. He said that this is the way it is in this land of ours today, this land that the Great Spirit gave to us. A lot of people came over here. They came over here into this part of the creation because they were not happy. They were persecuted and they were oppressed. They wanted to be free. So, somehow or other, they learned about this place where the Great Spirit had made everything bountiful.

They came over here, very pitiful people. They began to take all the things that were here. They made use of them. Pretty soon, instead of just being satisfied with the daily use of what they needed, they began to horde it up and began to become greedy and avaricious. Pretty soon it got to the point where they began to enjoy things so much that they just kept on creating things and taking things out of Grandmother Earth just for their earthly pleasures, not for spiritual improvement, not to lift themselves up as a race and as human beings. They just enjoyed the physical part of it. He said, "They're doing that right now, still, today."

"That is why it is like this way, nephew," he was saying to me. "That is why the Indian has a hard time enjoying this creation today the way that he did for so long. Because these people are leading us in that direction. We are on that river and we're heading for that waterfall."

"They hear the roaring noise now," he said. "They are hearing the roaring noise. They know that something very serious is going to happen. Now they are beginning to look around, and they are beginning to try to do something. But it might be too late, nephew," is what my elderly uncle told me. He said, "It might be too late." He said, "What we have to do is we have to educate them. We have to educate them on how to live in harmony with this creation, to live in harmony and not to subjugate it, as they have been doing."

That is my message here. There are a lot of you in this room that are concerned about the rights of Indians. But what we need to be concerned with is the survival of the human race. That is what the red man has to do for his fellow man, to reeducate him on how to live in harmony with this creation.

That is what I want to say to you good people. I appreciate all of you legally trained people, all of you who have studied the laws, the laws of man that have been created to govern ourselves.

What little I know about social structure is that we need order. And we have to make laws that we can all live by. But there are other laws above and beyond the laws that we make. There are the natural laws that the Creator made so that this creation of his could function. And as long as we are contradicting those natural laws, we are going to be in the situation we are in today.

We have to make some mental adjustments. We have to reorder and reorganize our thinking. Like I was saying, the red man doesn't believe that he is a self-made man. He understands that Somebody made him. He tries to respect that "Somebody." He tries to live according to the natural order of things.

Through that, many of us have come together to deliberate and to listen to all the learned minds that are in this room right now. So I am sitting in this room trying to listen to some of this, too, and trying to think about how it is going to help me and my people, where I come from. Because we are involved in some of this white man's litigation that affects the future existence of my people.

We have power companies back home that are trying to take our land. We have some power companies that are trying to take our land to erect these gigantic towers, these pylons that run the electric lines across our reservation. Right upriver from our reservation there are a series of power companies. They are playing a part in this. They want our land to build these power lines so they can sell electricity back and forth across the country.

These same power companies have been encouraging the United States Army Corps of Engineers to take some more of our land on the east side of our reservation, on the east banks of the Missouri River. They have been encouraging the Corps of Engineers to build gigantic water recreational complexes on some of the Oxbows that were left when the Corps of Engineers changed the channel of the Missouri River. They want to have the Corps of Engineers build this complex so that they can run their warm waters into these Oxbow lakes and have a cooling system. They have another plan in mind to build another power plant downstream from the reservation. They could run that water through the lakes and cool it off and reuse it down on the other end before they pump it back into the Missouri. Because the Corps of Engineers forget that Mother Nature is built a certain way, when they rechanneled the Missouri, they narrowed the flow of the water and, therefore, the bottom of the river is scarring out. It is an expensive proposition to pump water up out of the river. It is better to run it through these Oxbow lakes, they say.

Every time the Corps of Engineers thinks of something, they create another problem for us Indians. These are the kinds of things going on back home in relation to water.

We have a desire to be the way we used to be. Before anybody came into our lives, we lived totally self-reliantly. We were able to take care of ourselves. We didn't ask any other tribal people or any other race of man to look after us. Here today it's not like that. With all of these federal programs being cut, there are a lot of people unemployed on my reservation. We realize how dependent we are upon the handouts from our white brothers.

We are trying to rebuild ourselves into a certain system where we can take care of ourselves. That is going to require the use of this sacred gift, water, to make things grow so we can take care of ourselves. That is why I always think about these things.

The people that I walk around with in my everyday life, that's what we do all the time. We don't do that now and then. We do it all the time. We keep our mind in that direction so that we can influence other people's minds in that direction. That way, maybe we can all live on this Grandmother Earth in peace and harmony.

That's about what I wanted to say to you, my friends and relatives. May the Great Spirit be with us all.

BALANCING COMPETING INTERESTS

Moderator's Preface

A fact of life in the western United States is the premium placed upon water supplies and the fierce competition for those excessively appropriated supplies by a catalogue of water users. The list includes agriculture, mining industries, municipalities, Indian tribes, and a host of other users. Efforts to balance the various interests to water use in the West necessarily involves accommodations, concessions, and shifts in political power. Cultures and lifestyles hinge upon the future distribution of water wealth in the West. Are Indian cultures and lifestyles destined for destruction because of the water struggles in the West?

Certainly, Indian tribes possess water rights. Present and future possession of water is another issue. The entitlement of Indian tribes to reserved water rights has been well established by the United States Supreme Court in *Winters v. United States* and subsequent case law. However, entitlement is not enough to assure present and future water use for Indian tribes. Paper water rights do not convert to "wet" water upon command. The water resources to which many Indian tribes have legitimate reserved claims have been over appropriated through state regulating schemes. Although Indian tribes may possess senior claims, the intense competition among water users creates obvious resistance to efforts to settle conflicting water claims of the West.

"Balancing competing interests" is an illusory notion when applied to western water conflicts. Before balances can be effectively struck there must be understanding and appreciation between competing interests. Once there is understanding, resolution of conflicting issues has an opportunity to occur. In the past, complex, lengthy litigation has been the vehicle for resolving water conflicts of the West. Additionally, legislation has been employed to settle western water claims.

The results of litigation and legislation fall far short of any semblance of balancing competing interests. Obviously, litigation is a win/lose proposition and legislation is usually the product of particular interest groups.

In recent years, negotiated settlements have been used as an alternative to litigation and legislation. The caution flag that must be raised concerning this method points to bargaining power and preparation. It sounds simple enough but comprehensive planning for water negotiation involves knowledge and skills which are developed through special education and experience.

The panel presentation "Balancing Competing Interests" explores several perspectives of competing water interests. The panelists make no effort to engage in speculation of "balancing." The theme appears to be understanding competing interests.

JOSEPH A. MYERS
Associate Director
American Indian Lawyer Training Program
Oakland, California

MR. GARY D. WEATHERFORD

Center for Natural Resource Studies
John Muir Institute, Inc.
Berkeley, California

MR. WEATHERFORD: I would like to deliberately understate the issue of water competition, because I think often it is said that it is highly complex and even mystical. I would like to suggest that it can be reduced by sacrificing some of the finer texture to a few themes and issues. I would like to touch very generally upon the objectives, context, values, competitors, and choices involved in western water competition.

First of all, with respect to objectives, I think we have to ask: What is the social objective of the intense water competition in the West? Is it to balance the varying interests, as the title for our panel would suggest? Is it to reduce current conflict and prevent future conflict wherever it arises? Is it to maximize compromise and accommodation?

There really is no universal answer to this question, obviously. On an individual interest group or tribal level, the answer depends on who you are, what you have at stake, what you have by way of resources, and what you desire. When I say "desire," I am assuming that personal desires can include notions of social good.

Whether an outcome is balanced or not really depends on our perception of whether we have gained or lost in the process. In a broad social sense, the word "balance" implies the avoidance of both bloodshed and unilateral action—that is, a satisfaction of one's needs sufficient to avoid instability in the established order. That is a very minimal definition, obviously. This explains why the word "balance" has such positive trappings. It has the status quo and incremental change going for it.

Because it is viewed as such a good thing, it is used indiscriminately by people to characterize either what they desire or what they have achieved. A more apt characterization of the social objective of all this water competition might really be mitigating—hopefully democratically—competing interests.

What about the context? In what settings, under what circumstances is this competition occurring? It is happening most dramatically, of course, where water is approaching or has reached a condition of full appropriation—that is, a condition where water rights and claims exhaust reliable supplies. If you look at a map of the relative surface water depletion, you can see that in parts of Nevada, southern California, New Mexico, Utah, and Texas, the percentage of local subbasin water supply depleted actually exceeds 100. In other parts of California, Arizona, Utah, New Mexico, and Texas, as well as Colorado, Wyoming, and Nebraska, the percentage ranges from 76 to 100 percent for depletion.

In contrast, Alaska and all the states east of the Mississippi deplete between zero to 25 percent of their surface water supply. Significant ground water overdrafting is occurring in many areas of the West. And pollution problems, principally salinity, plague several areas of the West, particularly the Colorado River Basin.

The major consumer of water in the United States, to fill out the context further, particularly in the West, is irrigated agriculture. Approximately 85 percent of the water consumption is for irrigated agriculture in the West. The remaining 15 percent is divided between the other uses, consumptive uses: domestic, municipal, and industrial.

The seventeen western states account for 90 percent of the country's irrigated acreage, which totals over 40 million acres. About 68 percent of the ground water withdrawn in the country is for irrigated agriculture. So much of the competition to acquire existing water rights is centering on water now used for agriculture. The water that is not appropriated and consumed serves many social ends as well: fish and wildlife, hydroelectric generation, navigation, and recreation. Roughly 51 to 75 percent of the total stream flow in most of the subbasins of the West are estimated to be needed for aquatic life and outdoor recreation.

The competition for water, however important, is really occurring in the context of much larger forces and themes. I would number the following four: scarcity, sovereignty, stability, and survival. Water in the western United States, if not everywhere, cannot be extricated from these larger issues. Water, of course, is a valued good. It is wealth. Its possession—either consumption or in-stream preservation—adds wealth, generates wealth. Lack of possession limits wealth, and dispossession reduces wealth. There is a marked disparity in the economic conditions of people's working, living, and investing in the West. The allocation of water alters the comparative wealth or poverty of these people. In short, the growing relative scarcity of water is occurring against the backdrop of the relative scarcity of other indicators of wealth: employment, standards of living, land and mineral holdings, et cetera.

Water is also allocated within the ambit of sovereignty—the relative powers of government—federal, tribal, state, and local. The issue is: Which governments and branches of governments have the final say over the allocation and reallocation, the control and management, of natural resources, as well as over the standards for individual and corporate behavior and freedom with respect to those resources? The relative power of these various governments to influence or control water allocation and use is but a facet of larger sets of relationships and power positions of these governments. The present effort to shift more water development responsibility from federal to state government, for example, is part of what has been characterized as the larger movement to decentralize the nation. The fact that water is such a potent indicator of wealth makes it a potent subject and symbol of political power. Part of what is being fought out, then, with respect to water is really something much larger, namely, who controls.

Another overarching factor is stability: social, economic, political, and cultural. The dependency of our economic system and national defense on control of energy fuels has become painfully obvious in the last eight years. Energy development has become the most dynamic variable, other than climate, in the water management picture. Fossil fuel energy independence has become a fleeting goal, but greater domestic development of those fuels is widely viewed as a national priority of the highest order. Such development is perceived as critical to our stability as a nation. Water, in turn, is a necessary ingredient of that development. A good share of the syn-fuel resources is in the western United States and on Indian reservations.

Survival is a force that is difficult to discuss without appearing melodramatic. It is the raw end of the stability I just mentioned. There are struggles for survival going on quite apart from the quest for energy independence and national security. Anglo, Hispanic, and Indian interests are obviously involved here with rural cultures and lifestyles, struggles in which the mental and physical health of individuals, families, tribes, and communities are at stake. The availability of land, water, and air is indispensible to these rural cultures. To this lay mind, the thrust of social settlement and economic development in the intermountain western United States seems to be largely monocultural, overwhelming rural subcultures. Greater or less access to water is a condition that cannot be divorced from the active struggle for cultural survival, engaging many people in the region.

Now, I would like briefly to address the processes and forums central to the competition: lobbying, association, litigation, negotiation, condemnation, application, and nonparticipation.

Lobbying comes into play where public decisions are sought to satisfy one or more competitors. Legislation to build a reservoir or augment a water supply or to quantify reserved water rights are examples. The proposed Water Rights Coordination Act of 1980 is another example.

Association between interest groups, coalition building, can convert competition into cooperation on one scale but build larger competitive blocks of interest on another. The political association of the Navajos with the upper Colorado River storage legislation in the 1950s and 1960s, in which water projects were handed out, is an example.

Litigation, particularly through stream adjudications to quantify water rights, obviously, is another process central to competition.

The transfer of water rights by negotiation and sale or by forced condemnation is becoming an increasingly popular way of reallocating water and satisfying competition. A variant here includes the practice of offset, where a seeker of water invests money to help an existing user conserve water in order to produce some surplus to supply the new use. Some states require public agency approval for that process. Negotiation also underlies deferral agreements or covenants not to sue where existing water right holders or claimants agree for a period of years not to press their rights, allowing a new use to occur.

If unappropriated water exists, then the competitors seek to satisfy their wants through applications for water permits, licenses, or certificates, a process that also can be contested.

One response to competition, perhaps even a means of competition, can be nonparticipation itself, where a water right holder or claimant, such as an Indian tribe, decides that more can be gained by not bargaining than by bargaining, by not entering the fray or the market, at least for the time being.

Another aspect of the context in which water competition occurs in the West is risk. Risk faces water competitors at several levels. First, there is the risk that the supply of water will diminish through drought, or the quality will degrade through salt buildup or contamination. Then there is the risk of future social change, which will cause disruptions in supply.

Competitors seek legal, institutional ways of guarding against these risks, such as senior water rights, priorities, shortage-sharing agreements, preferences, and water-quality guarantees and controls. What assurance is there that property rights of water will not be redefined, regulated, or condemned? What assurance is there that water projects authorized by Congress or state legislatures will actually be funded and built? That contracts signed by one tribal council will be honored by the next? That energy corporations will meet their contractual commitments? Or that the federal government will stand behind its treaties and trust responsibilities?

Risk pervades the struggle for water. Efforts to reduce and hedge against physical and institutional risk occupy much of the attention of the water competitors. The minimum-flow priorities won by the lower Colorado River Basin—and most especially, California—in compact negotiations and statutes illustrate the importance both of understanding risk and of possessing the power and resources to minimize risk.

Finally, the context in which water competition occurs is value laden. At bottom, competing interests express values. Water is a premiere multiple value resource. It is valued for the sustenance of people and animals, production of food and fiber, the carriage and treatment of waste, the movement of commerce, the extraction and processing of energy fuels, the preservation of natural systems, the generation of electricity, and, of course, the recreation of the human spirit.

The competition over water involves interests clustered into interest groups, but, again, at heart we are talking about values. And conflict, compromise, and coalition between competing interest groups also means conflict, compromise, and coalition in values. Most of the values we are talking about are both persistent and, from a general social perspective, legitimate.

The front-line competitors in the water struggle, we all know, are farmers, growers, cities, tribal reservations, industry, recreationists, and environmentalists. Most of us as individuals find ourselves represented or benefited by many of these competitors. The urban dweller in California, for example, uses about 150 to 200 gallons of water per day if you add the share of water used for urban goods and services. But that per capita figure would exceed 2,000 gallons per day if you were to add the share of water used to irrigate food and fiber in the state. A lot of water is delivered to the table in the food we eat. If you were also to add the share of water dedicated for minimum flows for water quality, recreation, fish, and wildlife, the per capita figure would leap further. In short, individual interests cut across the broad sectarian interests of agriculture, cities, industry, et cetera.

In the struggle for water, a variant of Pogo's wisdom is very apt, namely, if not the enemy, we are at least the competition. The sectarian competitors line up depending on the setting. In Wyoming, a coal slurry company may join forces with the city to develop a new ground water supply that permits favorable private financing for the city. Elsewhere, a city may successfully defeat the efforts of a utility to acquire irrigation water that produces return flow of value to that city. Farmers in one basin may make it politically impossible for a water-thirsty power plant to be sited, but farmers in another basin may actively seek the power plant with the hope of selling some of the water rights at the right prices and obtaining capital improvements for their water system. Environmentalists may oppose irrigators in one area over the issue of minimum flows, but cooperate in another area to oppose water acquisition by energy developers.

Alignments of competitors, then, will shift over time and distance, and over issues. The social, political, and economic power of these competitors varies both over time and in relationship, one to another. Notwithstanding the general power of the group, the outcome of competition in any given setting is not a foregone conclusion. The buying power of energy development currently is very significant. When an industry can pay in excess of $200 an acre-foot per year for water and marginal agriculture can only afford to pay $10 to $15 an acre-foot for water, it is clear that the power of the dollar will weigh heavily in competition between those sectors. But if local interests or the state government places special restrictions on the energy developer, the economic advantage can cease or be offset.

Energy development is now supported by a national political commitment. The combined forces of the federal government, multinational corporations, and the national support of the citizenry make energy development one of the strongest interests in the picture.

Tribal governments have the constitutional relationship of the federal government, equitable claims, and national guilt, as well as long-term cultural commitment and endurance, on their side.

Municipalities have the urban votes and the capacity to pass on costs to consumers, as well as the considerable influence in state and federal capitals, on their side.

Anglo irrigation interests have longstanding political ties of local, state, and federal governments, as well as the sunken investments of publicly subsidized works and the role of supplying essential goods of food and fiber, on their side.

Environmentalists and recreationists have a broad base of support, particularly in urban populations.

Competing successfully requires information, experience, skill, staying power, and a measure of luck. Twenty and fifty years ago, tribes commonly were not directly represented in the water bargaining of the West. Today they are directly involved, but have limited resources to allot to the competitive struggle for water.

The arid West will continue to be a laboratory for experimenting with ways to expand water supply and to moderate water conflict and demand. According to John Folk-Williams, there are approximately seventy-five Indian water disputes pending in the West. The number of disputes predictably will increase as the factors of scarcity, sovereignty, and stability and survival intensify.

Outcomes will continue to be only partially conclusive, providing the basis for new variants of conflict and resolution.

Demands will continue to be mitigated through contractual bargaining, private and public arbitration, litigation, legislation, executive action, political organization and lobbying, and militant acts of self-help.

Lengthy stream adjudications will increasingly be a continuing backdrop in many basins, against which short-term and tentative bargains will be struck, such as convenants not to sue, waivers, deferral agreements, leases, and the like.

Conservation and water reuse will become more widely practiced as water becomes higher priced. There is even the possibility that technological innovations, such as a photovoltaic sun pump, may make desalination feasible, increasing water supply.

But the critical issue for affected parties will continue to be whether to compete actively, and how. The heightened competition should not blind us to the fact that some of the pressing water demands of the day could well be short-lived. Fifty years from now, alternative energy sources, independent of water, may be serving our primary needs. It is important that long-term social, cultural, and ecological values not be exterminated in the competition of the day. What is going on is a struggle between diverse values. Let us not forget that the competition for water, no matter how symbolic, dramatic, and intense, cannot be divorced from those larger forces that bear upon resource scarcities, sovereignty, survival, and stability.

The competition is stressing our political and social systems. What will result will be mitigation, not necessarily balance. And whether that mitigation is sensible in terms of both public health and welfare only history will judge.

MR. JOHN B. NARCHO

Papago Water Commission, Papago Tribe of Arizona
Sells, Arizona

MR. NARCHO: Litigate, negotiate, legislate—a study in frustration for the Papago Tribe.

You must realize that a tribe through the federal court system can acquire judgment after twenty to thirty years to water that no longer exists. This will not deliver one drop of wet water to our reservation. In fact, there could be more water in the ink of the judge's pen that signs the judgment than the tribe will ever see. Damages are what the court will award, not wet water.

I would like to give you a brief description of my reservation so that you can more fully understand and appreciate our problems with water and competing interests.

The Papago Reservation includes three reservations: the San Xavier Reservation, consisting of 71,000 acres; the Gila Reservation, consisting of 10,500 acres; and the Sells Reservation, consisting of 2,700,000 acres. This is the second largest reservation in this country.

The Papago Reservation is located in the extremely arid southern part of Arizona. It is so dry out there that even the rattlesnakes carry along water canteens. We have no rivers, we have no lakes, streams, dams or other types of stored water. Everybody in southern Arizona is wholly dependent on underground water.

In the extreme northern part of the reservation, or main reservation, large non-Indian agribusinesses have pumped most of the water from the reservation. This is in the Safoythick District; for the last thirty-four years, non-Papago farmers have pumped a million acre-feet a year from that water basin. In 1955, that district had fifteen wells and was farming roughly 1,300 acres. We only have one well working now, one good working well.

In the eastern part of the reservation, including San Xavier Reservation, where I live, the City of Tucson, large mining interests and agribusinesses have diminished the underground aquifer to the extent that many wells on this little reservation are now dry.

In 1928, the tribe at San Xavier was farming 2,000 acres. We had fifteen wells. Currently we have five wells. We are farming 500 acres. Our community well has been moved four times, closer and closer to the riverbed—not running river, underground river.

The amount of water that these competing interests pump from the aquifers is a little less than half a million acre-feet a year. Annual recharge to that aquifer is 80,000 acre-feet a year. They are overdrafting it.

All competing interests must look to the scarce underground aquifers for the necessary water to maintain a city population—water to manufacturers, utilities, the mines, and agribusinesses. There is insufficient water to satisfy these interests, and the withdrawal of water from the basins is many times the amount of recharge returning annually to the basin.

Substantial investment and the entire economy of these business entities in the City of Tucson are wholly dependent on underground aquifers, in which my tribe has an extensive water right. The assertion of our water right is a severe threat to the economies of these competing entities.

These entities have pushed the Papago water rights into the political arena. The political power is in the hands of these entities. The Papago Tribe might have 3,000 qualified voters compared to the million and a half voters that the non-Indians have. That political fact of life is probably the most serious threat to the Indians' ability to secure a water supply to which they are legally entitled. Legally, these considerations are irrelevant, but as a practical and political matter, these competing interests cannot be ignored.

Our experience with the role played by tribal leadership is encouraging. The tribal council, in setting priorities of the tribe, always considers its water right as one of the top priorities, but never seems to acquire sufficient money to adequately protect these rights. They feel, and justly so, that the federal government has the absolute duty to acquire and protect the Papago water rights. Politically, this is unworkable. The trustee is controlled by the political machine, and the political machine is basically not concerned with acquiring and protecting water rights for a few thousand Indians against the wishes of millions of qualified non-Indian voters.

If we are going to acquire and protect our water rights, we must do so ourselves. In 1974, my tribe passed a resolution requesting the Secretary of Interior to take the necessary legal action to acquire and protect the tribe's water rights in the basins under and adjacent to the San Xavier Reservation. After extensive prodding, a suit was filed in federal court to determine the tribe's water rights in the Santa Cruz Basin and to enjoin the pumping by non-Indians in that basin so that the Papago Tribe can utilize its water rights. The suit also contains a demand for damages suffered by the tribe for the past taking of its water by the non-Indians. Tribal leadership, utilizing this potential club over the heads of non-Indians, forced this group to the conference table in an attempt to try to find an equitable solution which, in the long run, would be beneficial to all parties.

The tribal leadership realized that these tribal lands were not situated on or near a river, a lake, or stored water, and that any water the tribe might receive must be taken from these competing interests, from the scarce amount of water available.

They also realized that what Congress giveth, Congress can take away. Sure, they have to use condemnation and award adequate damages, but our tribe wants wet water, not money. These negotiations are still going on. And as of this date, two bills have been introduced in Congress and withdrawn. Today, the third draft of the water bill is being circulated throughout the State of Arizona and the Papago Tribe for consideration by all parties. The bill does contain water and money for water development of the Papagos.

Where is the water coming from? First, after several years of intensive negotiations, the tribe acquired 45,800 acre-feet of Colorado River water, to be delivered to the Central Arizona Project aqueduct. Although the tribe has entered into a contract with the Secretary of Interior, the battle for this is still being fought. The non-Indians are still battling to keep this water from reaching the reservation. And if it does reach the reservation, then to restrict the tribe in its use of this water.

The proposed legislation would firm up this water and guarantee its beneficial use. Acquiring the additional water is much more difficult. Utilizing the only existing water source, the seriously overdrafted water basin, would only be a temporary solution, unless the City of Tucson moved to California and the mines and agribusinesses were shut down—the tribal leadership knows this politically is not going to happen. And I might say, too, that in the Santa Cruz Water Basin we have some figures that there is a 50- to 100-year water supply left in that basin.

The only other sources of available water that exist are under federal land in the northern part of the state and effluent water, which the Papago Tribe has continuously refused to accept.

The proposed legislation requires the purchase by the Secretary of Interior of effluent water of the City of Tucson, which he then can exchange with competing interests for pump water, Central Arizona Project water; or he is authorized to construct a recharge basin where the effluent water, after treatment, would be allowed to return to the water basin. The Secretary would receive a credit for this water and be allowed to pump ground water from the aquifer near the Central Arizona Project aqueduct and use this system to deliver the pumped water.

Even though the tribe has continuously refused to accept the effluent water, it is possible under the proposed legislation for the Secretary to additionally treat effluent water so it is suitable for agricutural purposes, and to construct a separate closed aqueduct and pump this treated effluent water 30 miles uphill to the reservation, at a height of 300 feet and, from what I hear, costs of $40 million. At the present date, this proposed legislation has not been accepted or rejected by my district or the tribal council.

As you all know, efforts by the tribes to force the federal government as a trustee to take an active role in acquiring and protecting Indian water rights are extremely frustrating and unproductive. It is true that the Department of Justice, along with the Papago Tribe, filed one lawsuit against the competing entities' using and depleting our water. But for the past four years, the Papago Tribe has used every means at its disposal to force Justice to file three more water lawsuits involving separate water basins under and abutting the Papago Reservation.

Due to the fact that these lawsuits would involve thousands of non-Indians as defendants, the Papago Tribe does not have the economic power to finance these lawsuits on its own. The Department of Justice has put all Indian water suits on the back burner. And Congress continuously refuses to make available the necessary funding for the Indian tribes to press this litigation on their own.

On the other side of the coin, the federal government for many years has appropriated and spent billions of taxpayer dollars to fund massive irrigation projects, taking Indian water and delivering it to the non-Indian farmers. This is something that has not happened in the past; it is happening today and will continue to happen in the future.

Any change in congressional action would create a serious threat to a congressman's political security. If a congressman dared to carry out this country's legal obligation to its Native Americans, he would probably be voted out of office and a substitute put in his place who was more responsive to the non-Indians.

What is true for Congressional leaders is also true for state leaders. There are many more non-Indian voters in the state than Indian voters. If the state leaders and lawsmakers were to support the tribes' legal water rights, they would find themselves out of office.

There are four options available to the Papago Tribe in regard to disappearing water: do nothing, negotiate, litigate, legislate. The Papago Tribe has chosen to litigate and negotiate at the same time, using litigation and the threat of litigation to improve their bargaining position and to keep the non-Indian interests at the negotiating table. Our bitter fight for water has not only involved the non-Indian interests, but also the federal government, the State of Arizona, and other states that worry about a legislative precedent being set that will eventually affect them.

For those Indian tribes who are fortunate enough to have water located on Indian land, we congratulate you and we envy you. For those tribes, like the Papago Tribe, who are unfortunate enough to have reservations located at the bitter end of the water hose, the problem of finding a solution to the critical water problem, whereby your tribe will receive wet water, is not only an absolute necessity but a worthwhile challenge that must be met today. For tomorrow that hose could be dry.

In closing, a threat to resolving all the Indian water problems is Washington State Senator Gorton's water bill, which would subject federal and tribal reserved rights to the coordination of regulatory powers of the state. The bill would require the quantification and exercise of Indian water reserves within an eight-year period.

Representatives of Senator DeConcini's office came to our tribal council last week. They have been approached by a western regional big interest on a similar type bill, where the states would have the power over Indian water.

Another problem concerns the Ak Chin Settlement Bill Act, requiring 85,000 acre-feet of water. The problem is: where to get that water. Leave it to the bureaucracy to mess up again. They want to get some of it from underneath our reservation. They will not go to the other water aquifers nearby because of the non-Indians. So who do they turn to? The Papagos. So we might be involved with another tribe over water. It creates problems, compounds problems, and they just don't seem to work out. It is very frustrating. We are at the point where we can't go anyplace. We're out of water.

MR. DOUGLAS NASH

Attorney, Confederated Tribes of the Umatilla Reservation
Pendleton, Oregon

MR. NASH: The complexity of water issues is almost overwhelming. Each reservation is different in its own circumstances and situations. We have federal and state water laws. We have federal and state water regulations. You stir in a little policy, a little politics, and a little economics, and you have the big picture. The big picture is so huge, it's almost unfathomable.

Talking about balancing competing interests, I suspect that what we are really talking about is dealing with competing interests. We are all well aware of the fact that there are many competing interests on water issues today. These interests can't be ignored from the tribal standpoint. They exist and they are very real. They have to be dealt with.

I am familiar primarily with one reservation setting in the context of water. Each setting is going to be different. I would like to cover four points with you. These four points are, first of all, an information base; secondly, dealing with state regulatory agencies; thirdly, dealing with competing non-Indian water users; and fourthly, and a special one to some tribes and us in the Northwest, fisheries' interests and how this ties into water.

Before I do that, let me give you just a brief scene-setting description of the Umatilla reservation. I'm sure it is a common one, one that many of you tribal representatives can relate to. The Umatilla reservation is set in northeastern Oregon in what is predominantly an agricultural setting. The Umatilla River, which is akin to a small stream or a large creek, bisects the reservation and is a direct tributary to the Columbia River.

This small stream at one time abounded with a number of species of anadromous fish. Now we have one remnant steelhead run, thanks to water problems.

The reservation has high-mountain timber country, it has foothills, grazing land, and, on the bottom, some very prime farmland. Farmland, as you might expect, is the major economic motivation of the area. This farmland was, and still is, primarily dry-land farming.

We have seen in recent years, however, a vast development of irrigation projects on this farmland, both on and outside the reservation. This summer provided us with a look at the economic motivation for irrigation on lands that in the past would yield on the average of 60 to 70 bushels of grain to the acre, lands that under agriculture this year yielded somewhere in the neighborhood of 130 to 140 bushels of grain per acre per year. The motivation is great.

We are also blessed to have a municipal well within the reservation's boundaries. This well provides, when it's operating, water to the City of Pendleton at the rate of 3 to 4 million gallons of water a day. Below the reservation, between the reservation and the Columbia River, there are four major irrigation districts. Each of these has its own diversion structure, its own state water rights. One takes its water from a permanent diversion dam near the Columbia River that totally blocks the mouth of the river.

With that setting, let me talk briefly about the four areas. First of all, work on water resources on the Umatilla reservation began intensively about eight years ago. The big question was: What do we have? We searched through state water records, through federal water records, through research projects, and we found, first of all, that very few people knew anything about water resources and that there was no data base for water resources on the reservation. We decided that this had to be a priority item. We did this through the use, contract use, of competent individuals—engineers, hydrologists, geologists—people who were of expert witness quality.

We initiated research projects and studies. We needed to find out how much water there is on the reservation, where it comes from, and where it goes. Basically we did a water balance, a water table, to find out the scope and extent of the water resources.

We initiated our own data collection system through the use of observation wells to monitor ground water levels, to see what ground water is doing; and stream gauging stations in the river system to see what the surface water is doing, to get correlations between the two and generally to provide engineers with some of the twenty years of data that they like to have to reach conclusions upon which to base their opinions. This can be very important.

This one step, this first step, I submit, is necessary to any tribe interested in preserving, protecting, keeping, or managing its water resources—whether you are on the verge of negotiation or litigation, or whether you are involved in management, you have to have the nuts and bolts figures down to engage in any of those activities.

Secondly, state regulation. You have to view state water regulatory agencies as competing interests. They are competing with the tribe for the regulation of water resources within a reservation, and competing strongly. They will continue to compete very strongly.

Years ago we had developed what we termed a comprehensive water management plan. It was, in essence, a water code for the reservation. It had both legal and administrative and engineering input into it; it was a very complex document, extending over some 200 pages, I would estimate. We wanted it complex. We wanted it comprehensive, I guess, and necessarily complex. It dealt with every aspect we could ever imagine in a water code, not only from the regulatory aspect, the technical aspect of wells and water diversions. It also dealt with the daily administration of the water office, the tribal water office as we envisioned it. It dealt with forms, it dealt with notification, it dealt with mapping procedures and policies.

We designed an implementation phase. You cannot simply adopt a water code and expect it to cure the problems. The adoption process itself, as we mapped it out on a kind of bureaucratic blueprint, required 450 days of implementation time from the time the code was adopted until there was a water office in place and doing business, staffed and ready to do its work.

We examined the potential and need for this kind of a document. We determined early on that it was needed and began debating about the feasibility of adoption. We looked at what state regulation had done for the water resources in the area. State regulation gave us a riverbed between the reservation and the Columbia River that has dried up three different times before the stream reaches the Columbia River. Irrigation diversion at one point dries the river up. Water seeps back into the stream bed, where it is picked up again by the next diversion, and so on down the line. This doesn't do great things for anadromous fish runs.

We looked at the ground water problem and found that, again, thanks to state regulation, there was a critical ground water problem that extends from within the reservation to the west about 50 miles—huge commercial deep-water wells going dry themselves—then, in turn, or early on, drying up domestic wells. Domestic wells within this area regularly have to be deepened for private individuals, private citizens, to maintain a usable water supply. The ground water table is declining, as was described earlier. The recharge rate is not the same as the withdrawal rate. It is vastly different, and the natural result is a vast decline in the ground water table.

While we were talking about this or debating this, we saw the *Walton* case decision and examined that and its potential impact on the reservation. We looked at what was available for alternative regulation on the reservation. If the state has absolutely no authority, we know the federal government has no scheme to fill the void; that leaves only one possibility and that is the tribe. If the tribe didn't do it, based upon the setting that I described to you, we could imagine the results. Competing water users are not ignorant or dumb. They are very wise people. They read the law books just like tribal attorneys or other people interested in water law. The potential at the time was basically unlimited, uncontrolled water development: irrigation wells, municipal wells, domestic wells. In a setting that was already in a critical state, the Umatilla Tribe decided that that was unacceptable, and we adopted what we called the interim water code, basically a status quo situation that asserts tribal control but puts everything in a holding pattern, requiring tribal permits for any new developments, and said that this would be in effect until the comprehensive management plan was enacted and in place. We announced that to the world, and the world raised its eyebrows locally. But it goes on. It is not without problems, but it is done.

I think one of the best ways to deal with the state regulatory agencies is to cut them out of the picture. The law abhors a vacuum, it is said in the law books. A tribe cannot stand a vacuum, a regulatory vacuum, over resources as critical as water in this day and age. It has to be filled. If you're going to assert tribal control, it has to be done with quality, has to be a competent scheme, a manageable scheme, one that at least rivals and preferably betters any kind of state regulatory scheme.

Thirdly, other users. We talk a lot about minimum flows, especially minimum flows for fish purposes. We are concerned with tribal entitlements. How much water is the tribe entitled to? How much do we have on hand right now? I suspect we have utilized somewhat of a different approach in this area. Instead of defining a minimum flow and going after it in full force, we have taken the approach of looking at what's available right now. What can we get our hands on? Then, taking the step of saying: What's the difference between what we have on hand now and what we require in the way of a minimum flow? Let's take the easy stuff first, save the general stream adjudication for later, if it's necessary. If it isn't necessary, fine.

We have, in fact, worked with some of our competing water users. We have talked with them about water savings, bad delivery systems in irrigation districts, delivery systems that leak and evaporate vast amounts of water just in the transportation of water by itself. We have worked with irrigation districts in finding them a different and more reliable water source than that which they divert from the Umatilla River, in order that their diversion dams and especially the permanent dam that is a problem to fish passage can be removed. We do that with their full cooperation, their consent. I believe it generates far better results, quicker results than had we gone to court for that particular process. We have worked with competing interests in an impoundment feasibility study, to find out who is interested in impoundment, flood control. The irrigator is always after more water, fisheries benefits, and so on. Again, these people are well aware of tribal rights and tribal law. They maintain a daily knowledge based on this. They are vitally interested. They have to be dealt with on that basis.

Fourth, special fisheries interests are of particular concern in the Northwest. The Umatilla Tribe is in the early phases of a modest fisheries enhancement program that will be expanded in the future. There are hosts of other agencies and groups that are vitally interested in the fisheries business: state agencies as well as federal agencies and many private organizations, clubs, and individuals. As we are seeing now, these groups are quickly coming to the realization that Indian tribes are one of the very last hopes to maintain adequate waters in the streams and lakes for fisheries purposes.

The *United States v. Washington*, Phase II decision, as you are probably aware, said the tribes that have a treaty fishing right also have a right to an adequate quantity and quality of water to maintain that fish life and maintain the fish habitat. It also said that the state cannot degrade nor can it authorize the degradation of fish habitats in those areas where treaty Indian fishing exists. The alliances this creates provide a situation where the political influences that are such a vital part of the water business can be greatly enhanced from the tribal standpoint.

There are, in the whole process, two dangers that I perceive facing us in the future. First of all, we are aware of the fact that there is a general rule, taught as the basis of tribal powers, that a tribe has sovereign powers, except as it has surrendered those powers or as Congress has taken those powers away by an express act. Unfortunately, we have to add a third process by which tribal powers can be diminished. And that is, whenever the Supreme Court says so. That concerns me.

Secondly, we are soon to face economic arguments—if you haven't already, and I am sure many of you have—economic arguments about water. We have heard some in the past about fish.

It is going to be said that tribes have a water right, for sure. But here, if we allocate water to this tribe for fish, for example, saving that fish is going to cost us "X" amount of dollars in irrigation losses, "X" amount of dollars in power generation, "X" amount of dollars in any number of other competing interests. These will be forceful arguments. But I think that most of you will agree, when you have read a treaty or reviewed your tribal documents, that the rights that come with treaties or tribal governments, whether hunting or fishing or water or whatever, didn't come subject to economic feasibility. They were there regardless of the economics that exist.

MR. RICHARD B. COLLINS

Visiting Professor, University of Colorado School of Law
Boulder, Colorado

MR. COLLINS: I am going to begin by disagreeing, in part, with Jim Johnson about the need for certainty of contract and other arrangements between development or investment companies and Indian reservations and tribes where they might wish to invest.

Some of those same energy companies are perfectly willing to invest in mines in the so-called Third World—in Africa or Latin America or Asia—under circumstances that are infinitely riskier in the terms he is talking about than investing on an Indian reservation.

To be sure, the calculus of the risk goes into the deal, but nevertheless, the very fact that such investments are made seems to suggest to me that certainty of contract is not the major problem. It enters into the equation, of course.

But the Indian nations do share something in common with those underdeveloped nations abroad in another respect. And that is that their principal problem in using water or any other resource is development capital. I would like to talk about the problem of development capital for a few minutes, because the real contest about Indian water rights is not about water that Indians are using, except for those places where Indians make a significant claim to in-stream uses, such as for fishing purposes. Those uses aside, the real contest is over the water that the Indian people are not using, the undeveloped water, the unused, unquantified water rights.

Most of the *Winters* rights claimed by the Indian nations of this country are rights that are defined theoretically according to developed uses, at least by irrigated agriculture, possibly by mining and other industrial uses, as well. And most Indian lands in those regards are completely undeveloped, at least compared with the other land in this country. They are the most undeveloped parts of this country, by and large.

Now, there are some people who like it that way, perhaps. And there are a lot of environmental groups who like to think that all Indians like it that way, which is an unfortunately patronizing attitude that one runs into now and again. But that is plainly not true. Most Indian nations wish to develop. They wish to develop in their own way, perhaps not in quite so rapacious a way as their white brothers, but nevertheless, they don't wish to starve in their splendor.

So the problem then is where to find the capital. In regard to water in particular, the problem is that undeveloped water, even if you have a prior right to it, a superior right to it on paper, can be used indefinitely by the junior right holder, as long as you have no way to use it. If you have no way to put the water to the use that defines your right, such as irrigated agriculture, then, in the meantime, the competing users may freely use all of that water, even though in theory their right is junior.

When we also consider that one of the major water rights problems in many parts of the West is uneven supply—not enough water most of the time, but once in a while too much water and coming at the wrong season of the year, and one year there is more than another year, and so forth and so on—it has been clear for a long time that the major problem in the West is the capital to develop the water in a way that includes both storage and application in the most beneficial way possible.

Now, the potential sources of capital to develop water obviously are the tribal government's own resources when it has sufficient resources to consider doing anything. But only in a very few cases are those resources sufficient in and of themselves. To private investors, at least in the cases of mining and other industrial users, especially in the energy field, this is a promising potential source for the capital development of water supplies. Finally, there is the United States government, which has been the principal source of capital for water development in the West for everyone for a long, long time.

Now, it's true, as Jim Johnson says, that the chances for wet bailouts of water disputes between tribes and others are reduced, but I do not think they are reduced quite so much as he says. Perhaps from an Arizona perspective they are, but from the perspective of the West as a whole, there are still many, many opportunities for federal projects that would solve, in a beneficial way, a number of the disputes that exist.

Historically, the projects that the federal government has funded have not benefited Indians very much. They haven't worked out very well from the standpoint of the Indian nations. Since 1902, the Bureau of Reclamation projects have only rarely served any Indian people. And even the much smaller special projects funded by the Bureau of Indian Affairs, the so-called

Indian irrigation projects, have often been focused on allottees and have tended to promote the alienation of allotment lands and therefore have wound up benefiting mostly the non-Indian successors to allottees rather than the tribes.

So the history of federal capital development of water resources in the West has not been at all helpful to Indian tribes, with rare exceptions. Recent history involves a new problem, and that is the policy initiated by the Carter Administration and continued by the Reagan Administration for very different reasons, to restrict very greatly the amount of federal development that they are willing to recommend. Whether that is going to be a long-term policy of the government or short term remains to be seen. Nevertheless, the fact is that since 1977 there has been very little federal money available for new projects. In fact, one of the ironies of the political landscape is that there is probably more water development going on in the wet southeastern United States right now than there is in the dry West.

The point I'm trying to make is that there is a need in many, many circumstances for political support on behalf of Indian tribes and by Indian tribes for projects that are designed to significantly assist tribes on Indian lands, along with their non-Indian neighbors—projects that are a wet bailout of the disputes. Because in this way the development capital is found. It is found in a way that the tribes cannot achieve on their own, as a practical matter, at least in the foreseeable future. It is found in a way that can fulfill the federal trust obligations toward the Indian tribes. If we are to have such a scarcity of funding of federal projects, one thing that should be politically supported is the notion that the federal trust obligation to Indian tribes should put projects that significantly benefit Indian lands at the top of the list. If reclamation is to have a list of 100 projects and only money for five, those five should have an Indian component, or at least that should be a major policy consideration in selecting the projects that are built and are funded. Indian projects should have top priority.

The problem in this regard in the past has always been the lack of political power of Indian tribes. The reason that the Bureau of Reclamation projects have not significantly served Indian lands has been that the political power lay elsewhere, and there wasn't sufficient political focus marshaled in favor of serving Indian lands in connection with these projects. In fact, as we all know, many of the projects have been at the expense of Indian reservations, because the projects have been in areas where the water for these Bureau of Reclamation projects was in fact taken away from Indian reservations.

But with the present situation of restricted funding of projects, there is, at least in theory, a possible way to build political alliances that can lead to a better formula for selecting the right projects.

The states in the West want these projects. The non-Indian potential users and existing users who want more water want the projects. In many instances, the projects could or will benefit tribes, if they are ever built. When we add the fact that the potential *Winters* rights claims of tribes lie as a sort of threat to non-Indian water users, there are the ingredients, it seems to me, of useful political alliances—to see to it that projects that do benefit Indians are at the top of the priority list, and to see to it that they are the ones that are built and that they are built in a manner that assure Indian communities are permanent homelands, rather than transient paths to individual farms, as they have in the past.

My own experience with this issue arises mostly in regard to the two small Ute reservations in southwest-Colorado. One of the reservations is served by a reclamation project, and although its participation in the project is relatively modest, it is very significant for that tribe. It is very, very important for a reservation that has never had any water development, and where, in dry years, even water to drink must be trucked onto the reservation. But much more significant is that for some years a reclamation project has been authorized that would serve both the Ute reservations in southwestern Colorado to a very significant extent. The Indian component of the project is quite large. Both tribes have strongly supported the project. It has, of course, some environmental opposition, as one would expect. But the main reason the project hasn't been built or isn't being built is the water development moratorium of the Carter Administration, now preserved again for different reasons by the Reagan Administration. The political argument that we are trying to advance in this debate is that this project ought to be at the top of the list, because it fulfills the historic federal obligation to these tribes whose reservations are very dry and useless without the development, and that it can provide a basis to see to it that the *Winters* rights claims of these tribes don't put them on a permanent basis of warfare with their non-Indian neighbors. The project is large enough, would store enough water, would serve enough Indian lands, that by serving some of the lands that would otherwise have a *Winters* claim, the project would provide a reasonable basis to settle other *Winters* claims in a manner that everyone could live with, and in a way that is not going to require somebody to be a loser in the sense that the prior appropriation system requires.

The point I'm making strongly here is that federal funds, I think, still will be available, albeit on a much more limited basis. The political support is needed for the argument that those funds should take into account Indian needs very strongly in their allocation. They shouldn't be going to Tennessee, they should be going to reservations in the West. And I hope everyone here supports that development.

FROM THE FLOOR: I should like to address this question to Mr. Collins. It was my understanding that he said the underdeveloped Indian water can be used by junior claimants. I would like to have a citation on that issue.

MR. COLLINS: I could cite any water law treatise. All I meant by that is that the theory of the prior appropriation doctrine and the reserved right doctrine is no different on this point, and that is, that even if you are entitled to some water, if you are not putting it to use you have no right to stop a junior user from using it in the meantime. You have a right, as soon as you put it to use, to tell the junior user, "All right, I'm going to make a call now."

When an Indian tribe's right is an in-stream right, that is a different matter. But the big right we are talking about in most instances is the right to irrigate. Again, what I am saying is that if an Indian tribe has a right to a certain amount of water with which to irrigate that is not presently being used, some junior user somewhere can use it. In fact, that is what goes on, for the most part, right now.

James W. Johnson, Attorney, *Fennemore, Craig, von Ammon & Udall*, Phoenix, Arizona, also delivered a presentation that has been withdrawn from publication at his request.

MR. JOHN A. FOLK-WILLIAMS

President, Western Network
Santa Fe, New Mexico

MR. FOLK-WILLIAMS: I have been asked to speak because I have been doing some research on Indian water rights, on conflicts around the western states that involve issues relevant to Indian water. It has been quite stimulating to listen to the range of views expressed here.

What is this balancing of competing interests all about? Obviously, there isn't to be a resolution of anything here. But I think it is useful to talk about the way the non-Indian system goes about balancing competing interests.

Some earlier speakers have pointed out that in their dealings with Indian communities non-Indians have been guilty of misrepresentation and immoral conduct. They have neglected to live up to the spirit of treaties. I am afraid that that is true. It points out a basic element in the way the non-Indian world goes about making decisions about important matters. It doesn't really operate according to the fundamental moral values, which is a little shocking. This doesn't necessarily mean that the non-Indian world is immoral or hopelessly corrupt, just strange.

I think it is useful to contrast with non-Indian methods, some of the traditional decision-making processes that Indian people have described to me, particularly a consensual process where all have a chance to speak and, in a cooperative atmosphere, gradually arrive at unanimity.

Well, we non-Indians don't like to do things that way. We do like to fight, and we respect opponents who fight back. The decision-making processes that are typically used to resolve disputes over water invest one institution with power to make the crucial choices. In other words, the power to decide is put in the hands of one institution, maybe one person, and everybody else who has an interest in how that decision is made competes for influence over that person or that institution. They are out there constantly striving, by hook or crook, to have as effective control over that process as they can possibly get. That is what balancing usually means in practice — getting control over decision-making processes.

In America, that system is achieved through conflict, continual conflict. You don't find people waking up one morning and saying, "I'm thankful for being alive on this earth, and I think, heck, let's live live up to that treaty. Let's share the water and let's knock down that dam and let it flow freely. Let the water flow again, and restore the fisheries. Let's give the Indians a fair shake." Instead, they wake up in the morning and strap on the gun and go out to intimidate—let's put it crudely, let me oversimplify—they go out to intimidate, to gain power, to wield power. You have to meet that process, accept it for what it is, realize that you are being invited to combat. That is what the balancing process is all about.

Now, what about the competing interests? What is at stake, basically, in these conflicts? Well, sometimes it's something pretty trivial. Maybe it's whether or not a building should be ten stories high or five stories high. There is competition about that, but nobody is really upset about it too much. When you get to something like water, though, you are touching on a different kind of issue. It is a resonant issue. Everybody talks about water in terms of survival. It is that basic. So there is the interest: water. But underlying that is a value: survival. In looking at the issues that Indians have been preoccupied with for so many years, you find water rights, you find land claims, you find jurisdictional issues, you find the effort to exert regulatory control over water resources. Those are the issues, those are the interests. But they are all facets of one crystal. The central thing is survival. It is the integrity, the permanence, the viability, the survival of Indian communities. That is what has been communicated to me time and time again by Indian leaders. Water is a means to that end.

Gary Weatherford has spoken of the difference between interests and values. I would like to emphasize that difference. When you enter the fray, when you approach this question of making decisions about a vital resource, you have to ask this question: What are the underlying values? Let's assume that it is clear to everybody that the underlying value here is survival—it is basic viability.

Does the other side know that that is what the real issue is, that that is the underlying value at stake? Or does the other side see it in terms of how many acre-feet of water they want? Do they perceive it as a numbers game? Do they perceive it as a purely narrow economic interest?

In the research we have been doing on Indian water rights, we have talked with a great many representatives of state government, of agricultural associations, of many of the non-Indian competitors for water supplies that Indians lay claim to. We have heard a number of strange characterizations of what Indians are after. It is a conviction among some that the Indian claims are okay if they basically relate to some sort of traditional past that is associated with subsistence, meaning less water rather than more. But some of the newer ideas about water use that the tribes have defined are sometimes greeted with hostility, and they arouse a skepticism in non-Indians, who say, "Well, you see what they want, they don't really want survival; they want to make money. They want to be successful. They're not interested in subsistence fishing; they are interested in a commercial fishery. and they are asking us to give up our water so they can make money."

Well, what is survival all about in the modern world? It is essential that every Indian community communicate to the other side what the conditions of survival are in 1981, 1982, 1990, 2000, and so on.

But, then, you also have to realize—and I am talking here for the sake of argument to the Indian decision makers in this very mixed audience—you also have to ask yourselves what do you know about the interests and the underlying values of your competitors? What is at stake for them? Here they are participating in a decision-making process—and they are asking the question: How long are they going to stick with it? They are running today and they look tough. They have a lot of stamina. But are they going to be running tomorrow? Are they running for a month? Are they running for a lifetime? They are trying to size you up, and you are trying to size them up. What does the conflict mean to them?

We have heard a lot of characterizations of non-Indians here, most of them pretty negative. But the fact is that survival is an issue, a social and cultural issue, for many non-Indian communities as much as it is for Indian communities. You have to take seriously and understand what is most important to your competitors. Otherwise you may make a mistake. You may misjudge the opposition. You may never be able to reach any kind of agreement if you don't understand who and what you are up against.

You also have to understand that you compete in different arenas at the same time when you talk about water. You compete, on the one hand, for the resource itself, for proprietary rights to divert, use, or keep in--stream a certain amount of water. These are proprietary rights. But you also compete for governmental authority with the states. We all have had experience with the opposition of western states to the use of taxing powers by Indian governments, various regulatory authorities, and now this is extending to the area of water resources.

Government, the state government, is quick to react, because you are talking here about the essence of government—regulatory authority or the power to collect revenue. These are the kinds of things that state governments often compete with Indian governments for. You can bet that the state governments see this as an issue of survival. It is the survival of a kind of government. That is what is most important there.

What about competition? Do you always have a true picture of the extent of competition? Are the competitors all lined up in front of you, or are there some who only cast a shadow between you and the others?

There has been a focus on the role played by non-Indian farmers and irrigators who were responsible for the very projects, with federal help, that actually diverted water away from reservation lands. And that is still going on.

As Gary Weatherford pointed out, the major part of water resources in the West today is used for irrigation. But are irrigators still the principal opponent, the principal competitor? Municipal use, energy development, environmental protection, recreation interests—there is quite a multiplicity of the interests to keep in mind today. All of them look at the statistics that 80, 85, 90, 95 percent of the water in a given state in the West is used by agriculture. The solution is obvious. There is no water supply problem in the West. There is a water allocation problem. So we have to reallocate water from agriculture to satisfy all of these other interests.

There is a case near my home in Santa Fe, New Mexico, that has been going on for some fifteen years now, litigation involving four pueblos in a very limited watershed that is tributary to the Rio Grande River. There is a conflict between, on the one hand, the pueblo people of these communities, who are simply trying to define their rights to water, and the non-Indian farmers, who in this case happen to be Hispanic farmers. These are very, very small-scale farmers, most of whom barely make a living but have small ditch associations and irrigation facilities. This complex dispute, which I will not try to outline to you, seemingly is a dispute between the Indians on the one hand and the non-Indian irrigators on the other hand. But, it is the observation of many that the real competitor is the city I live in, Santa Fe, which is in a neighboring drainage basin. It is not a party to this lawsuit at all. It already, however, has a well field on the edge of the neighboring basin. The city has been prevented by the State Engineer from pumping more than a minimal amount from that well field because it happens to drain out the neighboring watershed, which is at issue in the litigation.

Well, Santa Fe is a relatively small city, and was even smaller when the litigation started. It is perhaps 50,000 now, but it is growing rapidly. What's going to happen in ten, twenty, thirty, forty, fifty years? Santa Fe will grow and grow and grow. The assumption is that ultimately Santa Fe will buy out or condemn, or gain by fair means or foul, the water that the Indian and non-Indian communities in the drainage basin are fighting over. So do you know the true extent of competition?

In looking at decision making, you must understand another crucial factor. Decision-making processes don't work unless people *agree* that they are going to work. Indian people have a great deal of power. Even if they do nothing about water or land or their own property rights, they have great power by virtue of a very simple fact, which has been restated several times today. The Indian communities exist, they reside where they are. They aren't going to go away. Some Indian leaders will put it even more strongly than that, that this particular people have been instructed by the Creator to live in such a way, in such a place, forever. That is it. There is no debate about that. So that is the power in itself. In non-Indian terms, that is a power. People will try to use decision-making processes, but if you don't cooperate, they can't work.

In other words, by accepting a decision-making process, you give it power. This is visible in a very pure form in a process known as arbitration, where a number of competing interests agree voluntarily not to try to settle a dispute among themselves, but to submit it to a neutral party, an arbitrator. They empower the arbitrator by this agreement with the authority to analyze the facts and the issues, and then to determine and issue a settlement. And that settlement becomes binding on the parties. It is quite clear to everybody that the process wouldn't work if everybody didn't agree to it.

Well, what about litigation? When you submit to the jurisdiction of a court, you are very clearly conferring power on the court to decide about your water resources. That is extremely important to remember. We have heard of the situation involving the Gila River in southern Arizona. There was a decree: the Gila River decree in 1935. That decree resulted from a stipulated settlement, a negotiated agreement in which the Indians had no direct representation. They were represented according to the tenets of American law by their trustee, the United States. The United States gave away the rights of the tribes, from the Indian point of view.

The State of Arizona today says, "Look, that's settled. We can regard this as a sacred court decree, protected by the doctrine of *res judicata.* That is it. You had your day in court. That's what our system provides for." But from before the time the decree was formally entered, the tribe in question expressed its opposition. Its leaders tried to change the terms of the settlement. They established a very clear, very public record of opposition. They said, "No. We refuse to accept the results of this process. We had nothing to do with it. This entity, the United States, has given away our rights, no shadow of justice about it. We refuse." Well, what's the result? Does anyone think that the Indian water rights on the Gila River are no longer in dispute? Of course not. The dispute does not go away.

Here is a very obvious point about conflict over issues like this. Law does not always express what is going on. The laws are changed in response to pressure. Legislation is a decision-making process in which there is a classic competition among interest groups for control. The ones who win out write the laws. Let's put this very crudely: The rules of the game change. You bet they do. That is the nature of the combat that goes on in this country. If you have the power, if you can get the legislature to pass the law you want, you win. But in this case, although the law is complied with and seemingly the dispute is settled, and all the details are taken care of in accordance with the law, there remains a conflict.

The Supreme Court gave an opinion earlier this year in *Montana v. United States,* which in the view of the court, was based on precedent. But the Court's decision concerning the ownership of the Big Horn River bed was perceived as unjust. The conflict doesn't go away because of the legal decision.

The question of balancing competing interests is extremely complex. The competition must be understood. The interests must be understood. The underlying values of the interest groups that make them fight, that make them move with you or against you, must be understood. Your potential allies and adversaries must be understood. But, most importantly, the nature of decision making in this country must be understood.

MANAGING THE RESOURCE

Moderator's Preface

Indian water rights have been and will be asserted in a variety of contexts whose parameters are defined on the basis of tribal economic needs and aspirations, geographic conditions and political and legal considerations. While the Standing Rock Sioux Tribe's predominant concern is agricultural development, the Quinault Nation is concerned with in-stream flows and the quality of the water shed in order to protect forestry and fishery resources. The Yakima Nation in turn must be concerned with all three elements: fisheries, forestries, and agricultural development. Definitions of the resource management needs of Indian nations, as they struggle to meet the challenges of developing effective management systems, vary accordingly. Thus, rather than attempting to identify water resource management needs and capabilities by type of water use, it is first necessary to examine issues and considerations that are common to all Indian tribes, based on their dual roles as governments and owners of the reservations lands and natural resources.

As a government, a tribe is primarily concerned with protecting and exercising its jurisdiction over water use within reservation boundaries, whether that use is by the tribe acting in its proprietary/ownership role, by individual tribal members, or by individual non-Indians or non-Indian businesses. Water-use regulation in this context is simply another way of describing water resource management. The primary means of exercising the tribe's governmental role is through the promulgation and enforcement of a water code that in most cases includes a permit system. A water code must be based on an accurate assessment of the water system, both surface streams and underground aquifers within the reservation boundaries, as well as the interrelationship with neighboring off-reservation water systems. The code should specify the type of uses allowed, including adjustments for actual user needs, for example, adjusting irrigation and municipal/industrial needs to conservation values identified by the tribe. Some form of permit system must be in place as an essential element of the management scheme. Since few, if any, reservation water systems can be completely contained within reservation boundaries, tribal water management systems should also address the need to interface with neighboring jurisdictions or conservancy districts.

However, it should be kept in mind that only a few tribes have adopted water codes. In many cases, this situation is a result of the fact that the authority of a tribe to assert its governmental powers for the comprehensive regulation and management of all water resources within the reservation has not been clear as a matter of federal law. It is probably more accurate to say that this particular aspect of tribal authority has just not been adjudicated in federal courts, since the potential has existed as an inherent attribute of domestic, territorial sovereignty of tribes recognized under federal law for over 200 years. Recent federal court decisions, particularly the so-called *Walton* case involving the Colville Tribe of Washington State, have upheld tribal regulatory power over reservation water systems. Yet, there are many aspects of a tribe's jurisdiction, such as tribal authority over water uses, that have off-reservation impacts and that remain unsettled. The need to proceed with water code development and other management tools cannot wait for final clarification by the courts, but must be addressed by all tribes as soon as is practically possible.

In their proprietary capacity, tribes confront a need to develop and manage water resources to which they possess a claim of right. This urgency follows from the fact that the increasing scarcity of water resources in those states where most Indian reservations are located creates tremendous pressure on tribes to apply their water rights to beneficial uses. This situation places tribes in a dilemma, since putting the right to use involves project construction and other steps, which in turn call for monetary resources not presently available. A potential solution may exist in the form of leasing or conveying water rights on an interim basis to third parties until a tribe is in a position to develop the water resource for its own purposes. The ability to lease a water right and receive income from the lease is authorized by law, but only so long as the use of the water is appurtenant to the parcel of land involved. Marketing the water right separately from appurtenant lands is not presently possible according to prevailing legal theories concerning Indian water and land rights. However, a clear trend to rely on marketing mechanisms as a means of allocating scarce water resources appears to have been established in the western states. Marketing mechanisms have the advantage of inducing a greater degree of efficiency on an impartial basis, and the trend to rely on such procedures may very well beneficially influence the situation confronting tribes. Pressure to liberalize federal Indian law to allow the marketing of tribal water rights may well result in largely resolving the "use or lose" dilemma now confronting many tribes.

Development and implementation of effective water resource management systems is a very high priority for many tribes. Steps are needed not only to protect and preserve the jurisdictional rights of tribes as governments, but also to protect and preserve their proprietary rights to resources that are absolutely vital to the long-term future of tribal peoples. The most critical need, consequently, is to obtain the financial resources necessary to begin addressing the complex and enormous tasks associated with effective resource management.

ALAN R. PARKER
Counsel, Karl A. Funke & Associates, Inc.
Washington, D.C.

MR. RONALD B. ROBIE

Director, Department of Water Resources, State of California
Sacramento, California

MR. ROBIE: I think it is important to go through some of the framework of western water law in order to put into perspective the role of the state as a manager. Because, after all, in terms of administering water rights the state is really a manager of resources. It seems to me that there has been a real problem in how water resources are managed in the West.

I was interested in hearing someone on the previous panel talk about the Indian interests in these controversies as "the other side." You know we have a lot of different interests in California. You're now in northern California. For those of you who are new to California, northern California doesn't always agree with Los Angeles and Southern California. You hear all sorts of nasty remarks made about each region. And as I go around the state, I have to keep reminding myself that as a government official I work for the State of California, not just one regional group in California. But in the same way that I work for all of the people of California who are interested in water—to me at least, it seems that the basic perspective of the water rights mystery is that if Indians assert a claim, they are not "the other side." I don't think the government should automatically be on the side of whoever the other side is—and you never know who they are.

So I think I would like to bring to you a fundamental perspective that there is a need basically to look at government in a new way. I am not a typical water rights administrator—in fact, I am not one right now. I was for six years. Now I am on the development side. I would like to speak to you from the perspective of one who has administered water rights and who spends considerable time running around the West in the state dealing with real live controversies.

You know, when I consider the reaction of most state water rights administrators to the issue of Indian water rights, I am reminded of the parable of the blind man and the elephant. You have heard it many times. Several blind men fell to discussing what an elephant was like. To settle their argument, they decided they would test their conceptions by observation of a real elephant. One felt the elephant's leg and said the beast was like a tree. The other felt the animal's side and said the beast was like a wall. And the other, feeling the tail, said the beast was like a rope.

Well, I believe that we've all been somewhat blind in our reactions to the Indian water rights elephant and our reactions to state water rights systems.

Many western states perceive the Indian water rights elephant—again, the other side—as a monstrous threat to the future working of the permit system. After all, that is the most important thing to them, the permit system. The Indians, in turn, perceive state water laws as an adversary system, and justifiably so, designed to leave reservations with no water to develop. Both, I think, are trying to describe the elephant from the part they felt.

Like the blind man, state water rights administrators and Indian tribes feel the relationship between state and Indian water rights from their own perspectives. And these are perspectives that have been nurtured by the adversary relationship that has continued for several decades. I might say that one way we can break down this adversary relationship is for state governors and people in responsible positions to place Indians within the system so that there is a perspective brought to this.

Governor Brown, for example, has appointed an Indian to the Colorado River Board. This is the board that, in California at least, frequently is the principal representative of the interests of the water users of the state, all except, of course, the Indians, under the statute. The Governor has at least placed an Indian representative on the Board so that an Indian perspective is given to that Board.

The perspective of state water administrators has been especially biased. They have a propensity to see all Indian water users under their reserved rights in terms of the maximum possible amounts of water that can be claimed under the *Winters* doctrine. They have, it appears, been blinded by the claims of maximum amounts of water that would be theoretically involved, say, in a law suit. It is as though we measured everything by the plaintiff's prayer, although we should know that the amount awarded after the merits are heard is limited to the facts that can be proved.

It is normal in our legal system to state the claim at the outset. And, obviously, I don't expect the Indians to back off their claims. But if you look at the rhetoric of most western administrators, they have assumed that the use of water under an Indian water right will immediately reach the amount expressed in the claims—the maximum theoretical claims. Furthermore, the rhetoric seems to assume that the states are unable to forecast or accommodate the use of water on the reservation. They see Indian water rights as a lion poised to devour all entitlements granted under state law.

Well, the concern of states about federal water rights, in general, is prompted by two real factors. The first is the obvious scarcity of water west of the hundredth meridian. And the second, of course, is in response to this scarcity. The states have established a permit system that extends in most states—but not in California—to all waters, surface and underground. These permit systems, as you know, have distinguishing features. First in time, first in right, is the principal feature. The second, beneficial use, is making the water serve as many uses as possible. And the third is a concept of forfeiture. A right that is not exercised over a period of time is lost. The Indian reserved right does not fit tidily into this system. While it shares the principle of priority, having a priority in time—the date the reservation is established—the amount of reserved water is not identified and the principles of forfeiture do not apply. A reserved right is not subject to equitable defenses.

A major concern of water managers is to preserve what I call doctrinal tidiness. Reserved rights interfere with this process. If you have ever talked to people who run state water rights systems, you know it is just like in the early days, hundreds of years ago, when you had all these pigeonholes. If it didn't fit in the pigeonhole, then it wasn't a California water right or anybody else's water right.

Well, I would not recommend the entirety of the California water rights system to any state that is considering reform of its water laws. We are confounded in this state with strange legal creatures that keep jumping out at us. So we are different than most of the western states. We have riparians, appropriators—and old appropriators, prior to 1914—overlyers, who are ground water users who did something else, puebloists—only California has those and all sorts of other variations.

Yet somehow the system has managed to accommodate this variety of different beasts. Perhaps that makes us in California less afraid of this reserved rights elephant than states who have had more tidy legal documents, because the conflicts seem more accentuated.

Most people who look at California's water rights system can't believe it works. And when we try to explain how it does, they still don't believe it does. But, to a large extent, it does. It doesn't force all controversies to be immediately resolved in an adversary way. And, hence, most or many of them are resolved in other ways.

Well, the elephant in California can disrupt our system at times, but I doubt it can destroy us. Now, I am very concerned with the tendency of many state water administrators to believe that if they grumble enough, they can drive the elephant away. I am sure those of you here today don't believe that's true. But how this could be, given *Winters* and its progeny, escapes me. Ever since *Winters,* the courts have repeatedly held that treaties, agreements, statutes, and executive orders must be construed liberally, and any ambiguities resolved in favor of Indians. The decades of litigation over Indian water rights have not driven the elephant away, and, as was pointed out earlier, even if the Supreme Court decides against you, the controversy has not gone away. Yet, I think in most western states, there is the tendency to deny its existence.

Well, a more recent trend that I have been following is looking to Congress to drive away the elephant. The Western States Water Council has been considering, yet has not really supported, several legislative approaches to terminating reserved water rights. It is interesting to see how few opportunities Indians have to participate in deliberations of that group.

One, which the State of Washington is working with and some of you are familiar with, would extinguish unexercised Indian rights as well as other federal reserved rights. A seven-and-a-half-year period would be allowed under the bill's effective date to exercise Indian reserved rights, and thereafter they would be terminated. Senator Gorton of Washington has been considering a draft bill to be introduced for some time.

Congressional termination of reserved rights is, of course, only one sympton of the rumblings of the new federalism that stirs the western states these days. In the water rights areas, however, these general issues of sovereignty involve substantial issues of personal rights, both of the holders of state water rights and the Indian people. Termination of reserved rights wipes out one set of rights to afford security to another, without any comparison of the legal or equitable merits of each.

I would much prefer to see reserved rights considered on a case-by-case basis as the need arises. A case-by-by-case determination has two practical advantages over termination. The first is fairness. The relative rights of all parties are considered within procedures that should meet certain due process standards. The second is the avoidance of the rush to the courthouse.

If reserved rights are to be terminated at some date set in legislation, there would be a major effort made to quantify and establish reserved rights before the deadline. Quantification merely for the sake of quantification in beating a deadline would accomplish very little, and would be counterproductive. It would be a substantial burden on state water rights administrators, as well as the tribes, to handle the claims. And you might find that once something like that was done, the state would immediately move to repeal it after they realized all the work they had to do. Because the tidiness of their doctrine is also carried over into the tidiness of their processes. And one of the things we have in government today at all levels is a lack of funds to handle adequately the multitude of applications of one kind or another that the governmental bodies have before them. The filings for this and that have increased in the last few years.

A case-by-case determination of Indian water rights doesn't leave the states powerless to consider Indian rights in an allocation scheme. You know about the McCarran amendment and the other provisions that enable these things to be worked out. I personally have no problems with seeing Indian reserved rights adjudicated in federal courts. However, I realize that some administrators are concerned about state adjudication. I think the McCarran amendment, to the extent it covers them, gives state water administrators adequate tools that are far preferable to extinguishment. I think that state officials in this area simply have to recognize the federal nature of Indian water rights and not hold out forever for state adjudication. And I'm very much a supporter of states' rights. As any of you who know me know, we have been on a long-running feud with the federal government to try to get them to comply with state water rights law. I can understand why the Indians don't feel the federal government did a good job of their water rights over the years, because the federal government has managed to stampede over and trample state water rights in their operations in this very state.

In the long run, it is probably much fairer to all concerned to measure that elephant accurately, when it becomes necessary to do so in terms of reserved water rights, than to continue to drive it away with the fear that it is capable of devouring everybody's entitlements.

I do believe, however, that the United States has a responsibility to participate in the fair allocation of water, which extends beyond determining the relative rights of reservations and states' rights holders. Where an Indian reserved right actually cuts off a supply of water used under an existing state entitlement, the United States should help reduce the injury. This should be done with federal participation with the states and tribes in physical solutions. And many times, physical solutions are possible, for instance, lining of canals to conserve water, and dead leveling. We have to provide enough water to go around, to permit the growth and development of reservations, while minimizing the use of water and loss of water to others. This is frequently not even thought about, because everybody is hellbent on deciding it in a legalistic way.

This cooperation will be, in the long run, more productive to the states, the United States, and the Indian people than continuing to argue about the elephant. And I would hope that the United States in this regard would be more constructive and help the states who would also be constructive.

I would like to comment on one other aspect of water rights, because I have talked so far about the water rights system. I am now the operator of a large public works project, the enemy to many people, and in terms of doing this, we frequently flood out people of various kinds. The issue is: How do you approach this issue in a fair and equitable way? What is your approach? I mean, that is very frank. We go around California and flood lots of towns that used to exist. What are the responsibilities of a state public works agency with regard to the local communities and the associations with whom it must come in contact?

Well, these disruptions can result in direct disturbances, such as flooding an area, to more indirect disturbances, such as increased pressure on local schools and government, resulting from the people brought in by the project.

Right now, the only project that we are considering as having a major disruption on an Indian tribe is a project on Stony Creek in the Sacramento Valley, north of here. And depending on its location, it could flood an Indian rancheria. And we also have the option of not doing it, and that certainly would be a decision. We will abide by the decision of the people of the rancheria.

But the policy in our department is to negotiate long-term agreements, regardless of the impact, with affected local agencies, whether they be a county or an Indian tribe, and to provide measures to mitigate the impact of a public works project.

The basic principle we use is that the party should be made whole, and we expect to be good neighbors and good citizens when we participate in a community coming in from outside. We also have a special obligation to Native Americans, and we follow that guideline.

To give you an idea of an actual agreement that we have entered into, I would like to describe one we recently signed with Sonoma County and several Lake County school districts. These entities are affected by a geothermal plant that they are building in Sonoma County. In the agreement with the county, we promised to pay about a million dollars for some road repairs. We have also agreed to reimburse the counties for actual costs of emergency services, and make certain annual payments based on a negotiated formula for school students working in the community. We have also agreed to pay a lump sum to one of the counties, because they wanted to build some new schools with the money and not wait and get it over a period of time.

So the agreements also provide for a long-term continuing relationship between the public works agency and the local agency—a continuing process of living with your neighbors, not just building something and going away. And I think that this aspect of public works projects is something that hasn't been done too much in California. We are fortunate that Governor Brown sponsored, earlier in his administration, a commission to consider impacts of public works projects on Native Americans. It has rather strong powers to assure that these projects are undertaken in a sensible way and in a manner that is consistent with the objectives of the affected Native Americans.

I think the package of all of these aspects makes us all better citizens. And that, to me, is the most important aspect of the relationships between state government and Native Americans, just like it has always been with everybody else in the state. It is time that everybody includes Indians in California.

FROM THE FLOOR: I have one question concerning the administration of water resources, and that is: Can the states and the tribes integrate the administration of rivers and underground aquifers that don't recognize political boundaries? Has some sort of integrated administration been developed in California? If so, how has it worked?

MR. ROBIE: No, unfortunately, California's ground water law is one of those aspects of the law we don't like to talk about except when we're pushing for changes in the law. Unfortunately, our ground water law hasn't been adequately integrated with our surface law. We haven't had, I don't think, any conflicts of any substance involving the two. There have been some cases in which there have been adjacent surface water flows that have been related to ground water. As long as they are directly related, you can handle it under California law. But once you get to an indirect relationship, there is a big gap.

MR. DAVID GETCHES

Associate Professor, University of Colorado School of Law
Boulder, Colorado

MR. GETCHES: If you want permanence in your life, become involved in water litigation. It never ends.

I am going to take some time today to talk about the tribes' authority over water resources. There are at least two kinds of tribal authority. There are all kinds of water rights over which the tribe might exercise authority, and different types of uses and users.

The two kinds of legal authority that you should keep in mind are proprietary and governmental. Tribes are owners of water rights and, as such, they are proprietors and owners. That is a different kind of interest in water rights than a government ordinarily has.

Now, even within the proprietary rights of the tribe, there are a couple of subcategories. *Winters* rights are what we have been talking mostly about. But, in addition, tribes can hold rights that are pursuant to state law or defined by state law.

Governmental authority of the tribe includes the authority to determine the nature and extent of water rights and also the authority to administer or regulate the use of rights within a reservation.

Keeping those things in mind, it is useful to recall some of the reasons why a tribe might want to exercise authority. An obvious one and one that probably pops into your mind is a financial reason. Tribes are all in need of money, as any other landowner is, as any other government is. In order to provide for appropriate development of tribal resources, resources like coal, fish, and, of course, the land and agricultural resources, this all requires water. And in order to get a good financial return on all those other resources, water has to be used properly. Of course, another financial reason for controlling water is that water itself can be sold or the use of water can be sold to others who may want to use the right.

Reasons for exercising the governmental powers or the regulatory powers of the tribe include the assurance that a scarce resource will be capably managed. A resource that is in very short supply is vitally important to any government. Also, a government wants to be able to allocate water in a way that coincides with tribal goals and tribal values. That may mean balanced development or maximum economic use of the resource or assuring equity among tribal members and water users within the reservation. And governments are also interested in other goals related to water, such as assuring water quality, a goal that is very familiar to Indian tribes.

Let us look first at the authority of tribes based on their ownership of water rights, and look at the *Winters* doctrine water rights, those rights that are held by virtue of the *Winters* doctrine. The first right that the tribe has as a corollary to that ownership is the ability to demand that other junior water users on the same water body or stream system allow the tribe to use its water to whatever extent it is necessary for the tribe to fulfill the purposes of the Indian reservation. So the tribe can demand that it be able to get to the water it is entitled to.

Secondly, the tribe as an owner has the right to alienate portions of those rights. Now, when we think of a normal water rights owner, we think of someone who can exercise a water right just as a tribe can—that is, to demand that other users junior to them make sure that the water reaches them. We also think that normal water users, not in the Indian rights context, can alienate the rights, can lease them, or can sell them. But it is a little different in the case of Indian water rights, because Indian property, real property, can't be sold without Congressional consent. We know that the Non-Intercourse Act prohibits transfers of Indian land without the consent of the federal government and participation of the federal government in the transaction.

That principle probably applies to Indian water rights, as well. Congress has not consented in many instances to the conveyance of Indian water rights. It has, it seems, consented to the lease of Indian water rights along with the land. That seems to be implicit in 25 U.S.C. §415, the leasing statute. Also the federal courts, the Ninth Circuit, has held that lessees of Indian land can exercise the tribes' reserved rights while they are in the leasehold.

There is no authority at all, though, for a lease of Indian water rights apart from Indian lands. There was a recommendation along those lines by the National Water Commission in its report almost ten years ago, in which it said that unused Indian reserved rights should be leasable and leased by the federal government so that Indians would benefit as a result. We all know that non-Indians continue to use those Indian rights for as long as the Indians don't have an immediate use for them. Indians would have those rights identified as their own while they are being used by these other non-Indian interests. And they would also receive some income. Of course, there are quite a few problems with implementing the suggestion, because some quantification of the Indian rights is a problem that meets us at the threshold. No such law was passed, as recommended by the Commission.

That summarizes what Indian tribes can do with their *Winters* doctrine water rights. They can demand that they be delivered, that the water to fulfill the rights be delivered, and they can lease the rights under certain conditions.

Nonreserved rights are, similarly, fairly easy to deal with. First, you might wonder why an Indian tribe would have nonreserved rights anyway. One possibility is that the tribe could have acquired land outside the reservation to which rights might be appurtenant. Another situation would be that through the purchase of land to which rights were appurtenant within the reservation, Indian tribes might have state-created rights, or they might have a reservation that has a very recent establishment date. For instance, if a piece of land was acquired in recent years and established as an Indian reservation, the priority for that reservation might be later than many other rights in the area. So the tribe might want to acquire rights pursuant to state law, to purchase them from other water users with an earlier priority date. If a tribe does have these state-law-based rights, those rights will be subject to the definitional-type strictures that the state law imposes. However, regulation of those rights may be in the hands of the tribe itself.

We have been talking about the tribes' authority over water rights as an owner, first of *Winters* doctrine rights, then as the owner of state-created water rights. Now let us turn to tribal authority over water rights within the reservation that it may now own—that is, the tribe's governmental authority. The first type of authority that is exercised over Indian rights with which we become concerned is the determination of the extent and priority of those rights. Ordinarily, we assume that the determination will be made in a federal court. Federal courts have nonexclusive jurisdiction over such matters, and Congress has consented to joining the United States in state court proceedings to determine the extent of reserved water rights. That is the McCarran amendment consent, which has been held by the Supreme Court to apply to Indian reserved water rights. Presumably, there are circumstances under which either the federal or the state court might make this determination of the extent of tribal reserved rights.

The more potent question, a question that is going to see the most discussion in the future, is that of tribal regulation of water use once we have some idea of what the tribal rights are. I think tribes are, for the most part, content to have a federal court make the determination of their water rights, provided there is enough information around to have the decision be soundly based and provided that the decision is kept open. Because, after all, a reserved water right is supposed to fluctuate according to tribal needs and expand to meet future needs. So when we talk about determining the extent of the *Winters* right, we are talking about a temporary determination.

As I say, the more interesting and ongoing question is: How much can the tribe regulate water rights within the reservation? Well, we know that tribes generally have inherent sovereign power to regulate any Indian conduct or property within a reservation. The other side of that is that the states ordinarily can regulate conduct occurring outside the reservation or property outside the reservation.

We know that unless Congress assumes regulatory authority itself, this inherent authority of tribes within the reservation over Indian conduct and property will be solidly based and can be exercised by the tribal government. The Secretary of Interior has been given some regulatory authority over Indian water rights on reservations. The Allotment Act, in 25 U.S.C.§381, allows the Secretary to make some regulations concerning the use of water if it is determined to be necessary to secure a just and equal distribution among the Indians who reside on the reservation. However, the Secretary has not fully implemented that authority. So you won't see much in the way of federal regulation of water rights on Indian reservations.

Secondly, the Secretary should only exercise that authority according to the terms of the statute if it is necessary. And, presumably, it wouldn't be necessary if the tribes' own regulatory scheme did the job—that is, assure a just and equal distribution among Indians residing on the reservation.

We have a situation without the federal government very involved. On the other hand, we have an absence of federal legislation providing for state control of water use regulation on the reservations. In fact, as Public Law 280 states, the states have expressly been denied authority to affect Indian water rights.

So, given that situation, we can conclude that the inherent authority of Indian tribes to regulate water use on the reservation remains. The conclusion flows automatically that users of Indian reserved rights, whether they are Indians or non-Indians, can be regulated by the tribe. In other words, a lessee of Indian water rights ought to be regulatable by a tribe without legislation for that purpose.

What about non-Indians who use so-called surplus water on the reservation? Surplus water is water that isn't included in the tribes' reserved rights, water outside the *Winters* doctrine. It is water that the state, presumably, can allocate to water users according to its water resources allocation scheme. Well, those people may be, I submit, subject to tribal authority also. They are in Indian country, and they are dealing with the resource that has great importance to the tribe. Some important tribal interests may be implicated.

Now, most of you are aware that criminal jurisdiction has been denied to Indian tribes in most matters over non-Indians within the reservation. But although criminal jurisdiction over non-Indians has been denied by the Supreme Court, civil jurisdiction is viable in a number of circumstances. There are a number of early cases, most of them dealing with taxation, that have held that non-Indians are subject to tribal regulatory authority when they are on the reservation. There are more recent cases, some of them dealing with judicial jurisdiction, zoning, and more tax cases, that confirm that this proposition is quite true today.

Unlike the situation with criminal jurisdiction over non-Indians, there has been a long administrative history of the government acknowledging that tribes do have civil authority over non-Indians on the reservation. I might add a gloomier note, however, for those who would like to see tribal civil authority expanded, particularly in the water regulation area. The recent history of federal support for tribal regulation as it affects non-Indians on the reservation hasn't been very good. The federal government has failed to approve water codes submitted by tribes that provide for jurisdiction over any but reserved rights. In fact, water codes that have been submitted for departmental approval have been generally at a standstill altogether. This is because the last couple of administrations in Washington have been unable to decide what their policy is with respect to water codes.

Last January, the Carter Administration promulgated some regulations governing the approval of tribal water codes. Those regulations have never been made final. I understand they haven't been officially withdrawn, either. They are out in that great limbo with millions of other federal regulations that may never see the light of day.

But these regulations are rather troublesome in that they address only the tribes' authority to regulate reserved rights and don't seem to extend to regulating non-Indian exercise of rights within the reservation, both reserved rights and nonreserved rights.

To be sure, the full extent of tribal jurisdiction over non-Indians using water rights based on state law is very uncertain. I did point out that non-Indians on the reservation are in Indian country. Indian country is a concept that pertains mainly to criminal jurisdiction matters, but it has also been said by the Supreme Court to apply to problems of civil jurisdiction. It is a territorial type of definition and covers all fee land within an Indian reservation. Presumably, a non-Indian functioning on fee land would be within its compass. However, some recent cases have suggested that a determination of whether tribal jurisdiction or some combination of state and tribal jurisdiction applies to non-Indians on a reservation depends not only on whether the matter takes place in Indian country, but also on the extent of legitimate tribal concern with the transaction.

So we have to look beyond simple Indian country boundaries to find the dividing line for jurisdiction over regulatory matters, including regulating water use on the reservation. The approach of recent cases is for courts to examine the extent of significant tribal interests in specific circumstances, looking to see whether tribal laws can be applied to non-Indians consistent with principles that the Supreme Court has developed.

Now, it would be a very easy case if Congress authorized a tribe to regulate all rights, all water rights within the reservation. And certainly it is within Congress's power to do that. But Congress hasn't dealt with these matters very explicitly. As I mentioned, the only federal legislation authorizing any kind of regulation of water rights on the reservation is the Allotment Act provision, allowing for some federal regulation.

So the question is typically whether the tribes' inherent authority is sufficient to regulate non-Indians who are exercising state-created water rights. The Supreme Court has given us some signals on how to make that determination. A case that has been affectionately noted by many of the speakers, *Montana v. United States*, is an important one for this inquiry. That case, as many of you are aware, was one in which the United States Supreme Court found that the Crow Tribe didn't have sufficient interest in regulating non-Indian fishing on their reservation. Now, that came as a shock to a number of people. But what we have to do as lawyers and managers looking into the future is to figure out what impact that case has in the area of Indian water rights in particular. Can non-Indians, exercising state-created rights, be regulated by the tribe? Well, let us distinguish it from the *Montana* case. Remember, in that case, the bed of the river in question where the non-Indians were fishing was not owned by the tribe but was owned by the state. Of course, that was decided in the first part of the same *Montana* decision. Secondly, the land where the fishing was taking place, where the fishermen were standing on the banks of the river, was non-Indian-owned fee land.

Another distinction is that the Court found—and this may be the most important distinction—that for the Crows, the record didn't show a history of important tribal reliance on fishing and hunting.

Then, finally, the tribes' regulatory scheme in that case amounted to a simple prohibition against non-Indian fishing and hunting, and it wasn't a careful conservation scheme. Now, you can see here what the implications are for regulation of non-Indian water rights on the reservation. If these factors don't exist, if you can show, for instance, that it is vitally important to the tribe to have its own regulation of the water rights, the result is likely to be different. This is presumably not a difficult finding for any tribe where a case would likely come up, since it is likely to come up where it is important.

The door was left open explicitly in *Montana* for tribal civil jurisdiction over non-Indians on the reservation. Here is what the Supreme Court said: "A tribe may retain inherent power to exercise civil authority over the conduct of non-Indians on fee lands within its reservation when that conduct threatens or has some direct effect on the political integrity, the economic security, or the health and welfare of the tribe."

Does that sound like it could be talking about Indian water rights? The Court did note in a footnote in the opinion that the same rationale that justifies this statement I have just quoted justifies the *Winters* doctrine of water rights. Not an entirely clear reference by the Court, but I think it definitely leaves the door open for tribal regulation of all non-Indian water rights on fee land on the reservation.

Well, what are the tribal interests in regulating water use on the reservation? An obvious one is to prevent conflicts with federal statutes and policies. Statutes like the Allotment Act, which assure that there should be an opportunity for tribal members to become economically self-sufficient by using a parcel of land for agriculture. Statutes like the Indian Self-Determination and Education Assistance Act and the Indian Reorganization Act, which provide for Indian self-government. And the statutes that I mentioned before, which set up a very minimal scheme of water rights control on reservations. Public Law 280, that denies states the right to do anything that affects Indian water rights. And the McCarran amendment, which allows for limited state court jurisdiction in determining the existence of Indian water rights. This seems to define the limits of state interests in regulating Indian water rights on the reservation.

Another tribal interest is to protect conflict with the tribes' ability to regulate Indian water rights. So the tribe has to regulate non-Indian rights in order to protect the Indian rights. It often occurs that when parties competing for water use both need the water at the same time, somebody has to make the decision between them. On what basis is that decision made? The whole question is complicated when you add the fact that the parties are holding their rights pursuant to different systems of law, one pursuant to the state water rights laws and the other pursuant to the *Winters* doctrine. How can you treat them both fairly? It seems that some integrative function has to be performed by one government or the other. In the case of an Indian reservation, only one government can arguably have jurisdiction over both Indians and non-Indians. It is not the state government. The state government simply cannot get into the business of managing reserved water rights. So if one government has to do the job, it has to be the Indian tribal government.

The interest—and a very strong tribal interest—in having proper regulation and distribution of water was recognized by the Ninth Circuit Court of Appeals in the recent case of *Colville Confederated Tribes v Walton.* Here is what the Ninth Circuit said: "A water system is a unitary resource. The actions of one user have an immediate and direct effect on other uses. The Colville's complaint in the District Court alleged that the Walton's appropriations from No Name Creek imperiled the agricultural use of downstream tribal lands and the trout fishery, among other things. Regulation of water on a reservation is critical to the lifestyle of its residents and the development of its resources. Especially in arid and semi-arid regions of the West, water is the lifeblood of the community. Its regulation is an important sovereign power." That is the kind of interest that presumably the court in *Montana* was talking about when it said that there is a realm of tribal civil authority over non-Indians on fee lands on the reservations.

Now, in the *Walton* case it was found that the existence of the Colville Reservation preempted state law and allowed for tribal regulation. You might reply that, there, the stream was entirely on the reservation and maybe was an easier case. But this fact, the court said, wasn't determinative of its decision. Nevertheless, I would like to qualify what I have said by pointing out that the degree to which a stream or water source is located and used outside the reservation relative to its importance on the reservation may be determinative in individual cases of the degree of tribal regulatory authority. It makes for some very uncertain cases.

Ultimately, what a court is going to have to do is look at the *Montana* factors to determine whether the absence of tribal regulation or the presence of state regulation will interfere with important tribal interests, interests like maintaining a unified and rational water management scheme. Interests like protecting and developing tribal property and tribal rights, rights to land, fishing rights, and so on.

The extent to which a tribe attempts to exercise the authority that it has may determine how much of the tribe's authority is recognized. In other words, the tribe has to take some steps to exercise its authority if it hopes to have that authority recognized. The tribe is not going to succeed in controlling reservation waters if it limits its own jurisdiction in its own tribal constitutions and in its own tribal codes just to reserved rights. They must, at the outset, remove any legal impediments to their exertion of authority over all the water rights on the reservation.

Secondly, the tribes are going to lose in this battle if they have to rely on the regulations that were proposed by the Department of Interior for approval of water codes. Those regulations drastically understate the extent of tribal authority to regulate water on the reservation. It is a limitation on the tribes that doesn't exist inherently and is imposed only by the Department of Interior. The response to that is going to be a lot of opposition, indeed, lawsuits.

FROM THE FLOOR: How do you justify the state and federal water rights? I live on allotment land and I draw water from the same creek that the non-Indians draw from. How do you justify that under the state and federal law?

MR. GETCHES: The problem is that there are both reserved rights and nonreserved water rights on the reservation. One of the things I wanted to point out was that there is a lot of difficulty in managing two separate systems of rights.

MODERATOR PARKER: Your right as an allotment holder is regulated, if anything, by the tribe and, secondarily, by the Secretary of Interior or his agents. But somebody right next door to you who is a non-Indian who owns that land and who exercises a water right, his right is exercised by the state. If that land is within the boundaries of the reservation, then there could be overlapping regulation by both the state and the tribe.

FROM THE FLOOR: We have been led to believe for the last ten years that no Indian allotment of water will go off the reservation. We're involved down at the Chemeu Indian Reservation. We have had numerous opportunities to sell the water to people wanting to develop it outside the reservation. We got a ruling about five years ago that there will be absolutely no Indian water allowed off the reservation. We happen to have 11,000 acre-feet a year that we haven't been using, and we can't sell it or even give it away because it goes off the reservation.

MODERATOR PARKER: Now, this is the Secretary of Interior or the federal government who is imposing this restriction on you, is that right?

FROM THE FLOOR: It's out of Phoenix, as far as I know.

MODERATOR PARKER: Guy McMinds had a question, too.

MR. McMINDS: I guess I'm not really entirely understanding what the lawyer and economist are saying. I am afraid that that is a position all of us Indians are in a lot of the time. I am going to try to ask a question so that you can get my head straightened out.

One of the things is that I have a tremendous amount of fear about assigning, even through a lease, a portion of water to a non-Indian company, corporation or state, because they could manipulate the machinery to get a claim on the water. What assurance with the law do you have that this is not going to occur?

MR. GETCHES: Well, Guy, I am not sure you have any positive assurance. But you do at least have a contract. What happens now is that all the water in the stream is being used. Water rights that the Indian tribe would use and may in the future use are being used by somebody. Sure, they're down at the bottom of the list on priorities, but they're using them for free. And there's nothing on paper saying that they're really living on Indian rights. I think that it is a preferable situation to have a lease, something on paper, that shows those rights identified as Indian rights, which is more than you have now. And, secondly, to have some income, which you don't have now that the rights are being used by others for free. So I can't tell you that you have any absolute assurance that you will be able to enforce that contract later. But at least you will be one step closer to having a legally enforceable deal.

MODERATOR PARKER: Do you know of any law that would restrict somebody in the position of the Chemeus from leasing a right that has already been quantified?

MR. GETCHES: Yes. I think that that is the same problem of not being able to lease water rights apart from the land. That is the predicament you get in, the one the gentleman from Chemeu pointed out. They've got the water rights, they know what they are, but they can't lease them because apparently the federal government interprets the laws as I do, and that is that they can't be leased without some further Congressional consent. So, yes, I think that is probably what the BIA was saying when they denied authority.

MODERATOR PARKER: Is there a specific statute that they point to, or is that just their interpretation?

MR. GETCHES: It is based on the principle that you have to have Congressional consent to convey any kind of Indian property, and Congress hasn't consented to that kind of conveyance. It is a Non-Intercourse Act principle.

MR. BROWN: I might interject here, that one thing that can happen in that situation is that if you had an energy company or some entity that wanted to use that water that could afford to pay a lot for that water, then they might be willing to assume litigation costs associated with trying to force a change in that situation.

Obviously, you've got a similar situation in New Mexico now. El Paso is trying to take water in New Mexico and transfer it across the state boundary, which New Mexico is resisting. El Paso has already spent upwards of a half a million dollars litigating that suit, just trying to throw out the prohibition against that sort of move. It very well might be that you would be throwing the litigation cost onto somebody else that could afford it better, rather than having to absorb that sort of thing yourself.

MODERATOR PARKER: I would just like to close by emphasizing that we are not here to advocate a particular position or point of view or perspective. In terms of an exchange like we have just had, it is for the purpose of exchanging ideas, information, and explore these kinds of ideas for purposes of the record and the later report that will be issued.

MR. LEE BROWN

Associate Professor, Department of Economics,
University of New Mexico
Albuquerque, New Mexico

MR. BROWN: John Folk-Williams mentioned that we need to understand the tools, the mechanisms, the procedures used by your competitiors. As an economist what I'm going to principally address is one of those major tools that has been developing in the West, particularly with reference to non-Indian water rights—the market allocation of water rights. I want to make some general observations about water management in the West and lead up to the role of markets as they are developing generally here, then try to end up with a possible candidate of how markets might be usable by tribal water management organizations.

I would like to draw a distinction between the terms "water management" and "water development." The title of our panel is "Water Management." I would say that what we have been doing for the last century in the West really hasn't been water management; it's been water development. That is, we have been taking water in an unused situation and applying it to new uses. It is only in the recent decades, varying from basin to basin, that we have begun to reach a condition of full appropriation of ground water. At that point it no longer becomes feasible to talk about water development, but you are talking about water management in a larger sense when you talk about techniques other than developing new water.

Water development has included diversion projects from other basins. The terminology now also includes notions of spring flow augmentation, whether it be cloud seeding in the winter or whatever. Whereas management includes such techniques as conservation of water and, more importantly from the standpoint of markets, transfers of water rights from one use to another.

What I am principally interested in at this point, and what I think this panel is concerned with, is the management of water resources. To a large extent, the major development era in water affairs is behind us. I say that with some reservation, because since the moratorium on discussion of interstate transfers expired a year ago, there has been a revival of interest in major transbasin interstate diversion. In fact, the Governor of Texas recently has come out very strongly in asserting the high plains diversion, what used to be called the Texas water plan, to divert the Mississippi to the high plains of Texas, and which has now been broadened to include the high plains of the whole region. So there clearly is a revival of interest in development projects for water generally, but I don't see them as having either the political or economic future that they have had in the past.

Peter Drucker is an individual that many consider to be the dean of modern management. Most of the major textbooks in management techniques have some sort of role in it for Peter Drucker. Let me start with taking his definition of management in a quote. He describes management as "an organ of an institution." And the institution, whether a business or a public service, is, in turn, "an organ of society, existing to make specific contributions and to discharge specific social functions."

What I want to draw from that quote is that society establishes institutions. We have goals. We have talked about values here today. We have goals and values that we are trying to achieve. Whether consciously through design or unconsciously through evolution, whether through court decisions or through acts of the legislature, we establish institutions for performing the tasks and the functions that we want to have succeed.

By an "institution" I don't mean just an organization, a corporate entity or conservancy district or something—I mean the whole array of rules, practices, customs that we use to perform these functions. If I am right that the era of water development is behind us, then what we are facing in the future is the design of water institutions for managing the water resources, whether we do it consciously or whether it evolves through practice. That includes not just developing the water resources and putting them to beneficial use, but also actually taking, transferring, and introducing techniques that lead to conservation of water as we go through it.

The situation is very different now, from an economic standpoint, than it was in the first part of the century. In the first part of the century, water was what an economist would call a "free good" in the sense that there was more water available than there were users who wanted to put it to use. I don't mean by that that the capital to develop the water was ever a free good in the sense of being able to capture, store, move, and apply water—that has always been a very expensive proposition. But the water itself was a free good up until recent times. It is no longer a free good in the sense that now in most basins in the West if you want to have water for a new use, there has got to be a retirement of water from some other use, so that you give up something to apply the water to the new use that you have in mind. So it is no longer a free good, it is no longer a free good as measured in dollars and cents. For those of you who may pay much attention to water market transactions that are taking place in various parts of the West, water may be sold as the right to an acre-foot. Water may be selling for $100 to $200 an acre-foot in some basins, and it may have gone up steeply over a certain period of time and be selling for as much as $10,000 or $11,000 an acre-foot. That is a very dramatic increase. In fact, even with as much inflation as we have had in the general economy, there is nothing that matches the increase in the price of water rights in various basins in the West that have been fully appropriated.

So what we face is the task of designing either new institutions or modifying through practice the ones that we have, to face the new societal task of managing the water that we have and not just developing it like we have done in the past. In order to decide what sort of institutions you want to perform that task, you have got to know what your values are and what the institutions will do in achieving those values. I don't want to get into a long digression here about what the various values are that you would want water management institutions to apply in allocating the water among various uses. I think I can skip over having to deal with it in detail by asserting two propositions.

One proposition is that, whatever society we are dealing with, we want a certain degree of material improvement. I think it is the case that, whatever society we are dealing with, we are interested in material improvement in using the resources that we have—whether it is water or capital or labor or whatever—using them in ways that promote the material growth of the economy and the well-being of the citizens of whatever economy we are talking about. The second proposition is that there are nonmaterial values that clearly are as important, if not more important, than the material objectives that we have set for ourselves.

So on the basis of those two propositions, what I am saying is that whatever institution we design for managing water, whether it is going to deal with development or whether it is going to deal with conservation of water or the transfer of water, we want to ensure that we have economic improvement but we also want to make sure that we protect some noneconomic, nonmaterial values as well.

Against this background, let's look at what I consider one social technology for doing that, and that is the marketplace. The marketplace is a procedure that we allow to happen in the economy, and that we choose to use or not to use. Some of my economist colleagues tend to have more of a theological attachment to marketplaces as being the ultimate solution to virtually every problem. But even most of them would admit that the marketplace is not going to do much in solving the basic problem that we are talking about here, the quantification of Indian water rights. I don't see how the market is going to contribute to that in any way.

What are markets? The term "markets" conjures up everything from the New York Stock Exchange, which is allocating capital basically through shares of common stock or bonds, down to barter markets in developing countries, where you have a one-on-one negotiation over what the price of a particular commodity is going to be. Essentially, what we are talking about are the procedures, practices, and customs in which allocation of a scarce resource is determined through voluntary exchanges by individuals, with the price of the exchange being arrived at by those individual negotiators, rather than being set by some sort of outside authority.

Now, there are a number of characteristics that you could set up for judging the institutions. Drucker says that the key thing is: Do the institutions perform? Do the institutions succeed in bringing about the objectives that you have set up? I would assert that the value of markets is that, in fact, they do perform. If you want to see that a resource is going to be used in its highest value—its economic value, material value—markets will do that for you, with rare exceptions. The idea is that the highest bidder is going to purchase the resource and that highest bidder better be able to use that resource, whether it's water or anything else, more effectively than anyone else or he's going to lose money on the transaction and he's not going to be in the bidding game next time around. Markets do perform to the extent that economic improvement or material improvement is one of the goals that you want to pursue. Markets are very effective performers in achieving that sort of result.

However, my second proposition is that there are other values that are more important than material improvement. And markets are not going to handle this situation. There are difficulties that occur with markets. One of the major ones underlying the development of water law in the West is the fear of monopolization—that is, that one individual through the market process, will acquire control over all or at least the bulk of the water resources, and therefore will be able to dictate to everybody else what the price of water is, and will be able as well to charge abnormally high prices for the water. I think we have gone to considerable effort as a general society in developing water laws to prevent that sort of monopolization from occurring. But it is one thing that is beginning to happen in certain basins in the West, where either directly or through subsidiary corporations, particular water users have acquired the bulk of the water resources of that basin. I don't mean to assert any sinister motives to that trend. It has been done principally, I think, because particular water users had uses for most of the water of that basin, whether copper development or energy production or whatever. Nevertheless, it is a departure from the general rules of the competitive market that economists deal with.

There are third party effects. That is, if, in this voluntary transaction between two parties over water, there is a third party who is affected by the transaction but who does not have a role or a voice in that negotiated decision between the purchaser and the seller, then we raise the question of whether, in fact, that third party shouldn't have some sort of control or lever over the transaction.

As it is generally interpreted in western water law, if you have a transaction between water rights holders, Parties A and B, and Party A sells his water right to Party B, and Party C is damaged in some way and can't acquire the water under the same conditions he had before, then he has cause before regulatory or court judicial bodies in most western states to object to that transfer and be compensated, or actually to prevent the transfer from occurring. So, to the extent that there are third parties, we may not want to allow the market to operate.

The institutions that we set in place for the last hundred years, designed to develop the water, have worked quite well in a large sense. If the objective was to make the desert bloom and put the water to use, that is what has happened. The water is being used. In fact, that is one of the concerns that we have been talking about here today. That process of putting the water to use left a number of things outside the framework. It didn't deal adequately with Indian water rights and it didn't deal with in-stream values. There was no notion that you could leave the water that was of beneficial use over the last hundred years in the stream. It is only recently that we have begun to assert in-stream values as another use that we would like to have for water. And the markets haven't been handling that situation.

Lastly, and probably most importantly, there is a deep-rooted emotion, that has been expressed several times, about this attachment to water. Sometimes when I sit by the ocean, which I don't do in New Mexico, but I do try to get to California when I can so I can sit by the ocean, and can sit by it for several hours and just enjoy the movement of water, I sometimes wonder if it isn't genetic somewhere. It's down that deep in terms of our attachment to water.

One economist summed it up in a technical way. He described water as "the object of a very complex structure of evaluations, rituals, superstitions, attitudes, and beliefs. It has been the subject of sacred observances from very early times in human history." I think that has been reemphasized here several times today.

To the extent that water is something more to us than a commodity, then we may not want to have the market allocate it. So what I am arguing for here is that I think the marketplace can serve a useful role. In allocating the resource toward material improvement, it is difficult to rival how well markets function, as long as you control them. But there are other nonmaterial values that I think also have to be asserted. So in looking at institutions, what I am suggesting is that we see if there isn't some sort of a mixture of market and nonmarket considerations that we can bring in.

The idea in my mind—and it is a fairly rudimentary idea, not something that I have been thinking about for a long time—is that there are several ways you can introduce a market into a management situation. You can do what is occurring to a large extent in the West, which is the right itself being sold from one party in use to another party in use. That is one way to introduce the marketplace.

There is another way to introduce the marketplace, and that is to retain the water right. Some collective authority—a tribe, a conservancy district, a corporation—retains the water right and sells specified annual flows for specified periods to the highest bidder. That is an auction-type market. You are leasing the water right to the user. But you are still retaining the ultimate control to decide whether or not, in fact, to allow the market process to operate. That is, you can choose to let the highest bidder go on and take the water for a specified period of time. But given that you still retain the property right to the water itself, then you can choose to ignore or override what the market process is dictating. I think the value of that is its benefit to both sides. On the one hand, it introduces the economic goal of materia improvement into your management structure, because you are generally going to set the thing up so that the highest bidders, those who can use the water most productively in a material sense, are going to get the water. On the other hand, you retain the authority to refuse the allocation if there are other nonmaterial values that seem more important in this context to you than the material improvement that would go from allocating the water to the highest bidder.

If you think about this scheme, it is not particularly novel or new. Leasing water rights to the highest bidder is occurring to some extent in the West, though not as frequently at this point as the outright sale of water rights from one user to another. In public lands, such as grazing lands or forest lands from which timber is harvested, we use auction markets to a large extent to allocate the resources that flow from those public lands. We retain the title to the land itself and, if we've got some stronger political imperative or social imperative, we can override the result that would come out of market allocation or the bidding procedure.

Another characteristic of that approach to managing water is that the payments for the water are made to whatever central authority owns the water right. What is occurring frequently now is that water rights in agriculture have fairly low market values, while water rights for energy purposes have very dramatically high market values. So that in moving a right from an agricultural purpose to an industrial or municipal purpose, there is a very stark increase in the price of the water right, the proceeds of which go to the owner of the water right. As the right becomes more valuable, the proceeds, the actual dollar payments, go to the collective authority, whether a tribe or conservancy district, who actually owns the water rights. In an economic sense, the rents that are associated with water are being captured by the collective organization rather than by the individuals.

Ultimately, if you have a set of social values that you want an institution to fulfill, and if the technology of the marketplace fits into the way you look at evaluating things and looks like it would serve you, then you introduce the technology into your water management scheme. If it doesn't fit, then you look at alternative techniques.

MODERATOR PARKER: Let me try to make a summary of the point you were making. The Indian tribe could have the choice of simply putting its water right up for lease, receiving an income for a temporary or interim period or doing whatever it wants to with that income. One of the things that it might be able to do would be to build up a project so that it could put that water right to use on its own reservation. Or it could lease that water right for an interim period of time, and then, when that time period expired, it could apply the water to its own reservation.

MR. BROWN: After an initial lease period, if the tribe chose to use the water for internal purposes, the tribe could decide not to lease it again to an outside or non-Indian user. By having the auction process there, the tribe would always know what value it was giving up.

If you have two alternatives, of using it internally or leasing it and letting someone else use it if they are willing to pay a certain amount of money, then from a material or an economic standpoint, your investment had better be better than what you could make by leasing the water right, or you're going to lose money in the process.

MODERATOR PARKER: I think the only problem with that is that you have to know what right you're going to assert in terms of quantity.

MR. GETCHES: I think it is going to be necessary, before you engage in any leasing, to have some idea of the quantity. Now, I suppose if it were a small enough lease, you could assume that the tribe certainly had rights to that quantity. But, beyond that, some quantification is necessary. It is a lease apart from the land, I think, and there are differences of opinion on that. I think you need federal legislation authorizing that conveyance.

MR. FRANK TENORIO

Secretary-Treasurer, All Indian Pueblo Council
Albuquerque, New Mexico

MR. TENORIO: First of all, I would like to sincerely thank the American Indian Lawyer Training Program for according us the privilege of coming together on such a timely issue, the issue of Indian water rights.

I think the Indian people don't come together publicly too often. Yet we know, the full effect of knowing what the water rights are all about is something that we can't afford to leave behind. So I certainly am appreciative of the fact that I am here along with the attorney for the All Pueblo Indian Council, Joe Little, and my Governor from the Pueblo of San Felipe. I see several other Pueblo representatives from the Northern Area. Last, but not least, our friend, Mr. Chino's wife from Mescalero. She is a Pueblo. So I take this opportunity to recognize all of them.

As was brought out throughout the discussions yesterday as to the importance of water rights to our lives, go without water for one day and you'll know the effect of what it is to all of humanity. In that context, the Pueblo Indians are definitely a type of people that hold reverence to water. We hold such a reverence to water that we practice it in our everyday lives.

I can't help but be impressed by a slip of the tongue that Mr. Lee Brown made yesterday when he said that water was a commodity. And he apologized for saying that, to the extent that it was a word he did not like to use. But let's be frank about this whole thing. I think our non-Indian counterparts certainly do take water for granted. It is to them a commodity to exploit, a commodity that represents dollars to them — regardless of how you use it, regardless of how many ways you channel it. To these non-Indians, there are many facets of how you can wrest the ultimate dollar from water as a commodity.

I imagine that the Indian people perhaps are learning. I know that it is something that would not be their true frame of mind if they went ahead and grabbed it to the fullest context.

I would like more or less to qualify at the outset a lot of things I'm going to say. It will seem I am getting away from the subject of our panel here, "Managing the Resource." I would like to set a stage so as to qualify my remarks in regard to what we feel about water and how we came to this particular frame of mind.

As you know, I come from an area that is arid, an area that is lacking in abundance of water. So how we manage it and how we use it is definitely the key to our livelihood.

First of all, we consider water not as a commodity, but as a live spirit, a live spirit that has the necessary ingredients to be all things to our people. I say that because when a child is born in an Indian setting, a Pueblo setting, he is turned toward the very essence of what water means. My people didn't settle where they did settle because there was no water there. They settled there because they saw an abundance of water. They saw the topography. They saw the countryside that is conducive to carrying out their role in life, which is definitely practiced right at this time. Every Pueblo individual is well aware of what his role in life is. The most basic is a wholesome respect for water and all that water makes and all that water does to make life beautiful and possible. The trees, the sky—just look around you: everything is dependent on water. That is the reason why we like to say that we talk to water as a deity, as a being that has the supernatural powers that we derive, that we take, that instills us with powers that make us live, even in the bleakness that sometimes the world confronts you with. With water we say that we will make it. It also provides for us that cleansing nature that we take from water. It has a way for us in our everyday life.

Our Pueblo people are basically agricultural people. I believe that managing the resources as an agriculturally oriented people, we have had to do something right in order to maintain the lifestyle that was evident in our country for so long.

The Pueblo San Felipe certainly takes pride in still maintaining one of the original man-made, handmade diversions on the Rio Grande. We use that. We continue to use that, even though advice from the Washington area agency says that it is not economically feasible to run, that it's something archaic. But we say, "Let us be the judge," and we put into play those things that we consider valuable to us.

As far as the Pueblo Indian water management is concerned, we certainly are under numerous pressures that came about by decisions that have been handed over in the courts. There are definite ramifications that the people had to contend with as a result of some of those hallmark cases. We are certainly no different in our state, where the state engineer seeks to adjudicate all water and seeks to declare that they have a definite hold or rights over Indian lands, Indian water. We don't agree with that concept, and we will do whatever we can to dispel any control that the state would want over our lands. We drill our own wells and we divert our own water. We use our water in any way or manner that we see fit, because our lands and our waters are within the boundaries of the reservations.

I think it is incumbent on the Indian people, especially where I come from, to be definitely aware that managing the resources from here on out will be a task that will be hard to attain, because we find cities adjoining our reservations that more or less deplete our underground supply to a point that something has to be done to stop it.

I have several examples. One is on the Rio San Jose that has been dammed for Anglo agriculture at San Rafael and now is dry due to uranium mining and milling. Things of that nature are prevalent around Pueblo country and are responsible for the depletion of the underground water. We all know that Albuquerque is growing by leaps and bounds. The vying for water will become acute as time goes on.

During the early twenties, the Pueblo country was definitely in the way when a plan was developed to dam up at Cochiti to provide the middle Rio Grande people with some irrigation water. And the Middle Rio Grande Conservancy District was born. Agreements were made at that time to make that project a reality.

The Bureau of Indian Affairs at that time was representing the Pueblos in its negotiation. The Bureau said they did the best they could when it was conceded that the Pueblos were entitled to 8,844 acres of prior and paramount water rights. Some of us that live in the valley contend, why just 8,844 acres? We feel that these lands are the same parcels of land that adjoin the ancient lands. The Bureau of Indian Affairs conceded to end that agreement, saying that this 8,000 acres had the same right as any state land. In other words, it goes by the prior appropriations doctrine. I believe that in that instance we were sold down the river.

At this time the agreement is still in force whereby the Middle Rio Grande Conservancy District is managing our resources. They are operating under an agreement that was signed in 1928. At times, the agreement has been updated. But even though the language is explicit as to what the provisions of the agreement are, providing that water will be delivered to the lands of the Pueblos, we find that they still do as they please. In other words, our advocate, the one that is supposed to ride herd over that agreement, our trustee, is remiss. Our trustee takes a low-key position in this particular agreement.

A designated engineer is in place in order to monitor how effectively the conservancy district lives up to the provisions of the agreement under this contract. However, at this time there is an appeal by the district claiming that they don't believe that the designated engineer can tell them what to do or, to put it bluntly, they don't recognize the designated engineer's role in this particular agreement.

So it is not new to us that certain things have been tried in order to undermine an agreement that guarantees that we have a right to the water and that we can use the water in a manner that would enable the people of the six Pueblos to consider the water theirs from time immemorial and for all time.

There have been continuous problems with this particular arrangement. Right now we are in a position to try to come to some conclusion whereby both the district and the Pueblos can certainly live by this agreement. So we have tried within our area to go with those things that are in place. But when you have these types of organizations trying to help each other, it a very, very hard thing to do. We relied on the Bureau of Indian Affairs to advocate our position. It's a thing that I guess most of you have experienced—if you don't have the right kind of individual in there, or Indian advocating your position, it's an exercise that is not desirable.

We have often chastised the Bureau and its efforts here and there throughout the years. I, for one, am very, very cognizant of what the Bureau has to contend with from Indian leaders.

Someone a while ago told me, "If you don't tell a joke while you're up there, I won't speak to you for a long time." So I guess this leads me to a little something that I heard that was going on in Indian country, and that is that the federal bureaucrats for too long have acted on their own, as they saw fit, where Indians are concerned.

It seems that there were five people in a chartered plane going from Albuquerque to Window Rock to attend a BIA training session. There was the Director of the National Congress of American Indians and the President of the National Tribal Chairmen's Association and the BIA Area Director, the pilot, and an old Pueblo man. The plane developed engine trouble, and the pilot announced it was necessary to bail out. The problem was that there were only four parachutes. The Director of NCAI immediately grabbed a parachute and said, "I can't afford to die. My tribe needs me." And he jumped out. The President of NTCA grabbed a parachute and said, "I can't afford to die, my tribe needs me." And he jumped out. The BIA Area Director said, "I can't afford to die. Those two guys and all the Indians count on me to take responsible positions for them." And he jumped out. The old Pueblo man turned to the pilot and said, "I'm an old man. I've lived a long time. So why don't you take the last parachute?" "There's no need for that," the pilot said. "That guy you guys needed to make responsible decisions for you jumped out without his parachute."

So sometimes, it seems to me, that we Indians might just survive in this crisis we are now in if only the federal government would forget its parachute. I think we are at a time and place where we must get on top of our resources. We must learn all the ramifications that result from ignorance, that result from nonparticipation, that result from somebody else doing your thing for you. I can't stand still for one minute in wanting to put these words across to you.

Hopefully, the words will fall on ears that will listen to our plight. Because our plight is real. It just so happens that whenever we talk about something important, we have to go 10,000 miles to discuss it. I think it is important that tribes in regions within walking distance or within a stone's throw begin to talk to each other and begin to communicate with each other. Communication certainly is one thing that is dear to us—we definitely have to communicate in order to do things.

When I talk about communication, it reminds me of one of my Navajo friends that was in the Hopi country. There was a fork in the road. He was going back to the reservation. Just about that time, there were a couple of tourists that came upon him. They wanted instructions on how to get to the place where they wanted to go. So they said, "There's a young man over there. Let's ask him. Maybe he can lead us out of this place. We sure don't know where we're going. The maps don't do us justice. I might as well ask that man. He must be from here. Let's ask him." The driver of the car, the tourist, said to the gentleman standing on the corner of the road, "Hey, fellow. Can we take this road to Flagstaff?" The guy says, "No. Belongs to the Hopis." "Well, then, does this road go to Flagstaff?" "No. It stays here."

This is an example of the local ideas that we have about water. The Pueblo Indians are no different. We feel about water like I told you at the outset: We revere it, we talk to it, we love it. Anything that's done to corral it, control it, or bottle it is something that we will definitely fight.

I didn't say much about managing the resources because the Indian people like to see things in their original state. We like to see the birds fly free. We like to see the water roll down the river on its course, the way it was intended.

I know it is a far cry ever to attain that particular point in life again. But certainly we do yearn and do wish that people would understand us, because the way we see water is definitely different. Maybe it is because we are looking through a different window pane. But certainly the things that we see are meaningful to us and our way of life. I hope you do have the visions that we do, because it is really worth something. It goes toward longevity, longevity as it is expressed by the Indian people on this continent. We can stand the onslaught of three or four different kinds of civilizations. We will sustain. I think we do that because we remember where our roots are. We do the least we can to bother those roots.

FROM THE FLOOR: I just wanted to ask Frank, are you aware that Secretary of Interior Watt has stated his position on Indian water rights? In the United States Court of Appeals, Sixth Circuit, they interpreted the duty of the Secretary in the case of *United States v. State of Michigan* [653 F. 2d 277 (1981)]. They said, "Indian fishing rights and water rights are inseparable." And that's the way we see it. The Secretary of Interior allowed the regulations in question to expire on May 11th of this year, apparently on the grounds that he and the Bureau of Indian Affairs should defer to the states in connection with the regulation of Indian treaty fishing rights in the Great Lakes. That was the Secretary's feelings in this particular case.

The court goes on to say, "The protection of those rights is the solemn responsibility, obligation of the federal government, and no principle of federalism requires the federal government to defer to the states in connection with the protection of those rights. The responsibility of the federal government to protect the Indian treaty rights from encroachment by state and local governments is an ancient and well-established responsibility of the national government."

MR. TENORIO: That is true. I certainly don't agree with the concept that the state has any business in determining our water rights. The Pueblo Tribes have definitely resisted, and we will do what we can to withstand that particular edict. We don't agree with the states having any control whatsoever over anything that we do.

MR. GUY McMINDS

Director, Department of Quinault Natural Resources and Economic Development, Quinault Indian Nation
Taholah, Washington

MR. McMINDS: It's always interesting to see that the federal government has very unique ways of bailing out on the Indians. I guess the reason that I'm here is to try to acquaint you with the problem of managing water resources in an area that has an abundance of water resources. We have so much water on the Quinault Indian Reservation that, for example, from one stream we could in one day recharge some of the wells down in Papago country in the amount of water you need to use for one year. But, by the same token, we have many obstacles. We're the guys that have Senator Gorton.

The reason we got a Slade Gorton is that we've got big companies. The big companies want to use the water. Big companies supply a lot of jobs to a lot of non-Indians.

Let me give you a list of the companies that are competing for our water. A list of companies was very conveniently provided by their lawyer to the tribal chairmen in our area, so that they could try to entice the tribal chairmen and the Northwest Indian Fish Commission to negotiate for that abundant supply of water. These companies are: the Associated General Contractors, Boise Cascade Corporation, Burlington Northern, Chevron U.S., Incorporated, Crown Z, Garrison Sandlen, Georgia-Pacific, Entalco, ITT, Rainier, International Paper, Kaiser Aluminum, Longview Fibre, Puget Sound Power and Light Company, Rainier National Bank, St. Regis Paper Company, Scott Paper Company, Seattle First National Bank, Shell Oil, Simpson Timber, Washington Cattlemen's Association, Washington Contract Loggers, Washington Farm Bureau, Washington Forest Products, Washington Land and Title Association, Washington Women in Timber, and Weyerhaeuser.

Even though we have 84,500 acre-feet of water passing at one point in one day on the Quinault Reservation, you can see why our rights are sort of cloudy right now. With that kind of economic muscle—banks, major timber companies, mining companies, energy companies, and the like—the future of northwest water for Northwest Indian people is just as much in jeopardy as that water down there in the Southwest.

Now, before I begin, I would like to thank the American Indian Lawyer Training Program, for gathering this array of experts so that I could listen to their problems and their battles as they fight in an area where there is a scarcity of water. I think that I, from the Northwest, can learn from some of your mistakes and carry the message north so that we can prepare to battle those companies that I just listed.

In the technical reports and testimonies that I heard yesterday, I was extremely frustrated, extremely annoyed. Because I couldn't put together a game plan from what I heard. And until I heard Pete MacDonald last night, I couldn't respond to what I heard yesterday. I think he put it into context, and that's what leadership is all about. I think Peter MacDonald took the lead yesterday. He pointed out to the group that this water battle is like a ballgame—and it is. John Folk-Williams stated yesterday, "It's a war." A ballgame is a war. And you're out there to win. You're not out there to talk to that lineman across the line from you, to negotiate out a gain. You're out there to punch out a gain. And that's the name of the ballgame. I used to be a lineman, and I never let the guy across from me outgain me.

I think the idea of negotiation, however, is a good idea if you're battling, and only if you're battling. The guy from the Arizona mining interests [James W. Johnson] is in there battling. I hope he's here today, because I disagree with what he says wholeheartedly. On the Quinault Reservation—and I agree with the other people from the other reservations—we're here to stay! We will stay. Our interests always will be long term. They are not the interests of a short-term investment program that most United States companies have. These people who are investors in mining companies don't live in the area we do. They are there to do just what they say they're going to do—they are there to mine and get out. They are there to use your water and get out. And you have to protect against that.

I enjoyed Peter MacDonald's statement, because we are in a ballgame with the competition, who have a a very limited amount of time to make money for their stockholders. So, it is like a ballgame for them, and we have to recognize that.

I was very interested to hear people discuss the concept of negotiation. That means that they're going to put us in the mainstream. If that's equated with in-stream flow, then that's my water. But I hope I'm not like some of the Papagos who have a river under their reservation. It seems to me that these people are up a creek. I don't want to be up the creek. I don't think the Papagos want to be up the creek. So the ballgame is all about putting us in the mainstream. Our job is to keep us in stream, because Indians use water in stream. Our water is to keep us away from being up the creek.

I tried to put on paper this morning what I felt about the discussion yesterday. I felt my job to the Indian people was to convey to them what I thought about yesterday. My job is to try to put together what I would do in the Northwest, if I had this reservoir of talent that's in this room at my disposal to build myself a management plan for that 84,500 acre-feet of water that passes one point in my reservation every day. I would have to acquaint myself, as a manager, with the special characteristics that water has and try to refer that to my frame of reference, my Indian frame of reference, not that competing-interest frame of reference. I would have to understand that water is a renewable resource, although that renewability is very fragile. Once you use water, a special characteristic of water is that it is the universal solvent. It, by its nature of use, gets impurities as it is used. So it really is not renewable on the same scale or reusable on the same scale as it was prior to the first use.

In recognizing that, I have to go back to a principle that we have in fisheries. In fisheries we always say that we are managing the fish to get the maximum amount of fish back with the maximum harvest, so that we can have a continuous supply of fish year after year. I don't know how practical it is in the Southwest to have a continuous supply of water year after year, but I do know from what I heard yesterday that the Indian people want to be on their reservations for a long time, and they want jobs all year around.

So the technician—that legal technician, that engineer, that water technician, and those other people that are associated with the tribe—are going to have to find a way to fulfill that obligation to the tribe they work for.

In fisheries, we haven't done such a good job of renewing the fish supply every year, because that company that has short-term investments has developed terminology to keep the fish away from the Indian people. I heard discussions in here that all of the water was used up. The mining man from Arizona [James W. Johnson] claimed that all of the water was used up. I went back in my memory, and I know how that ballgame of paper fish and paper water goes. In the fish business the federal managers in the ocean continuously overpredict the runs so that they can harvest the fish destined for Indian fishing grounds. If I was a water manager in the Southwest and dependent on state law to predict my right, I'd probably develop the technique of underpredicting the water supply so that the Indians couldn't get involved with its use.

I think it takes technical people on the side of the tribe to get out there and in fact examine what's going on with this game of underpredicting. There might be some of that game going on for ground water.

The next characteristic of water that is important to us in the Northwest is that it is impoundable, and thus transportable, and, consequently, marketable to an area that has a scarce supply of water. With the probability that the Southwest is going to continue to grow, we are just like that Papago Indian who is competing with his Ak Chin brothers in the next basin away. We are several basins away, up in the Northwest, but we understand the scarcity of water and those of you in the Southwest who may be competing for the water.

Now, we want to keep that water in the Northwest, just as the Great Basin people in the central part of the United States want to keep that water in their area. But we understand the tremendous economic bite that is being put on the sources of water that seem to be in abundant supply.

Let me give you an example of what I consider the economic bite. Since I'm a rookie, and most of us from the Northwest are rookies in this ballgame, excuse me if I don't get all my calculations correct. If I have 86,400 acre-feet going by a point in the Quinault Reservation at flood time and I multiply it by the value of $2,250 per acre-feet of water—that's what industrial interests are willing to pay in the Big Thompson Project in eastern Colorado—I come up with a market value for that water of $194 million.

Now, I talked to our young people from our reservation. That's raw resource dollars, then, 194 million bucks. And the one-handed economists that I talk to—who don't use the other hand—tell me that in a normal economy that raw natural resource will manufacture you eight to twelve times more money. Do you know what that figure turns out to be? This is the kind of economic ballgame we're playing. It's over 8 billion bucks.

The pipelines across Alaska are built on the basis of the scarcity of oil because then it becomes extremely marketable. If I had to make a prediction about the scarcity of water, I would say that there will be water pipelines, just like there are oil pipelines. And I, in the Northwest, am going to have to prepare for the time when there are going to be water pipelines. Can you envision the United States of America with a series of water pipelines? Someone is going to have to be able to predict what that will do. The mass transport of water over the United States of America is going to be nothing that's inconsequential. It may change the entire weather pattern of this area.

So in my plan I'm going to want to consider that as a very probable alternative, because of those characteristics of water and because water is worth that much money.

In fact, I think the fifth characteristic of water, if I had to assign a characteristic to it right now, is that it's not only scarce, it verges on being precious.

If we believe that water is that valuable, then we're going to have to try to pull together the skills to protect that water. A number of the skills may be in this room. The tribal governments want to maintain that water to maintain our way of life. You heard Russell Jim say, "Leave us alone. I want to maintain my way of life." Well, I want to be able to protect our water so that our fishermen can maintain their way of life. But if they value their way of life, given that the federal government is bailing out of its financing programs for us to protect our rights, some of our leaders in that game plan at half time are going to have to go down to our people who have economic stakes in these waters and say, "Hey, if you're making money from these waters now, in order for you to protect your water you are going to have to contribute so that we can buy the expertise that we need to keep our fishery whole, and it may even mean that you as a fisherman have to compromise to protect your fishery. Because without some form of compromise, you may not be able to stem the tide of the radical right that is radically trying to come in to take away your right."

Now, by "compromise" I don't mean arguing verbally. A compromise comes very hard. You have to slug and punch just as hard as you can to maintain that right. In the art of compromise, you do need to know what you are doing. In our area I'm reminded of some of the recent compromises that were outright thievery because the Indian people couldn't control the federal system. The one that comes to mind right now is the Columbia River agreement with the states of Washington and Oregon and the federal government regarding their fish on the Columbia River. The Indian people thought they had an agreement for a certain number of fish, and the white guy said, "No, that was just a goal, and we can work toward that." Not only did they not work toward it, they almost took all of the fish away from the Columbia River people. The Columbia River people had to go to court again to "win their fish." And they did that. But the judge is telling them that they have to sit down again with the states of Washington and Oregon and the federal government to negotiate a solution.

What they need right now is the best technical experts they can find and a commitment from their lawyers to make the fish business a top priority. They need to sit down and negotiate using the best technical advice they can, to carefully read the words, make sure what they are getting, and to carefully study the numbers from a biological point of view.

To me, that is the kind of ballgame we are in in the water business. Tribes need to go back and define the skills and need to get people with reputations in advocacy to sit down with them and go over the various strategies and skills that they need to firm up their water rights in the Northwest.

An area I think is too often lightly touched on is the tribal purpose for allocating resources. What are the purposes? We need to specifically outline how we intend to protect that fisherman on the Columbia River or that old man who is living down the street. Those purposes really need to be outlined. They're the things that Russell Jim and others were talking about. That's the job of the owner. The owner in this case is the people who make the tribal government the responsible entity for carrying out this activity. The tribal government, as a good owner, needs to select a good coach, a coach that will be able to pick the material the tribe needs to defend its ground on that field. That coach has to be given the latitude to do that. Tribal personnel, policies, and procedures should not apply when you are battling against non-Indians in this ballgame. A lot of times we may select somebody who is not qualified to do the job. We need the best, because the stakes are high—1 billion dollars for one day's water—that is no small ballgame.

These technical people need to get everything squared away for us so they can acquaint the tribal council with the knowledge of that resource. And that coach, whoever is put in charge of these technical people, has to be able to come to the tribal council and say, "This is the resource, these are the kinds of policies we need now to protect our resource." And this coach needs to go over these policies and strategies with the tribal government, so that they are in tune with each other and so that they can go ahead. The tribal government needs then to get out to its constituency and advocate a course of action to protect this right. The reason it needs to do this is that the guy from the mining company is standing outside the reservation, figuring out how he can split that tribe up so he can take the water away.

When it knows the game plan, the tribal government has the responsibility of getting out with the constituents and acquainting them with that game plan. When you have an idea of what that game plan is, and the technicians and the coach running those technicians have some experience with playing with that game plan for a while, they are going to have to return to the council with any modifications in that game plan they have to develop a better strategy.

The commitment for developing internal tribal legislation so that you can finance a good water game plan has to be there. Once the commitment of the people on the reservation to finance their own game plan is there, larger money interests will begin to take a look at you, because then you are generating an economy and you will be able to get financing from outside of the tribal community.

The name of the game right now to defend your water rights is financing your own game plan. I don't think the government is going to be in the business of trying to defend water rights. That is the tenor of the government now. The strategy I would use if I were them and wanted to take away your water rights would be to give you lip service and keep you off balance, but not give you anything.

Wendell Chino is on the right track. He knows this. He knows the government is not going to give him anything. And he is going to protect his people.

Our ballgame as tribal leaders is now to go and convince our people that we are going to have to pay for some of this ourselves. If you don't have massive stands of timber, the question of how you pay for it is going to have to be discussed in pueblos in New Mexico, in the long houses in the Northwest, and other dwellings in the Midwest.

In closing, I want to acquaint you with the dangers in the Northwest by telling you that on my reservation on any given square mile we can have between 70 to 200 inches of rainfall a year at any given point. Streams on my reservation can go from 150 cubic feet a second—there are 7½ gallons in a cubic foot—to 55,000 cubic feet a second. There are 412,500 cubic feet of water going by one point at one time in one second. In one second, 412,000 cubic feet of water goes by one point on the Quinault River at one time. That translates into more than an acre-foot per second, which translates into 84,500 acre-feet per day.

Now, there are over thirty streams in western Washington that have the capability of generating energy, power, hydroelectric power, or of generating some transportable water that can go to the arid Southwest.

The users of our water in the Northwest are just using it for that property called solvency right now. They want to take the impurities out of their stuff and dump it back into the streams. They haven't quite figured out that it is more valuable in other, different ways.

So, back in the Northwest I have to recognize that there are people planning for the use of that water. And if I don't get into the ballgame, they will, and they'll take it away from me.

To summarize my discussion, water, no matter where it is, is extremely valuable because of the properties I mentioned. The key to the survival of the Indian communities is not to capture the experts in this kind of a meeting, but to capture them where the real ballgame is, so that we can develop an effective game plan. I thought Peter MacDonald's speech was excellent. If we develop a SCWRT [State Confederation of Water Resource Tribes] on a statewide basis, we may be able to make a bigger SCWRT. That is the challenge to the Wendell Chino's, the Joe DeLaCruz's, the Peter MacDonald's, and the other national Indian leaders: to develop that SCWRT, to coordinate that SCWRT, to begin to get the technical expertise we need to protect that water. Maybe we can even have our own intertribal water inter-ties, because water is valuable. And if we can cooperate with each other, we can have a better long-term existence.

In closing, I would like to thank Frank [Tenorio] from the Pueblos for starting out the morning, getting our feet back out on the ground from a tribal perspective. A lot of times Indian people are carried away in the tide of technical promotional activities, and they refuse to evaluate what the technical people say, to work it into a game plan for their own purpose. I hope I've at least got people to think in that vein today.

FROM THE FLOOR: Guy, do you own that amount of water you were talking about? Do you own it? Or does the water just flow through there? Do you claim ownership?

MR. McMINDS: That is on the Quinault Reservation, and it is our position that we own all of that water on it.

FROM THE FLOOR: I know it's your position. Are there any decisions, governmental or any other thing, that you can get that water?

MR. McMINDS: There is not a whole fleet of water decisions on the coast of Washington because of the abundant supply. My pitch is to get us into a position that allows us to make sure that nobody takes it away from us.

MR. CHRIS E. McNEIL, JR.

Corporate Secretary, Sealaska Corporation
Juneau, Alaska

MR. McNEIL: I want to take this opportunity to express my appreciation for being able to be here to share some of my ideas with you concerning Indian water policy and how it may relate to the Alaska Native Claims Settlement Act.

I think it is entirely appropriate that the title to the conference is "Indian Water Policy in a Changing Environment." We are certainly aware of that particular situation in Alaska, as things are changing very, very rapidly up there. No matter what the perceived problems I might discuss today concerning ANCSA may be—any ambiguities in the bill, whether or not it is perceived as a termination kind of bill—these are still very exciting times for Alaska Natives right now. The wheels of change were set in motion in 1971 by Congress and by Alaska Natives. I think it is a challenge for Alaska Natives now to manage that change.

I am here not to give a discourse in any sort of way on the history of the Alaska Native Claims Settlement Act, but I would like to highlight just some of the prominent issues I see that may relate to water rights issues.

The Claims Act, of course, is an extremely complex

piece of legislation. It creates corporations that are organized under state law. It creates some mandated and discretionary relationships among them and with the shareholders. You will have to excuse me for the way I will be using the term "shareholders." I know you are not used to it. It took me a long time to get socialized to using that term rather than "tribal members." But the owners of the Alaska Native corporations, of course, are shareholders, and that is the way we now refer to them.

The Claims Act has been a long process, as Mr. Angapak has described. The implementation has been arduous and complex. There are issues say, just in one paragraph, such as in section 7(i), mandating certain resource sharing among all of the regional corporations, over which the corporations have spent a great deal of time and, I must say, have spent literally millions of dollars. This is something that is rife through the act, and it's just a part of it.

If nothing else, I can say that all of the regional and village corporations can take the credit for supporting untold numbers of accountants and consultants and a lot of unnamed law firms I'm sure we are all familiar with.

Some of the key issues that I think are important in terms of water rights issues for us are the global issues: On the up side, whether or not these corporations will be able to flourish; on the down side, planning for survival, both financially and culturally as a people in Alaska.

One of the things that is prominent is that these corporations were incorporated under the state statutes as profit-making corporations. That creates a presumption and a set of circumstances that sets some of the tone insofar as the way the corporations operate. It creates expectations on the part of the tribal member-owners of the corporations, which are very high. The shareholders expect that the corporations will provide profits, profits on a large scale, and very quickly.

To give you some idea of the initial distribution of funds in round numbers, about half of the Alaska Native fund was distributed directly to shareholders, and the other half was distributed to corporations for future investment and growth on their part. Now that we have reached a point where half of the money is in effect distributed, it is left to these corporations to produce profits in order to provide any benefit to shareholders.

In order to provide just $100, in effect, on a per capita basis in a year, it would require our corporation to earn a million and a half dollars in after-tax profits. Those are really fairly big demands. I think the underlying problem is that the general public, Alaska Natives themselves, have been led to believe that the corporations are extremely rich. That really is not the case.

As an example, the per capita distribution under the Claims Act to at-large shareholders over a ten-year period has been approximately $6,000. This is really not very much when you look at it in context—ordinarily people discuss the billion dollars that you have seen in the media, the 44 million acres of land—we don't deny that these are all of great value, but once you break it down among the approximately 80,000 Alaska Natives, it really doesn't come out to what you might think it would.

We also have as another issue an underlying cultural concern. The Alaska Native leadership doesn't want to see the situation where the mere existence of these American-structured corporations would in any way lead to the demise of our cultural way of life. There are many cultures in Alaska. I am from the part of the country where there are Tlingits and Haidas, and there are many Eskimos and Aleuts and Athabascans who live in other parts of the state.

Another issue concerns a trust and tribal relationship after ANCSA. There is a major provision in ANCSA that provides that the land claims settlement will not result in reservations or racial enclaves. At the same time, ANCSA did not repeal any of the then-existing tribal relationships. In fact, it has gone the other way by express Congressional action in the Indian Self-Determination and Education Assistance Act, the Financing Act, and the Marine Mammals Act, and most lately in the amendment to the Alaska Native Claims Settlement Act under the D-2 bill.

The result of this is that there doesn't seem to be any single answer to the question of tribal status in our post-Alaska Native Claims Settlement Act world. Each issue seems to be dealt with discretely, depending on the total circumstances.

Another large issue that we face is a 1991 issue. One of the provisions of the act states that the stock that is given to each shareholder can be allowed to be alienated after a twenty-year period. The provision of the act dealing with this was amended in December 1980, and it still allows this stock to be sold, but under very specified conditions. The obvious concern is that this is the real termination, this aspect of the bill, and this is something that is of deep concern to Alaska Native leadership right now. It is something that is a high priority with the Alaska Federation of Natives in the near term.

In sum, the ANCSA corporations are structured like American corporations. I don't think there is any question about that. But their ownership, their politics, and their very souls are very distinctly Alaska Native. I think that is what creates the difference. They are hybrids.

As a final note, insofar as these issues are concerned, I want to point out that the Alaska Native leadership affirmatively chose this structure in 1971. It wasn't entirely something that was foisted upon the Alaska Native leadership. What it provides is a great deal of freedom, of flexibility, a little bit less intrusion on the part of the government; but it certainly also raises the spectre and the risk of failure for some or all of the corporations. It is something we are very cognizant of. ANCSA is a hybrid; it is an experiment. I don't think the judgment is in at all on the ultimate success or failure of these corporations.

I must point out that when you look at the act's complexity and ambiguity, one thing that is actually certain about it is that it was created by a committee.

Insofar as water rights are concerned, this issue, as Nelson pointed out, has not really been prominent in our minds. One of the reasons is that the conveyance has been so slow—in Sealaska's case it has taken virtually ten years to convey over 200,000 acres of land. It's still going on. It is apparent now that as the Department of the Interior has interpreted "immediately" in the act, it really is going on Indian time.

The Sealaska Corporation is composed of approximately 15,700 Alaska Natives. Most of the shareholders are Tlingits, Haidas, and Tsimpsians. The corporation is organized in such a way that we have a parent corporation, Sealaska, and four subsidiaries. Our subsidiaries are the Alaska Brick Company, which is a building supply company that has about $30 million in sales. We have a very large fish company in the Pacific Northwest, which I believe is about the third largest. It's called Ocean Beauty Seafoods. We expect around $200 million in sales this year. And we have Sealaska Timber Corporation, which is also a subsidiary, designed primarily to market, to export the timber that we own, also in conjunction with the village corporations in our area. We expect to be harvesting in excess of a hundred million board feet per year. We also have created another subsidiary called SBIC, Sealaska Business Investment Corporation. That corporation was specifically designed to provide investment opportunities for our own shareholders. That is, it is a venture capital firm and provides loans and equity investments on shareholder-owned businesses. We also have a heritage foundation that is a nonprofit foundation we incorporated in order to provide an organizational means to take care of the many issues of cultural survival and language, providing scholarships to our shareholders. So we have created a whole host of organizations to deal with these implementation problems.

By way of the land itself, we have gone through a process over the last ten years that has been very lengthy and expensive just in relation to the land. First of all, there were some deadlines that had to be met concerning the selection of the land. The general guidelines were set out by law and regulation about which land could be selected as a part of the act. But many discretionary decisions were made concerning evaluation and overall long-range economic needs in order to make these selections.

The next phase involved the inevitable contest and litigation with the government. Much of this litigation involved issues of easements. Some of the earlier litigation involved plans that would, in effect, turn much of this land into easements, and much of the value of it would be lost because of that. Finally, the conveyances came.

It has only been in the last two years that we have had any real, significant, actual development on the land. I find that in describing the land at Sealaska, it is much like our brothers on the Quinault, where we have a tremendous amount of rainfall. We have in the neighborhood of 150 inches a year. It tends to distort and diminish the importance of the issue when, in fact, it is really quite important. Right now, in southeastern Alaska, we have not had a substantive dispute concerning the ownership of the water resource. We don't know the full extent of the rights of ownership and control of that ownership. One case that has come down in the Alaska Supreme Court dealt with a third-party contest over the ownership of rights of a small lake that was providing water to a cannery operation. The court there held that those third-party appropriations under 43 U.S.C. 661, which is the Federal Appropriations Act, constituted a valid and existing right pursuant to Section 1603 of ANCSA. What this meant was that those previous interests were recently held to be good, as against the Native corporation who contested it.

The next thing I'd like to discuss is what we can expect by way of water development in Alaska and, more specifically, in the Sealaska region.

We have competing interests, both within Sealaska Corporation and with external parties. As I mentioned before, the corporations are set up to make profits. It means that they are highly developmentally oriented. We have competing needs internally, which we perceive to be extremely important. Those are the subsistence needs of our shareholders. We don't want to do anything to the environment that would in any way jeopardize the rights of those shareholders and tribal members to continue to be able to take fish and game from the land. We also have the environmental concerns within the corporation, and these relate mostly to fisheries.

The important thing is that the Sealaska Board of Directors, all of whom are Sealaska shareholders, have a real concern with the environment. We live in the environment of southeastern Alaska, and we know we are there for the long term. We are not an ordinary corporation that wants to come in, take everything out you can, and leave it.

Internally, though, we have a classic competition for resources that relate to water. The timber industry naturally cuts the trees down and, in our case, exports those trees. This has an effect on the land, particularly with reference to the streams that provide the abundant fishery resources in southeastern Alaska.

On the other hand, we own a substantially large fish company that also reaps the benefit of that water by way of the streams that exist there. We find ourselves in the position of balancing these interests, so that we are able, on the one hand, to have a controlled development over the timber industry and still maintain the viability of the streams for the fishery in Alaska.

As I mentioned before, there is quite a profit motive involved. There are high expectations. On the other hand, the fundamental decisions concerning the management of these resources are handled by the Sealaska Board of Directors. The Board will not allow the pollution of these resources. They want to maintain the historical conservation that Alaska Natives have had.

Our management is structured in a way that allows for this. We have extensive land use planning. We have hired individuals who have expertise in the environment—timber specialists, fishery specialists, and hard-rock mineral specialists—all of whom work independently of the corporations and the subsidiary corporations that we have created. This is not intended to be an idyllic structure, but we are attempting to manage these resources in such a way as to maintain the long-term benefit.

Over the long term, we have a lot of developments, and we know right now, even though we have these abundant resources, that there are going to be competing needs and that there, in fact, may be circumstances in which shortages arise. We have the timber-cutting needs, we have the expectation of hydroelectric power, we have fisheries, we have the infrastructures that invariably come with the development of any of the industries that I am talking about. We have the development of hard-rock minerals coming along the line.

I hope that my short discussion here has led to a little understanding of where we are in terms of water resources right now. While I know there are many differences—and substantive differences—between our situation and yours, I am sure that there are enough common issues that will be helpful if we are all able to continue to discuss these issues in forums like today's.

MR. NELSON N. ANGAPAK

Chairman of the Board, Calista Corporation
Anchorage, Alaska

MR. ANGAPAK: Let me preface my statement by saying that we Alaska natives are relatively new in the ballgame insofar as water and land resource management is concerned.

As many of you are aware, the Alaska Native Claims Settlement Act was passed ten years ago. The act promised us 44 million acres of land, but to this day only approximately 13 million of that land has been transferred to us.

While the act states that the settlement of the Alaska Natives would be accomplished rapidly, I guess everything is relative. Perhaps to the federal government, 13 of 44 million acres transferred is rapid. At the present rate that the land is being transferred to us, it's going to take another twenty years until such time as 85 percent of our main entitlement has been transferred to us. And none of us will be alive on that day if the actual amount of time required to transfer the land remains the same. We have very conservatively estimated that it is going to take another 100 to 150 years until all of the land that was promised us has been transferred to us. I guess that is a very rapid settlement of our claim.

At any rate, the Native corporations in Alaska made their selections. We had deadlines to meet. The final deadline of the land selection for us was five years from the time of the passage of the act. By then we were required to select all of the 44 million acres. Recognizing the fact that we must have a strong land base if we are to become successful companies, it took us all five years to make our selections.

The selections have been made. All the deadlines were met. We met every deadline. But along the way we have found that the Claims Settlement Act is a promise that has yet to be fulfilled. Long after the lands that were selected and the natural resources associated with them have been conveyed to us, we are going to be responsible for the management of those lands.

In our area, scarcity of water is not a problem. Roughly 30 percent of our whole area is water. Consequently, its abundance is really a blessing and a curse at the same time. A blessing because we can find it whenever and wherever we need it. A curse because—I hate to say this, but it is a reality, it is a fact—we have begun to take water for granted.

But over the last couple of days I have come to the realization that if we continue to take water for granted, we may not have it in the future.

One of the basic things we have been doing over the last couple of years is trying to acquire skills. I'll agree with Mr. McMinds here, we need the skills. We are in the process at this point of building technical expertise that will enable us to develop a sound land and water resource use management program.

How are we doing this? We are picking the brains of the technical experts. We are in the process of getting together a group of people, some with backgrounds in law, some with backgrounds in water resource management, because we feel that water is one of those resources that's going to make our lands a little bit more valuable than they are at this point.

One of the things we have found over the last couple of years is that when reviewing legal interpretations of water law and other laws that are associated with it, and I believe you will agree with me, we must get away from the traditional form of western interpretation of the law. Because if we stick to that and stick to the western interpretation of the law, we might find ourselves cornered.

As an example, section 4(c) of the very same act that created the regional corporation states, and I quote, "All claims against the United States, the state, and all other persons that are based on claims of aboriginal right, title, use or occupancy of land or water areas in Alaska are hereby extinguished." We are not disputing that language at this point. But our interpretation of that language is that while the Alaska Native Claims Settlement Act expressly extinguished all our claims based on aboriginal title, which may have encompassed water rights, the Claims Settlement Act converted that aboriginal claim into what we now call legal fee title.

We have not fully developed a comprehensive legal argument for this concept, but we feel very strongly that we can develop that language so that our interests in land and water will be protected.

Lastly, recognizing the fact that the American Indian tribes of the mainland states have been continually faced with the problems of water resource management, one of the things we are in the process of doing is reviewing the land management and water resource management programs of the mainland states, because we know that you are way ahead of the game insofar as that area is concerned. We feel that we can benefit from some of the lawsuits that have been filed, where there are legal decisions on behalf of the American Indians. I will be the first to admit that I am going to go away from this symposium by saying that I will have gained more knowledge from this symposium than I contributed.

One of the things we are doing in the meantime in our company is a quasi-water management program. It is, very simply, as follows: We are managing our water resource in conjunction with the management of our natural resources. In other words, while we recognize the importance of our water resources, we are managing that resource in conjunction with the other resources because, at this point, we know of no other way.

With that, I will close my statement by saying that Mr. Chino, as well as Mr. MacDonald last night, stated it very eloquently: We are faced with a problem of such magnitude that unless we attempt to unite, and do unite to resolve the problem of water resources, we may find ourselves in left field.

I think at this point there must be a total unity amongst us if we are to resolve this problem either through the courts, legislatively, or through negotiations.

Dinner Address

MR. KENNETH L. SMITH

Assistant Secretary for Indian Affairs
U.S. Department of the Interior
Washington, D.C.

MR. KENNETH SMITH: First of all, it is a pleasure for me to be here tonight. I want to congratulate the American Indian Lawyer Training Program for initiating and organizing this symposium on a topic of vital interest and importance to all of Indian country. The exchange of information, ideas, and philosophies among this group of knowledgeable people should be of great value to us as we go down the road.

Clearly, there is a need for tribal leaders and government officials to be informed about the complex issues pertaining to Indian water rights. Increasingly, decisions about water issues are being required of us. We sometimes have no choice, we have to make a decision. It needs to be a sound, sensible decision with all factors, past, present, and future, considered.

Most of you know that I am not a lawyer. So I am sure that I was not invited here to discuss fine points of the law or otherwise intrude into the lawyer's domain as an interpreter of the law. I think it is safe to assume that I was invited here as the Interior Assistant Secretary for Indian Affairs to tell you what I can about the Department's and the Administration's policies and plans, and perhaps a little of my own thinking and how I plan to function in this particular job that I presently hold.

There are a lot of lawyers here, so let me tell you right away that one of the things I do regularly in my job is listen to lawyers expressing opinions about the law before I make policy or program decisions. So, one of the things I will do here is listen. What I hear may be more important than anything I say.

Before discussing some specific water issues, let me say a few words about my responsibility as an advocate for the Indian community. I consider it a major function under my responsibility as trustee to be an advocate for Indian causes and rights. This, of course, does not license me as some maverick champion of unpopular causes. To be an effective advocate within the Administration, I have to be a member of the team. This means I can fight as hard as I am able in staff session and in the internal councils of the Administration. But when the President or the Secretary makes a decision, then I have to support it and implement it.

I am realistic enough to know that we aren't going to win every battle, but I will say this to you: We live in a political world. We all have to be politicians in one way or another. But we still need a solid framework of principles that support us and that we hold to. We may negotiate about the application of a right or the effects of a right, but it is my job to protect and defend those rights.

As an advocate for Indian country, I can't let the popularity of a position be the determining criterion of my efforts. I certainly intend to listen to and consider the recommendations of the Indian leaders, but then I will make my own decision. I feel that it would be an abdication of my responsibility if I did otherwise.

I think some of you have heard some of my speeches about consultation and that I feel I have a responsibility. I am held responsible for that job, and I am going to try to carry it out to the best of my ability. I will protect Indian rights to my fullest! On the other hand, I was appointed to the job, and I am going to listen, I am going to learn, and I will be the first to say that I don't know all the answers. I wish I could have spent two days listening to all the experts out there. I consider you the experts. Hopefully, I would go back with a little better wisdom about water rights.

I think it should be noted that there can be situations in which I, as trustee, might feel obligated to act in a manner different from a tribe's formally expressed will. We are facing this kind of dilemma right now in Montana.

I'm sure that some of you are aware of an issue called S.B. 76. It is a Montana legislative act that requires all water users who claim a right to water to file a claim in state court by January 1, 1982. Under that law, there is a presumption of abandonment if one does not file by the first of the year.

In addition, the Northern Cheyenne Tribe filed a water rights suit back in February of 1975 in a race to the courthouse because the state was about to enact its own water adjudication statute. The United States filed on behalf of the Northern Cheyennes the following April and then on behalf of the Crows in May of that year.

In April of 1979, in anticipation of the enactment of S.B. 76, the United States filed in the federal district courts on behalf of the Flathead tribe. The Montana legislature passed the bill the next month. Then in November of 1979, Judge Battin and Judge Hatfield dismissed all of these federal lawsuits in favor of state court jurisdiction. That dismissal order was appealed and argued last July. If the Ninth Circuit Court of Appeals reverses Judge Battin, then we stay in federal court. If they uphold him, I will recommend an appeal to the United States Supreme Court. However, if the Ninth Circuit doesn't make a decision by the end of December, then we are left holding the bag. Then we have to decide whether or not to file at least a protective filing in state court. We would, of course, disclaim jurisdiction and argue that the state doesn't have jurisdiction.

I hope that you appreciate the dilemma that I am in. I hope that the Ninth Circuit will hand down a decision, and I am reliably informed that it looks good for us. But we do have to have an opinion in hand in order to be certain of what the law is. I assure you that I will do the right thing as trustee for our Indian people. But as of now, we have to live with Judge Battin's decision.

Before discussing some specific issues, let me make clear that, unless I indicate otherwise, I will be speaking only for myself and not the Department or the Administration. I can tell you what I think, the positions that I am going to support, but until a Departmental or Administration decision is made, my positions remain simply mine.

I have no intention whatsoever of trying to push tribes into negotiating water settlements if they do not want to negotiate. But I most certainly do want to make it possible for tribes to negotiate a settlement when they believe it is to their advantage. I can appreciate that some tribes might think they have ideal conditions for successfully litigating their rights, but my general approach would be to encourage negotiated settlements. My basic reason for this position is that I think the tribes, speaking generally, can get greater benefits through negotiation than through litigation.

One reason is that litigation, after years of effort and great expense, may win you "paper water" that you can't use. You have won a legal battle, in short, but lost the political war.

I recognize that there can be lots of problems in working out negotiations that are not sellouts. As we have seen in the Ak Chin situation, there can be problems after negotiations. Nonetheless, I think the negotiated settlements generally have a better chance of producing real, wet water for a reservation. That's the only kind of water that is really useful.

As a matter of opinion, I think that the time element is important. The claims on water are going to increase with each passing year. One hundred years ago, the person who recognized the precious value of water in the West was a person destined to become rich. Ten years ago, the demand for water was not nearly so pressing as it is today. Ten years from now, the need for water will be immensely greater.

I am aware, of course, that the increasing need for water by other entities does not affect the legal rights of tribes. But realistically, we know it has a very definite practical effect. Right now, according to our calculations, the Central Arizona tribes have potential rights to most of the water there is in Central Arizona. But we know that this is not going to turn off the taps in the homes of non-Indians in Phoenix or Tucson. I think there are good reasons for the tribes to work for agreements and settlements as quickly as possible to turn paper water into wet water, producing benefits for the reservation. This is only my opinion. The individual tribes will seek their own counsel and make their own decisions on whether they choose to negotiate or litigate.

Since I favor negotiated settlements, I am willing to accept quantification. I know that there are tribes and individuals who want to cling to the open-ended position. However, I believe that quantification is inevitable. Through litigation or through negotiation, Indian tribes are going to have to quantify their water rights. The tremendous economic pressure of water will force the end of open-ended rights. Consequently, my recommendation is that tribes focus on maximizing what they can get in the quantification process.

Government provision of attorneys' fees to tribes has become a matter of Congressional scrutiny and controversy. Constituents have complained to members of Congress about our funding of tribes to hire private counsel to prosecute claims against the constituents. They feel that this practice is unfair because it provides federally recognized tribes with an advantage to which they are not entitled and places the enormous resources of the federal government at the disposal of the tribes and against non-Indian constituents.

There is no doubt in my mind that treaties and federal law have made it the responsibility of the United States to see to it that Indian resources are adequately protected in court in all matters involving the trust responsibility. It also seems clear to me that representation by the Justice Department may not always be adequate.

Where there would be a clear conflict of interest between the United States and a tribe, I assume there would be no problem in employing independent counsel for the tribe. Beyond this, however, I believe that there are times when subtle but important differences may arise between the prosecution of individual tribal interests by Justice Department attorneys and a tribe's private counsel. Therefore, at the present time I am actively working with the Solicitor's Office to draft regulations which will ensure that the tribe's position will be adequately represented in court when these differences arise.

The jurisdictional issue of water regulation and tribal water codes is important in Indian country. As you know, former Interior Secretary Morton imposed a moratorium in 1974 on the approval of any tribal water codes. To date, this moratorium has not been rescinded by the Secretary.

Water codes which would place non-Indians under tribal jurisdiction raise many legal questions. However, it is my position that the state has no jurisdiction to regulate reserved water on the reservation, but that such jurisdiction is vested jointly in the federal government and the tribe. The recent *Walton* decision supports this position in certain circumstances. It is my position that water regulation, like land use regulation, is an appropriate function of tribal government. I believe the function can best be exercised with the adoption of appropriate safeguards for the non-Indian resident water users on the reservation. I am now working for the adoption of this position by the Department. I must advise you, however, that the Solicitor does not concur with my feelings.

The Senate Appropriations Committee deleted President Reagan's 1982 budget request for implementation of the Ak Chin Water Settlement Act of 1978. The committee's rationale was that revised estimates showed the expected costs of the project had risen to $80 million, while the act authorized only $43 million. We have appealed this deletion. In this instance, we are dealing not only with a law, which the lawmakers might feel free to change, but also with a contract pursuant to that act which the tribe can enforce in court. In a memorandum to the Secretary, I pointed out that the Ak Chin community was authorized by the act to seek damages if the United States failed to deliver water to the reservation at the specified time. For a total breach, these damages could be almost $15 million annually. I also noted that any failure by us to pursue the timely funding of the Ak Chin project would seriously damage our credibility and our ability to negotiate settlements with other tribes. As you know, there are other tribes talking about settling their water issues throughout the country.

Though the Orme Dam is not, strictly speaking, a water rights issue, it is related. And I want to say a few words about Secretary Watt's approach to making a decision on that matter. I do not know yet for sure what decision Secretary Watt will make about the dam. But I do know this: When he makes his decision, he will be fully informed and aware of the concerns and the rights of the Yavapai Indians whose reservation is threatened with inundation by the proposed dam.

The Secretary not only kept an open mind about Orme Dam, he kept his eyes and his ears and his heart open. He met with the tribal chairmen in Washington on two occasions. He promised he would go to Fort McDowell to see the area and to hear the tribal members. He was very sympathetic with their appeal. He told me afterwards that he was deeply touched by their concern about their property and about their rights and about their land.

I think that on these water issues where there are differences of opinion, Indian and non-Indian positions, that we can be confident that the Secretary will listen to us and that our concerns and interests will be fully considered when decisions are made that affect our rights.

I have felt all along that I, as Assistant Secretary, and the staff that we are trying to bring on board, know the water issue is a big issue, a tough issue, but I think we have got to be prepared to strategize on how we are going to win that battle. If we do it properly and if we do our homework, I think we will succeed. If we don't do our homework, then I'm going to holler for help real fast.

I want to conclude by stating that I feel very strongly about the Department's trustee role. I intend to strongly support this position. But I need your support and help.

Dinner Address

MR. PETER MacDONALD
Chairman, Navajo Nation
Window Rock, Arizona

MR. MacDONALD: I really enjoyed listening to Ken Smith give us a message, not only from his heart but also from the Department of the Interior, that the Secretary will listen to us and will work with us in fighting for our water.

Normally, I, like Wendell Chino, also like to tear after BIA. But I am not going to do that tonight. I am going to do something a little bit different.

Tonight is Monday night football. I guess all of you know that. In some ways, this conference on water can be likened to a football game. When I looked at the program for tonight, I noticed that Ken and I were scheduled to speak here. I guess you could consider that as the half-time entertainment. The teams are in the locker room. The marching band is out on the field. The cheerleaders are twirling their batons and strutting their stuff. And everyone is relaxed, going to the restrooms, getting their hot dogs, and just hashing over the first half's events.

Down in the locker room, the team that's leading is figuring out how to beef up the defense, put a few more points on the scoreboard, and hold on to the lead. But for the team that's trailing, the coaches are desperately trying to figure out what went wrong with the game plan and what changes they need to make to shift the momentum and turn things around.

You, the experts here, are our offensive squads, our defensive squads, and our special teams, as well. But this is hardly a spectator sport for me or for the Navajo Nation for that matter. The way I read the scoreboard, I think it's time we overhauled the whole game plan.

At the start of the game, things started off real well. We won the toss and elected to receive. The special teams went in, made a fantastic kickoff return, and put us in scoring position with the *Winters* doctrine. But we haven't been able to move the ball since then, in spite of some brilliant punts and kickoff returns that we owe to our special teams.

That is why I believe we need a basic change in the game plan. When we started the game, we started out with three basic offensive strategies: (1) litigation in the courts, (2) legislation in Congress, and (3) negotiation. Let me be blunt with you here and tell you where I think things stand here at half time. None of those three basic strategies is working. Believe me, they just aren't enough.

First, litigation. The courts are not providing us with the gains we had counted on. The costs of water suits are staggering, not just for the lawyers, although they cost plenty, but also for the technical experts we need for soil inventories, economic studies, hydrologists, and the like. They are mighty expensive and hard to come by.

In the past, the BIA has adopted a posture of encouraging us to go forward with vague offers of funding and technical assistance. To date, I can tell you that the Navajos have spent over $2 million of our own money for water studies and litigation, while the BIA may have provided us with as much as $250,000. The BIA has yet to say a single word on our behalf in any court. Now the BIA is asking us for our technical research so that they can use it, supposedly for our benefit.

In Arizona, we are in federal court on the Little Colorado River Basin. When we argued this matter in the Ninth Circuit Court this last April, our trustee, the federal government, the Department of the Interior, the BIA, claimed it had sovereign immunity under the McCarran amendment and asked to be dismissed from the suit. That issue has yet to be decided.

I know that while some tribes, including the Navajos, must bear the continuing burden of litigation for our own benefit—and we hope for yours, too—many tribes simply can't afford the lawsuit. So it is foolish to believe that the BIA, even before the second round of budget cut proposals, would adequately represent those who cannot afford to slug it out in court at $150 to $300 an hour for legal fees.

Even if we could afford it, we need to be realistic. As has been said here throughout the day and, I'm sure, tomorrow, you can't drink paper rights. On the Big

Colorado River, the flow of the river is about 9 million acre-feet. The Indian claims alone on that river are in excess of 11 million acre-feet. The same is true when it comes to the San Juan River Basin. Just the claims of all the Indian tribes exceed the size of that basin. And we are competing with the State of New Mexico in New Mexico's own courts. So they literally have "home court" advantage. You tell me: What legal doctrine is going to give us more water than there is in that river or in that basin? Clearly, then, the first basic strategy, litigation, isn't enough. So that brings us to strategy number 2.

The second strategy available to us is legislation. Congress often defends us against state and local interests, because it represents the collective national conscience on some issues dealing with Native Americans. But water is not one of those issues. Every region of the United States wants our water—for development, for industry, for hydroelectric power, for irrigation, for recreation, for tourism, for use in secondary and tertiary oil recovery, for urban expansion.

Right now there are two unsigned, unnumbered water bills circulating in Congress to "remove the uncertainty associated with reserved water rights and confirm state jurisdiction over Indian water rights." They want to clarify the situation completely, by eliminating our rights! The bills provide that Indian water rights not exercised—meaning not used—within the next eight years will expire forever. If we had all the money in the world, none of us could complete a major water project in eight years. It takes that long just to plan and build one electrical generating plant or one coal mine. One of these bills waives the sovereign immunity of tribal governments and subjects us to state court jurisdiction. Both draft bills provide for compensation—spelled M-O-N-E-Y—if our water is taken.

If we rely on the second major strategy, legislation, and stick to our initial game plan, I predict the day is not far off when we will all be filing claims before a new Indian Claims Commission, the Indian Water Rights Claims Commission. That new Claims Commission will not have the power to give us back our water any more than the first Claims Commission could give us back our land. Instead, we will be offered shrinking dollars for perpetual water rights that are invaluable and irreplaceable.

So much for the first two strategies, litigation and legislation. We can't abandon them, but they just aren't enough. That brings us to the third and last strategy built into our original game plan, negotiation.

I hear Ken [Smith] and others say, "Negotiate." What do we negotiate with? Winston Churchill once said you can't win at the negotiating table what your troops couldn't win on the field of battle. So what do we have to negotiate with? For almost ten years, each and every year, we approached the Arizona State legislature to do just that. Several laws were drafted. No laws were passed, except for one. This was a ground water law that gave no, I repeat, no recognition to Indian water rights.

The states, in most cases, don't want to negotiate. They figure—and they are no dummies—that they are better off avoiding us and continuing to use more and more of our water. After all, possession is nine-tenths of the law, and maybe ten-tenths in this case.

So what are we going to do? Threaten to place a news article in the *Washington Post* or the *Navajo Times*? That should really throw a scare into them.

We did try negotiating once before, for the right to use our own water. In 1962, we were "given" 508,000 acre-feet of our own water from the San Juan Basin in order to start our Navajo Indian Irrigation Project. The quid pro quc was funding for the project. Twenty years later, the funding for the 110,000-acre farm is fifteen years behind. But the water we had to give up to get the Congressional approval for the project has been taken each year. Now we are being told that our irrigation project is so efficient we can get along with less water—not the original 508,000 acre-feet, but a mere 325,000 acre-feet. When we disagreed, the Bureau of Reclamation simply proceeded to downsize the delivery system so that physically we couldn't even get the water we were guaranteed by statute. That's what happens when you negotiate and get the negotiations embodied in law by the Congress of the United States. No one can make Congress appropriate the money needed. We have to live up to our part of the bargain, but the United States does not.

So we have tried negotiation from strength, from weakness, even from explicit Congressional statute. It doesn't work when delay favors those on the other side of the negotiating table. And most of the time, you can't even get them to the negotiating table.

That means that the three basic strategies we have relied on, litigation, legislation, and negotiation, are not enough. That's why the game plan has to be changed. And that's the challenge I want to throw out right here and now.

My proposition is very simple. We either use the water or we lose it. I challenge you all to find a way to enable us to use the water now, right now, legally, or at least not illegally, so that we can stake out for now a level of actual use that approximates what our people will need twenty years from now. Because we don't have twenty years to work our way up to that level of use.

There's no point in announcing a real game plan now. Because that's what we've been doing ever since the Supreme Court handed down the *Winters* doctrine. That's why we're in the jam we are in now. The other side has had our game plan.

Starting right now, before the teams go back on the field, we need to come up with a new game plan based on one simple principle: Use it or lose it. That's the challenge.

What does that mean? I have one suggestion. I propose that we establish a National Indian Waters Trust. If we're going to get serious, we had better start pooling our water rights first, on a state-by-state basis, then as part of a national confederation.

I'm not trying to set up another CERT [Council of Energy Resource Tribes]. Oil and water don't mix. But maybe we could figure out a way to pool our water, trade our water, lease our water, but use our water.

I read in the *Washington Post* the other day that the State of South Dakota has just entered into a $1.4 billion deal to sell Missouri River water to a private energy corporation to move Wyoming coal slurry 1,300 miles to ports down in the Gulf of Mexico. If they are clever enough to come up with something like that, why can't we come up with something just as smart to protect our rights by using them?

We shouldn't scare people by saying we are going to set up a water OPEC like CERT. But maybe we could just set up a State Confederation of Water Resource Tribes. That spells SCWRT—pronounced "squirt." No one would take a little squirt seriously, unless we did. And that's the challenge I put to you this evening.

To sum up: Our original game plan isn't working. We can't continue to rely exclusively on the three basic strategies we started with. I don't mean we should abandon them, but we have to add new offensive and defensive strategies, and we have to do it fast.

There are a lot of lawyers here. You lawyers shouldn't just have one-track minds. Don't just sell us rights and lawsuits. We can't drink them. We can't afford to assert them, in some cases, in court. And we won't have them very long. We need you to be more innovative, rather than just saying it's unconstitutional, it's this, it's that. Yet the game continues to go on.

And you water experts. Don't just sell us long-term plans. Because the water won't be there unless we can find a way to use our water now. Besides, even the best plans, short- or long-range, won't work unless money can be found to finance them. So you have to come up with both the plans and the financing strategies.

Finally, I am not interested in claims awards. I am interested in water. I am interested in survival. So let's figure out a way to use the water now, to commit it now.

Half time is just about over, and we had better have our act together before the team goes back on the field. Because if we lose this game, there won't be another season for any of us, ever. We're counting on you. Good luck.

Luncheon Address

MR. JOSEPH DeLaCRUZ
President, Quinault Indian Nation
Taholah, Washington

MR. DeLaCRUZ: It is really a pleasure and honor to address such a distinguished group of people regarding such a crucial issue as Indian water rights.

It seems like the issues and problems that we as Indian people and we as Indian leaders have to deal with have been with us for a long, long time. With all the studies and all the papers that have been put together, even before some of our times, the policies that we are dealing with as a people, our forefathers were dealing with. It is a policy that has not changed since the United States became the United States, since before the United States was the United States. It is called colonialism.

With some of the studies that have been done by our Indian organizations and by our tribal technical people through the years, it has become very obvious what colonial governments do to Indian people or native people, whether it be in the United States or in other parts of the world.

When we are talking about water rights or the rights of our Indian people, whether they be reserved through treaties with the United States or be aboriginal, there is one thing we can't forget as leaders of our various tribes. We know clearly the history of how they dealt with us. We know clearly why each piece of legislation was passed. We know clearly why most of the time we are forced to go to court against the state or the United States. It is because for the past 200 years or so, what we had other people wanted. You don't have to look too far back into our history to see what were Indian lands, Indian resources, a couple of decades ago before what we know today is part of history, the termination policy. Our reserved lands as Indian people in the United States were in the neighborhood of 160 million acres. We have seen what has happened going through a couple of administrations. They were going to make up their minds to terminate us, they were going to liquidate us. We ended up after that short period of time with about 55 or 60 million acres of land left.

It is clear to me that Indian people and Indian nations have always had our position. We have always had our policies as Indian nations of what our rights are and what our ideologies are.

A few years back, after the American Indian Policy Review Commission did research and study of 200 years of the federal-Indian relationship, you had a Congressional committee admitting all the past wrongs in writing. The Commission's majority report made some specific recommendations of what needed to happen to make what was reserved by our forefathers become a reality.

It wasn't too long after the American Indian Policy Review Commission that some Indian leaders, including myself, started advocating that we needed to begin talking to the states. We needed to begin talking to other people. Because it is very obvious that for almost five generations, and at least the last three generations, America—the United States government and the states—and their educational system have programmed people into believing that Indian people, Indian tribes, and Indian rights were really myths.

We find Americans in the state legislatures that have no idea what an Indian tribe or an Indian government is. For the tribes that have treaties with the United States, those treaties put us on a government-to-government, nation-to-nation relationship. It was their courts that changed that relationship, not our courts. It was their Congress that changed how we deal under that nation-to-nation relationship. It has only been after the American Indian Policy Review Commission, and the National Governors Study, and some of the work of the National Council of State Legislatures that you have federal people talking about government-to-government relations with Indian tribes. But that relationship will not become a reality unless tribes begin doing some of the things that we have talked about at this conference, when it comes to your property rights.

At most of the water conferences I have ever gone to, and I have gone to almost every one of them in the last ten years, I have heard the *Winters* doctrine talked about and preached about. The United States Supreme Court said that the *Winters* doctrine was the law of the land in 1908. Historically, this has been the law of the land relating to Indian people and their governments and their nations.

Administratively, however, we have got this huge bureaucracy that has every way that a person could think of to manipulate the result that that law of the land never becomes a reality. Today we are dealing with an administration that does not even realize there are Indian people and Indian tribes out there, and that does not even realize that those Indian tribes have treaties with the United States. It does not realize that past administrations have recognized this. It does not realize that its own State Department recognizes this.

People who work for the United States government, because of their own educational system and process, don't realize that Indian governments are governments, and that there are certain things that have never been taken away from us.

I'll say the State Department recognized that a couple of years ago, and a lot of people, misunderstanding what was happening, took issue with some of those people to get certain things in the record when the United Nations' Helsinki Commission was meeting. The United States was coming down pretty hard on some countries regarding the human rights of people in those countries. The question was raised, "What about United States policy towards the native people of that continent?" I wasn't there, but people that were there, I imagine the State Department people, said, "Who are they talking about?" A recess was called. Immediately, wires were being sent over the cable that comes across the Atlantic. These people were asking, "How do we look at our relationship with the native people," meaning the Indian people, "of the United States?" They went to the place that I guess is supposed to be the closest to us as far as the trustee goes, the Secretary of the Interior. And they wired back a cable that said, "Yes, the United States recognizes that it has these treaties with these sovereign Indian nations. And we have to develop a mechanism, to develop a consultation method, with these Indian tribes." Man, this is 202 years after the United States, and they're out there telling the world that. How many Indian people knew about that? How many people in the United States? Not too many.

We have had court cases and we have had decrees on many, many issues in this relationship. A lot of them were not by our design or by our request, because we were dragged into court because somebody wanted something. The court case I can speak to probably better than any court case I know is *United States v. Washington*, known as the Boldt decision. Looking back at what happened to the supreme law of the land of *Winters v. United States* and some other cases that went to the Supreme Court that nobody implemented, when Judge Boldt ruled in 1974 on *United States v. Washington*, it became very apparent that the tribes that were involved and their fish commissions had to become a part of a process to make what the Supreme Court said was the law of the land become a reality. When we started into the process after the Boldt decision, the first steps were not steps by our design—they were at the manipulation of powerful Congressmen, all the the way to the White House level. They suggested a Presidential task force, and it was set up by President Carter at the request of some powerful Senators. It was a negotiation that we didn't set up, and a negotiation we didn't have much control over. But we were on a football field, as Peter MacDonald was saying. We were holding our own through that process.

Our leaders recognized what the law of the land was, that 50 percent of the resource was our property right. So we ended up trying in several processes to make what that law of the land was into a reality. The Columbia River tribes and tribes in our area ended up back in court, and a lot of people have misunderstood the nature of the court order that was issued as a result. We have got until February of next year [1982] by that court order for the state, the United States, and the three tribes from our area to develop a management plan to carry out what the Supreme Court said is the law of the land. That is not very long. The Columbia River tribes and the Indians that fish the Columbia have ninety days to develop their recommendations for the Columbia River.

The reason I bring this up as an issue relating to

how we are going to have to deal with water is because of things we have had to go through; we have learned how they manipulate us. I believe in this final process we are going through, because our people have set up the mechanism of how we deal, and although it was by a federal court decree, we control the process and the mechanism. It is interesting to see people agreeing with what Indian people have been saying for 200 years when it comes to managing natural resources.

We have had a *Winters* doctrine since 1908, and we have had tribes stampeded into other court cases. With all that planning and everything that we have experienced with all these meetings, what strategy has been developed to circumvent the manner in which opposing parties seek to prevent administratively the law of the land from being carried out? When you look at what the United States Congress' American Indian Policy Review Commission has said, when you look at what the National Governors have said in their report, when you look at what the Commission of Tribal Stipulations has come up with, and when you look at the document that Guy McMinds read about the corporations that were up against us and want to sit down and talk, you find that they are all admitting these things have been wrong in our past relationships with the Indian people. And they are saying that we have got to find a different mechanism to work these things out so we can live together or at least live as neighbors. It has only been because of some of these crucial rights issues and current trends in America today that they are really looking at some of our last resources.

The American Indian Policy Review Commission recommended about ten or twelve pieces of legislation that would have dealt with some of the issues that we are in court with today. Those were tough issues. They are issues that people were a little bit afraid of. We end up dealing with these issues piecemeal in the courts, where they are pecking us away.

When people mention negotiations, a lot of people get a little fearful. When you look back through some of the relationships that Indian tribes have had with other governments, there is a whole trail of various types of negotiated agreements or documents. They may be only short term, some may be long term, but there is always a clause to get out of a situation like that. I believe that with the history of what has happened to our people, if we are going to put together a team that is going to turn this situation around, we have got to look at some of these past documents. A few of us took a look at twenty or thirty years of resolutions of Indian tribes or national Indian organizations a few years back and found that before our time those resolutions were the same resolutions that we were dealing with every year in convention.

My point is that the Indian position has never changed. Our position and our relationship with the United States has been pretty well distorted. I don't like to look at what we are dealing with as a football field, because we are in the day of computers and space science and technology. When you see these games where you have a spaceship with all these things firing at it from every direction, your reflexes have to be pretty good if you are going to survive in that situation. Those games are more like what our Indian people are dealing with. I can't play that space game—all my children can beat me when it comes to flipping those levers and firing that gun in that machine. But that is what has been happening to Indian country. You have to sit back and analyze the different directions that we have been pulled and try to figure out why these people are pulling our chain this way, jerking our chain that way. They are getting down to the final thing, our resources.

I don't need to go into the history of how they took our land or how they tried to make farmers of us, all the way down through history. These were policies designed to take from us.

I sincerely believe that if it wasn't for some people four or five years ago who were talking about taking a look at the relationships that Indian governments and Indian people have with the governments around them, meaning the counties and the states, you wouldn't have had Mr. [Henry] Loble today talking about developing some type of mechanism for the states and the seven tribes in Montana to live compatibly side by side.

I disagreed with one of his comments. I think that first of all as Indian people we are citizens of our own tribe, then citizens, if he wants to call it a state, but also citizens of the United States. And in this process, when people are speaking of negotiations and working things out, I have to take a hard look at who is representing Indian people, and the premises on which we are going to negotiate, and what type of control we will have, because we have got to recognize that they are talking about our property rights and our resources. In most instances, we have not had that type of control. We have had a fragmented trustee that has been able to laterally pass that ball around, back and forth, when it comes to crucial Indian issues.

We have all experienced it. You go to what used to be the Commissioner. Then you have to go over to the Solicitor. The Solicitor says, "Well, I think you had better go talk to the Justice Department." We have been around that circle so many times. That again comes from, I believe, a designed United States policy of not recognizing Indian governments as governments and of not recognizing that the United States has treaties with Indian tribes.

Believe me, the United States knows that. But if they can continually peck away—and we are talking about water rights at this conference—river by river or river basin by river basin, we are not going to have any water. They are going to continue to be in control of the situation that they have been in control of for 200 and some years.

But I believe, from what I have heard going on at this conference and the people I see here, that that game plan that Peter MacDonald talked about can be put together. I believe that the Indian nations have policy positions on what the law of the land is. Our task is to continue to educate the people around us, those people in the state legislatures, those Governors, those Congressmen. And whether it be a court arena or a bill back in Congress, before we panic, we have got to learn how to sit down and analyze that bill. Is it something we must have a lot of discussion on or is it something we can keep on ice and just quietly bury and kill forever? Sometimes we have given a lot of credibility to things people are doing that don't deserve that credibility. I think we can win this battle.

I haven't been involved in them, but when it comes to Indian treaties, reserved Indian property rights as the law of the land, I know that people, our Indian representatives, are working in the United States–Canada negotiations trying to develop a fishery treaty with Canada. I know that the United States representatives and the state representatives are very well aware of the strength of that Indian treaty. I know that we have a lot of allies out there who are non-Indian people, people who recognize that the Indian ideologies of managing and utilizing Indian resources are probably going to be the ideologies that are going to save America.

The Western Outdoor Association, which is all the environmental groups, came to us. There are areas on which we disagree with those people, but there are many areas we have in common. Once they begin to understand what Indian treaties are about and what Indian people are about and what Indian governments are about, we become more than ½ of the 1 percent of the population that are understanding what is happening when they are talking about piping water all over the country, talking about developing power at the expense of Indian people's lives and other people's lives—again, for economics, for the almighty dollar.

I don't think Indian people should forget our history: that one of the first things they destroyed with each tribe as they moved west were the key animals or fishes that were the major part of the economies that made each tribe strong. They destroyed our economies. We have been under five generations of paternalism.

It is amazing. We are still here. We have not gone away. I believe that we survived for a reason. I think that reason is here today for America. I think we have got to use our treaties, we have got to use every skill that we can put together to make America, from the White House to the Congress, realize what we are talking about.

I have often thought that it would be more inexpensive and a lot less controversial for the United States and the state governments and these big multinational corporations to get their heads together and appropriate the dollars—although they might have to displace some people, and other people don't understand displacement, but our people do—to get Indian territory back to what it was before they passed all the legislation to take the land away from us. We are only talking about 160 million acres. Get those lands back in Indian names, under Indian governments, and let Indian people manage those resources instead of continually trying to take them from us. I believe that would be a lot less expensive than the process they have gone through in taking Indian resources. Although some people that were part of designing the legislation to get title to Indian land might not want to be displaced, I believe there are enclaves in this country called Indian country that are going to provide some answers in the future to the insanity we have all lived through.

If this conference doesn't do anything else, I would hope that some of our technical people and legal people would go back and look at some of the documents that were based on our treaty rights to see exactly what was reserved and what we came up with at that time as a policy or position of the Indian nations. If those documents need to be improved on, improve them. But then let those papers be our message, no matter who we talk to. Believe me, I think we will win.

STRATEGIES FOR CLARIFYING AND PROTECTING INDIAN WATER RIGHTS

Moderator's Preface

Water is a scarce and precious resource in the arid West. Survival and economic development depend on having an adjudicated water right that can be protected judicially. While the parameters of Indian water rights were laid out by the Supreme Court in 1908 in *Winters v. United States,* most Indian water rights have not been adjudicated.

Vacillating federal Indian policies, which at various times have encouraged or discouraged Indian tribal existence, have contributed to the delay in clarifying and protecting Indian water rights. Today, the pressures of growth and development in the West require the adjudication or definition of Indian water rights, rights that have been ignored or disregarded by the federal government and state governments for so long. Indian water rights under *Winters* may well be substantial and superior to state-created rights, and it is this uncertainty that makes adjudication or definition inevitable. The issue for each tribe then becomes finding the best strategy to clarify and protect its water rights under the *Winters* doctrine.

Litigation has been the traditional method of defining water rights and many tribes are involved in this process today. Court proceedings, however, are lengthy and expensive, since they involve the joinder of all competing water users. They also involve the resolution of some uncertain aspects of the *Winters* doctrine, which may or may not be resolved in favor of the tribes.

The key issues in litigation thus far have been whether state courts have jurisdiction to adjudicate Indian water rights cases, and whether tribes are free to institute litigation at their own initiative in federal courts, which they view as more favorable forums. Depending on the ultimate resolution of these issues, tribes may or may not be forced to settle their rights judicially. The Supreme Court in 1976 in *Colorado River Conservation District v. United States,* known as the *Akin* case, held that Indian water rights could be adjudicated in state courts under some circumstances, but the case did not involve a state that specifically disclaimed Indian jurisdiction in its constitution, as most western states have.

The time, expense, and uncertainty of litigation may lead some tribes to consider negotiating a settlement of their water rights. Such negotiated settlements would either be approved by a court or would require congressional ratification. Achieving such settlements, however, will depend on tribal assessments of whether the process allows them to meet their goals, and perhaps, ultimately, on how those settlement proposals are received by Congress.

JOHN E. ECHOHAWK
Executive Director
Native American Rights Fund
Boulder, Colorado

MR. CHARLES F. WILKINSON

Visiting Professor, University of Minnesota School of Law
Minneapolis, Minnesota

Currently Professor, University of Oregon School of Law
Eugene, Oregon

MR. WILKINSON: The water crisis of the American West is similar in a number of respects to the energy crisis. For one, I am convinced that they are of similar magnitude. We hear more about the energy crisis because of the higher gas prices and the long gas lines that we have faced and the commotion that those problems have caused.

For reasons that I think are not good ones, those kinds of problems attract more public attention than low or warm flows in our rivers that cut off the migrations of salmon and steelhead and that leave major spawning beds dry. But in spite of a level of public awareness that I think is not high enough, we are moving toward water rationing, toward higher water prices, considerably more environmental damage, and other consequences that, to me, taken as a whole, are as legitimately serious as the energy crisis.

The two crises are also similar because one part of the solution to each is conservation. Saving energy is effectively a way of creating energy, and the same is true with water. In addition, conservation of water is a matter of special importance to Indian tribes. It has been made abundantly clear throughout this session that you have a tremendously difficult practical problem in turning your unused *Winters* rights into real water. To do that, you are often working within the context of a watershed that is already overcommitted, and the fact is, it is going to be easier, both legally and politically, if the requirements of your reserved rights can be met by disturbing as few existing uses as possible.

Conservation of water, and I think this applies to most of the watersheds you are in, can literally create all or part of the water necessary to fulfill your reserved rights and yet not impinge on legitimate established uses.

Conservation of water, like the broader energy crisis itself, is a multifaceted problem. I would like to talk about just one aspect of water conservation that I hope will be of some use to the tribes.

I have suggested that legitimate, established uses of whatever the technical law may be have equities that tribes have to recognize. But, foremost among those established uses that are not legitimate is the waste of water. John Folk-Williams mentioned yesterday that too often we tend to focus too much on the irrigators—the large, large agricultural interests—and he cautioned us not to oversimplify the problem as a battle between Indians and agricultural interests. I think it is true as a general matter that we are seeing a swing away from overwhelming water use by irrigators, a swing over time to an increased use by energy.

At the same time, we are still in a region where 80 to 90 percent of all water use in virtually every western state is by irrigators. It is easily far and away the largest water use in the West. We need to focus particularly on what, at least in my judgment, is not a legitimate use, and that is waste of scarce water by non-Indian irrigation interests.

We see it all too commonly: outmoded irrigation practices that include earthen irrigation ditches that leak; water-loving plants suck into them, take the water out, and water is evaporated. We see too much water applied on the fields, putting on more than is needed under modern technology. And we see a failure to use modern techniques such as center-pivot irrigation, trickle irrigation, and other technologies that are available.

In all, a reasonable, respected estimate is that 24 million acre-feet a year of water is wasted by western irrigation interests. If the entire flow of the Colorado River each year is 13 million acre-feet, then almost twice the annual flow of the Colorado, a figure of 24 million acre-feet, is more than all of the water used by all of the cities and all of the industries in the United States. That is the magnitude of the amount of waste that now exists.

Now, there are ways to cut back on water waste on the irrigation fields. Irrigation canals can be lined with plastic or concrete. They can be piped, which would eliminate the evaporative loss. Some of the on-the-field techniques could be used that I just mentioned. And, importantly, in California they have found that this is a big part of the problem: The fields can be leveled better, can be contoured so you don't have pockets of water running off the fields in a wasteful way.

Well, the farmers argue, and obviously there is merit to this and it needs to be respected, that these kinds of practices are too expensive. But I hope that Indian people particularly fully appreciate the irony of the argument — not in all cases, but in most cases — that water-saving practices are too expensive. As you well know, and it is worth doing further study on for those of you who do not, non-Indian irrigation projects have been heavily subsidized by the federal government. They used *Winters* rights in those projects in many cases. They did so at below market value. Today, they have that cheap water, and investing money to save the cheap water is in fact not economical to the farmers. So the result is that to wash out at least some of the economic arguments, the farmers are arguing that they had the projects built at low cost, using Indian water rights, and now the water is so cheap for them that it is not economical to reform and to save water today. I think that is an argument that Indian people need to be making in public forums.

Farmers also raise a fundamental point of water law. It is one that those of you who are nonlawyers should appreciate and understand as well as any lawyer, because it is central to the water issues. There are two elements to a water right: the quantity and the priority date, the time. Take a farmer who tapped in on a stream in 1905 and had 160 acres. Suppose that farmer took 5 acre-feet a year on those 160 acres on that quarter section. Well, that's 800 acre-feet of water a year. Under state law, that farmer stands at 1905 with a right to take out 800 feet over anyone junior, 5 acre-feet per acre. Importantly, that is a vested right under the United States Constitution, not just under state law. And if a state wants to take, say, 400 acre-feet of that 800 acre-feet, the state has to pay for it. You have to figure how much an acre-foot of water is worth on the market, and the state has to pay for it. That right is normally evidenced by a permit issued by the state that will say "5 acre-feet" on it, 160 acres, or some other unit of measure, and will state the priority date, the time of 1905. And often, now that we are adjudicating more and more streams, that 1905 farmer will also have a court decree acknowledging that right.

Well, to the farmer, that right is the key to the prior appropriation system. That is why it was adopted, this system of water law in the West, because it provides certainty—a fixed right, a right that farmers can build a farm around and irrigate on and be certain that that water will continue to flow. That water right is central to that farming operation.

Suppose, however, this situation: That even in 1905, that particular farmer only needed 4 acre-feet per acre instead of 5, and that that extra acre-foot per acre was just let run on the ground and was not needed or used, and that that farmer, with more efficient practices, could have used just 3½ acre-feet. Or suppose further that today, in 1981, with new technology, 3 acre-feet would be sufficient, that with piping, sprinklers, and good contouring that same land could be watered, the same crops could be grown, with 3 acre-feet. And suppose further, as you know to be the case, that that farmer is not alone, but rather that that farmer is in an irrigation project, so that you are talking about literally tens of thousands of acre-feet.

So, we have questions about what that water right is under state law for all those acres. Is 5 acre-feet the amount that was actually taken out? Was 4 or 3½ acre-feet the amount needed then? Or is 3 acre-feet sufficient, using today's technology? Well, as one might expect, state courts, particularly early in this century, were very tolerant of the irrigators' arguments that their right was 5 acre-feet, the amount that was actually applied to the land. But while I don't believe there has been a complete breakthrough, we have seen an important development, particularly over the last twenty years or so in state courts, in which the judges have begun to oppose waste and get tough and say, between the lines in their opinions, that no one wastes water in this court.

The extent of a water right is defined by beneficial use. And beneficial use has always meant two things. It means, first, the kind of use that is allowed in western states: industrial, agricultural, stock watering, domestic, and, in most states, recreational. That is an important meaning of beneficial use.

But beneficial use has also meant another thing. It has meant that water can't be wasted. So the quantity of water you are allowed to take out of a stream is an amount that can be used without unreasonable waste. That branch of the beneficial use doctrine that prohibits waste really has begun to pick up steam recently. One recent Colorado case—for lawyers it's 633 Pacific 2d 1064—said that in every water right that is issued in Colorado, whether it's a permit or even a court decree, that water right is only a maximum, and that if water can be saved there is an implied limitation on every water right granted under state law. There are other authorities suggesting the same concept.

I think it is most important, as one of the many strategies that we are discussing here, to make it clear that the farmers' rights are often not what they think they are. You have got to look further than an administrative permit or even a court decree specifying certain quantities, you've got to see if there is waste there. And if there is waste there, that is water that can be legitimately sprung loose and used to fulfill the reserved rights that are so important to the tribes.

I think to take full advantage of an Indian attack against waste, the state forum does need to be utilized. State legislatures can regulate against waste, and I think the tribes can make a difference there.

I think, too, you can make a difference in the state agencies. The procedures will be different in the various agencies — public hearings, rule-making proceedings, or even general stream adjudications on streams other than your own. I am suggesting that developing good water waste systems in your states is important, even though you may not have a case pending now.

I take no issue with the general points that were made last night by Chairman MacDonald. I think tribes do need to develop. I continue, however, to believe that we must not have a phobia against negotiating with the states. It is not 1960 any more, it is not 1970, it is not even 1975. We no longer have Attorneys General, either in Maine or Washington or states in between, who dare to advise their Governors that Indian rights don't exist. There is a very important difference today, I think, which is that the states now respect Indian tribes as the possessors of rights. The extent of those rights may be in great dispute, but it wasn't so long ago when you as a group went through many years of not being recognized as governments by the states or as possessing any rights at all — and there has been a shift. While I feel the same sickness in the pit of my stomach over the *Montana* decision that came down last spring that so many of you feel, the fact is that tribes have won more than they have lost, by far, over the last decade. There is a generalized impact from that Indian litigation offensive — you are now groups that states recognize as possessing some power and legitimacy and that they are willing to talk with.

Reuben Snake yesterday was too modest in talking about some of the things the Winnebagos did, because the fact is that he and Louie LaRose and other tribal leaders caused both the States of Iowa and Nebraska to come to them. In my home state of Oregon, I have seen the same result at Umatilla with the work Doug Nash has done, and perhaps especially at Warm Springs where the Warm Springs Tribe recently got the state to float a bond issue to help fund a Warm Springs re-regulating dam. I think that that kind of state cooperation on terms acceptable to the tribes is something that we need, that we must not ignore as part of the solution.

I see part of the solution of the broader problem as being conservation. I see part of that solution as being an Indian war against water waste, and I see part of that as an attempt to work within state law to limit non-Indian water rights under state law. That is one way, it seems to me, to begin to obtain some of the water rights that were promised to you so long ago.

DR. HELEN INGRAM

Professor, Department of Political Science,
University of Arizona
Tucson, Arizona

DR. INGRAM: I am an observer and interpreter of the patterns of water resources politics. I have been at this business since I did a study of the Colorado River Basin bill in 1967. Although my background is in political science, I must tell you honestly that the most important reference book that I could find to explain the Colorado River Basin bill in water politics was *Alice in Wonderland*, written by Lewis Carroll.

Now, I was afraid to tell you that. I thought you'd laugh, and you really did. It seemed that it really wasn't right to tell Indians and lawyers that pursuing a water right is like an English school girl having a bad dream. I thought at the very least I should be like John Folk-Williams and tell you it's like shooting it out with a gun and marching in there antagonistically. But it really isn't like that. It's like seeing things that you think are one thing, then they turn into something else. There is that wonderful part of *Alice* where the queen and the nurse have a baby, and they treat it like a baby and they say to everybody, "This is a baby." Like, "This is a reserved water right." And everyone believes it's a baby until Alice is given the baby, and it turns into a pig and jumps out of her hands and runs out. It wasn't a baby at all, although it was a baby to the Red Queen and to the nurse.

Indian water rights and the pursuit of water politics is like a game where the rules are constantly changing. That is precisely what Wendell Chino told us yesterday. There is a section in *Alice* where she is playing a game, and she has to keep running all the time just to stay where she is. She doesn't get anywhere. What makes matters worse, the Red Queen, at a whim, changes the rules of the game. She says, "You're not fair!" And they all say, "Keep running, keep running. It's your turn. Move, move!" And she doesn't have an opportunity not to play.

All right. For a few brief minutes, I would like to share with you my ideas of the western water game, which is changing very rapidly. The only constant in it is that Indians never seem to win. Perhaps my idea of how the game is changing may be useful in formulating a strategy to clarify and protect Indian water rights. Certainly, that is my intent.

To begin with, Lee Brown was very right in saying that the old game is not with us any more. I am most certain in describing the old game, because we have all described it here. We all understand it. We can all tell pretty well why Indians didn't win at that game. That game was called water resource development, and the objective of the game was to build projects that physically diverted water and put that water to beneficial use.

In that game there were such things as paper water rights, but that's not real wet water. Sometimes having those rights is a precondition to getting real wet water, but it is not the same thing. The State of Arizona struggled twelve years in the Supreme Court in *Arizona v. California* in order to get a paper right, which it then bargained mostly away in the subsequent struggle to get the Central Arizona Project authorized and finally funded. We have not yet gotten one drop of water to Tucson. A very good friend of mine tells me that we never will. That is the objective, however.

In that objective, how water was put to use, whether or not it was an economical use, was not very important. Uses were determined more on how you went about building a political coalition than making the best use of water. Putting water to use from that objective pretty much ignored physical limitations of water. How much water there really was in a river basin didn't matter so much, because when there was political consent we would build yet another project, which would divert more water in that direction and satisfy new claimants. Also, environmental concerns were pretty much ignored.

Indians didn't do very well in that game. They ended up with excellent paper water rights but not very much real water. And although we don't have a lot of time to talk about it, there are some clear reasons why. For one thing, the federal agencies, the Bureau of Reclamation and the Bureau of Indian Affairs, didn't help very much in planning Indian water projects. Indians weren't necessary in those coalitions of projects put together by non-Indians. You could find a majority and leave the Indians out. Indians didn't have a veto position because, even though they had large reserved water rights, the presumption was that there was going to be enough water to go around. Besides which, Indian claims were never going to be very large, it was thought.

The second period was a bit of a transition. It was the development period. The big change was that there was some chance, once in a while, that Indians perhaps would win the game. As Wendell Chino said yesterday, for a little while it looked like Indians were going to win. Then they changed the rules. I am talking about this little period of time when it looked like Indians were going to do better at gaining water development projects. One analyst has called this period "riding the Indian pony." It is kind of a piggyback game where you use an Indian water project to build consent for other non-Indian projects. Professor Collins suggested that, as a strategy that might have been pursued, yesterday. The period came about when Indian reserved water rights became a real element in water planning, because demands were pushing close upon supply and it was clear that those Indian water rights might be a barrier. So, as a sweetener to get Indians to willingly quantify their water rights, a project for Indians was thrown in.

We are now in a third period where all the rules have changed. This is the period that we could call the reallocation of water resources from one user to another. The era of developing large water resources projects, I think, is dead. Now we are moving water from one use to another, presumably to a higher use.

In this particular period, it matters very much that water be allocated to an economically beneficial use. That is significant. I suggest, therefore, that in pursuing Indian water projects, if it looks like Indian water is going to be used for an irrigation project at the same time as irrigation is being cut back all over Arizona, it is going to be really difficult to sell that project.

This is a time when the question of security of water rights is terribly important. Everyone is concerned about having to cut back, being held short in a situation of shortage or drought. Therefore, holders of senior rights are in a very good position. Their rights are negotiable. You can sell them for money. You can probably even use them. However, if those senior rights look as if they are going to really threaten other water rights holders, there is going to be a real attempt at taking those rights away, either by forcing some quantifications or by termination of those water rights through Congress. That is a real danger.

There are three options, it seems to me, today. One is to continue to play the game as if it were a development game—perhaps pursue the "ride the Indian pony" strategy game. I think that that strategy is dangerous because, to some extent, unless you can find a really high-valued Indian water use, it's going to be troublesome to try to get support for that.

Secondly, you can simply just not play. To an extent, that means that you come out of this period with an unsullied paper right, which may be better than no right at all or something you sell for a pittance. You stay pretty pure that way, but you are not, in the end, much better off.

The third possibility is that Indians participate in the exchange that's going on among holders of water rights. I think there are some real possibilities for leasing reserved water rights. It may take some changes through Congress. That is the third alternative. And, to me, it is the most exciting.

MR. HENRY LOBLE

Chairman, Reserved Water Rights Compact Commission
State of Montana, Helena, Montana

MR. LOBLE: I'm not appearing here as a lawyer, although I would be willing to wager that I've tried as many water suits as any lawyer in the room. I cover a long period of time. I'm doing what I'm doing, and that is negotiating tribal rights in Montana, because I want to do it and because I'm hoping I can solve what seems to me to be a very pressing problem.

Water is an emotional issue, particularly when you have ethnic overtones such as you have here. But don't think for a minute, those of you of the Indian race, that arguments over water are confined to Indians and non-Indians. Peace is in the grave as far as water law is concerned. I have tried many water suits, and they are not between Indians and non-Indians. You always have to be vigiliant about your rights. When your rights are settled, you are still going to be having arguments about water because it is a highly emotional issue. I recall one time I was interrogating and cross-examining a witness on the other side, and he jumped off the witness stand and took a swing at me. Fortunately, he missed me. The judge broke his gavel trying to restore order, but that is the type of emotion that you arouse when you are talking about water.

Also, beware of people who are your paid advisers and who say something to you like this, "We'll take this to the United States Supreme Court if it costs every nickel you've got."

The Montana Water Rights Compact Commission was created in 1979 by the Montana legislature. It has one purpose and one purpose only. It is totally unique amongst all the western states. I don't know of a state that has a similar commission. I don't think there is one. What we are trying to do is clarify and quantify Indian and federal reserved water rights, both Indian and non-Indian reserved water rights, by negotiation, by compromise, by settlement, and by entering into compacts.

Now, this had a background of litigation between the state on the one hand and the tribes and the federal government on the other, which resulted in the *Montana* case, whereby the district court dismissed the case and said, "This properly belongs in the state court rather than the federal court," where it was. That is on appeal, as you heard the Assistant Secretary last night say, to the Ninth Circuit.

The commission was created with the hope of entirely eliminating the litigation, and instead negotiating settlements of water rights. Our mission is: "To conclude compacts for the equitable division and apportionment of waters between the state and its people and the several Indian tribes claiming reserved waters within the state as well as similar compacts with the federal government on their non-Indian reserved rights." It is a nine-member commission. It is totally nonpolitical. I couldn't be removed by the Governor if he wanted to remove me. The only way you can get off the commission is via the Grim Reaper or resignation. I am going to try the best I can to negotiate the water rights of the seven Indian tribes in Montana and the federal government as well.

Negotiations are commenced when the Indian tribes choose to commence them by naming representatives. When we decide upon a compact, when written up that compact is effective and binding upon ratification by the legislature, the tribe, and the Congress, as well as having the blessing of Montana's adjudication process.

You would not have a paper right if you had a water

right that had been entered into in a compact, approved by Congress, approved by the legislature, approved by the tribe, and blessed by the court. You would have a real wet water right, and one, I think, that would be, beyond question, valid over and above the average water right. That is the type of water right that I am hoping we will end up with.

Of the seven tribes in Montana, we have negotiated with four of them. We are currently under way with three: Fort Peck, Fort Belknap, and the Northern Cheyenne. We were negotiating with the Flathead. The Flathead chose to terminate negotiations, however, and start litigation.

We are negotiating regularly with the federal government on non-Indian reserved rights, and are making a great deal of progress. With the various tribes we have negotiated with, we have covered all preliminary and procedural matters and we are proceeding to substantive matters. Both sides are now gathering factual materials for further substantive negotiations.

As far as coming to a conclusion, we don't sit around and argue about the fine legal points that you have heard discussed here. What we are trying to do is decide how much land the parties have, how much water they need, how it can be developed, and their plans for the future. Then we see if we can't sit down and write a compact that will permit both Indians and non-Indians to take care of those matters. We try to ascertain the facts without philosophical policy arguments.

There are questions of priority dates, quantities, purposes, and uses, but all of those things can be resolved by negotiation. The nice thing about the negotiation is that it is flexible. You can do things with negotiation that you can't do otherwise. For instance, we are talking very seriously with three tribes about utilizing stored water so that they will have a certain absolute year-round source of water. That source can be used as a substitute for other waters that are not convenient. We can change diversion points. We can even swap lands, if necessary. So you can come up with a really equitable decision and one that is beneficial to everyone.

I would like to see everyone given a chance to develop his water. I don't want to see a lawsuit where somebody wins and somebody loses. I think there are a lot of Indian tribes who don't have the money to fight those kinds of lawsuits, like they are doing in Wyoming, where one side alone is spending $8 to $10 million just to litigate.

As far as I'm concerned, Indians are citizens of the State of Montana, and valued citizens. I don't think it serves any point for the State of Montana or for those in authority there to stand in the way of the economic well-being of the Indian tribe. I think if the Indians can develop their lands with water, that is a real economic benefit to the State of Montana. I would like to see it brought about.

We recognize *Winters* water rights. We know the Indians have very definite water rights. What we are trying to do is enter into a compact that will give the Indians and the non-Indians absolute, certain water rights, so that they can start today or tomorrow, or as soon as we can get the job done, in their planning and developing. We do not want to spend any more time, if we possibly can, in fruitless litigation which lasts . . . how long? The Big Horn litigation is being adjudicated right now, but they don't expect to have a definitive decision for at least ten years.

Some of you think negotiation is a four-letter word. All right. Maybe it didn't work in Arizona. I don't know anything about that. I am not negotiating in Arizona. But I am going to do my level best to try to make it work in Montana. I think it is worth a try. I hope you will work with me.

MR. SCOTT McELROY

Attorney, U.S. Department of Justice,
Land and Natural Resources Division
Indian Resources Section
Washington, D.C.

MR. McELROY: I am pleased to be here today. I am a trial attorney with the Indian Resources Section in the Department of Justice. Our work, or at least a portion of our work, is relevant to the assertion of water rights by the United States on behalf of Indian tribes and their members, whether the federal government initiates the litigation or whether we are the defendant in an adjudication brought by a state party or some other non-Indian water user.

What I would like to talk about today is that work in litigation and what we do in terms of preparing cases for trial and in trying them.

Last night Chairman MacDonald talked about game plans and how to go about preparing for the future. I think that litigation is going to continue to be a critical part of the game plan. It is not one which I advocate for everybody, but I hope that by explaining to you some of the things that the government does or does not do, it will assist you in deciding what game plan is appropriate for you.

Many of you, of course, are very familiar with this and have been intimately involved in such litigation in the past. I'm going to try to stay away from the substance of particular cases. I cannot offer you any revealing insights on the advantages or disadvantages of litigation in formulating your own game plan. That varies from reservation to reservation, from state to state. It depends on the physical characteristics of your reservation and the physical characteristics of competing users. I hope to give some explanations about how the bureaucracy functions, and I hope it will permit you to evaluate in a more realistic sense what you may or may not be able to achieve through litigation.

We heard a lot yesterday, and we have heard again today about the problems of litigation. I would like to suggest that litigation is not always as troublesome as it has been made out to be. Sometimes we think it can work in an efficient, effective manner.

For an example on that, I would cite to you the second phase of *Arizona v. California*. In that case, the government and the five tribes along the lower Colorado River have sought to allocate additional water to the tribes in addition to that granted to the tribes in an earlier 1964 decree of the Supreme Court. The tribes were very perceptive in realizing that litigation was perhaps a wise course to take in that respect. They moved the Supreme Court to recognize additional rights for them, and under that kind of pressure, the government responded and filed a motion of its own in December of 1978, seeking additional rights for the tribes. Since that time, we have tried the case and we hope to have a decision from the Special Master of the Supreme Court soon. We expect that we will have a decision from the Supreme Court by the end of this term.

All in all, the time frame there is not nearly as drastic as it has been in other instances. We had a number of circumstances that contributed to the speed in which that matter proceeded. I think everyone, including our opponents, wanted a decision on the scope of the tribal rights in addition to what they already had. We also had a judge who tried very vigorously to expedite things. The judge was eighty-four years old, and any time any of the lawyers would begin to delay or procrastinate, as they are apt to do, he would remind us that he intended to finish the case before he died. He was very effective in keeping this going.

On the other hand, of course, litigation does not always work well. I have also been involved in a general-stream adjudication on the Carson River in Nevada. It is of great importance to the Pyramid Lake Tribe, not because they have rights in the Carson River, but because that adjudication will go a long way in defining the rights of their principal competitor to water from the Truckee River, the Newlans Project. That case was filed in 1925, and we have only recently gotten a decision from the District Court. We are still proceeding up through the appellate process on that case. So litigation doesn't always work well.

I would like to discuss a number of factors that come into play in litigation. I would like to start first with trying to explain, as difficult as it is, the role of the United States in litigation where Indian water rights are at stake.

The Justice Department for the United States is charged with representing all federal interests in such litigation. That is not necessarily an easy task, but it appears to be what both Congress and the courts have charged the Executive Branch with doing. That requires a number of difficult tasks by the government. It requires the government to evaluate all the different interests that the United States has and essentially to come up with a ranking of which ones they are going to advocate and how they are going to go about advocating.

This takes place in kind of a cumbersome, bureaucratic way that involves a number of different agencies in the federal government. Some of these we refer to as client agencies, such as the Department of Agriculture, which has the primary responsibility for deciding what rights will be asserted for national forests. We have the Corps of Engineers and other establishments within the Defense Department. And, most importantly, for what we have been talking about here, we have the Department of the Interior, which has as its critical function, as you all know, representation of Indian interests within the government as well as the competing interests of the Bureau of Reclamation.

The first cut, staking out the position that the federal government is going to take in litigation, falls on these client agencies who make a recommendation to the Department of Justice as to what position ought to be asserted.

Now, it is not quite the same as when a tribe deals with its attorney or any other private individual deals with its attorney, because the Department of Justice is charged with the responsibility for the litigation, and we look to the Interior Department for guidance in Indian matters. But our client is that great unknown, the United States. So we have a little more independent responsibility than does a private attorney. Essentially that is how the position is established in litigation. There's lots of going back and forth between client agencies and the Department of Justice.

The other important thing is tribal participation in that process. Once we get into litigation, that participation can take place in a number of ways. Obviously, the tribes consult with the Interior Department. We at Justice try very hard to consult with the tribes and their attorneys on matters of litigation. Apart from consultation, tribes have their own ways to participate. They can participate in litigation as a party. They can try to keep their eyes on the government to see that they do a good job while not participating directly. Or they can stay away from the litigation and see what comes.

Perhaps the most crucial part of preparing litigation for a trial that involves Indian water rights is the preparation of evidence necessary to support claims. Sometimes, that again becomes a bureaucratic nightmare because no one has the clear and plain obligation to prepare that evidence. It involves participation by the BIA, by the Solicitor's Office at the Department of Interior, and the Department of Justice.

The BIA is charged with the task, among other things, of coming up with the funds to support the litigation. You have heard how expensive it is, and that is correct. The studies that we undertake have proven to be very expensive in terms of preparing for litigation. The BIA is not necessarily structured in a way that facilitates funding for those sorts of things. Litigation sometimes makes very untimely demands on people. And the BIA, like other government agencies, has to program ahead if it is going to get money. Sometimes you just can't anticipate what is going to happen in litigation.

We also have problems because, as you have heard before, we know that Indian water rights include sufficient water to provide for the present and future needs of the tribes. That is a very general standard. We have to develop evidence that we can take to court to prove that water right. For that, we need objective standards. There has been a great deal of dispute about what the correct objective standard ought to be. We know in agriculture that we can refer to practicably irrigable acreage. But, as Mr. Chino told you yesterday, that is not a very helpful term all the time, either. There have been a lot of disputes about what that means.

All this ends up making the process very expensive, because we can't go out and hire an expert who has done the same study before. We need to develop a study that fits within an objective standard that is appropriate for the reservation at hand. In most instances, that has never been done before. Experts charge money. I can hardly blame them for that. It gets more and more expensive. We are confronted over and over again with this problem, but we are trying objectively to define "future needs." That is a very difficult task.

We have got to take what we come up with, take it to court and prove it in a forum that sometimes is not very favorable to what we are doing, because it is liable to have an impact on much of the surrounding community.

It is not always easy to decide, when we sit here and talk among friends, what that standard is and how we ought to go about it. It becomes even more difficult to come up with an effective standard when you have to prove it in court, subject to cross-examination and subject to all the other trials and tribulations of litigation.

As we know and as was mentioned earlier, litigation can take a long time and it can be costly. It is not unique to litigation that involves Indian water rights—it seems to be the history of water litigation. There is a variety of reasons for that. One is because in most water litigation there are a great number of parties and it's very hard to get agreement among 2,000, 3,000, 4,000 parties on anything. That factor alone lengthens the whole process.

Once you get into court, it is also hard in water litigation to come up with a physical solution. In many instances, there may be ways in which a variety of competing users can be satisfied if there is another dam or any of the other physical solutions that we have heard about today. It is difficult to articulate those alternatives in litigation. It is hard to present them to the judge as solutions from which he can select. Instead, once you get to litigation there tends to be polarization. People are on different sides.

Of course, litigation has been the traditional means

of resolving these kinds of disputes. There are reasons for that. There are rules for proceeding in court. We have heard that the rules change, and that is true, they do. But at least there is always a rule at any given point in time that you can argue.

There is also a judge who generally is interested in making the matter move along and who is charged with reaching a decision. So sooner or later you know you are going to get a decision. There is pressure on people to proceed, because they are in litigation and just can't talk and talk; they have got to produce.

In closing, I would like to suggest that in developing your game plan, you may wish to consider ways in which you might facilitate litigation if you are interested in resolving disputes over water rights. There are a number of factors, I think, that tend to contribute to the delays that we see in traditional water suits.

First, over the last ten years there has been a tremendous debate over what the appropriate forum is. I think it is safe to say that if either party to the litigation is dissatisfied with the forum that they are in and feels that they are not going to get a fair and impartial judgment out of the court, you wind up with a lot of delays, a lot of stalling, and a lot of posturing. Whether or not those concerns are justified, the result is delay.

I would suggest that if there is room for some kind of agreement with your opponents, perhaps one thing you might think about is choosing an appropriate forum for resolution.

Another thing you should think about is how many parties you want to have involved in the litigation. I think this calls for some creative lawyering by attorneys for all sides as to ways in which you might have only the parties who are really interested in the dispute appear in the litigation.

Finally, I would suggest that if there are some things that you agree upon, try to find ways to narrow the dispute that you take to court. Lawsuits traditionally involve both facts and law. If you can agree on the facts, agree on them. If you want to fight over the law, fight on the law. If you can agree on the law and you can't agree on the facts, fight on the facts.

In closing, I would just say that I appreciate the opportunity to appear here and speak. I have enjoyed listening to the other speakers. It gives a different perspective to those of us who participate in litigation.

I hope that these comments will contribute to your understanding of the game as it is now played. Thank you.

MS. SUZAN SHOWN HARJO

Legislative Liaison, Native American Rights Fund
Washington, D.C.

MS. HARJO: My name is Suzan Harjo, and I am legislative liaison for the Native American Rights Fund. I am what Mr. [Henry] Loble referred to as an "ethnic overtone." I am a citizen, not of the State of Oklahoma or the District of Columbia, but of the Cheyenne-Arapaho tribes of Oklahoma. I am Cheyenne and Creek.

I am reminded by something someone said yesterday of my Uncle Philip Deer, who once said, in discussing a treaty provision that talked about ownership of the river from bank to bank, that what was not clarified was that the provision meant from the Indian side of the bank of the river to the Bank of America.

I like Peter MacDonald's football analogy. I kept waiting for him to move to the wishbone and talk about it in terms of the conflict of interest.

Ken Smith was very interesting to listen to. I was pleased at his reference about conflict of interest and the Administration's review of conflict-of-interest procedures. I do hope this means that the Administration will be going forward with standards to govern the United States' conduct in cases and in instances involving conflicts of interest with trust obligations.

I was also glad to hear the positive leaning toward Orme Dam being constructed at a site other than the Fort McDowell Reservation, where the people have not wanted it and have made that desire very clear for almost a decade.

In looking at that decade of struggle by the Fort McDowell people, I would like to contrast that with Ron Robie's statement yesterday, which was so different from the experience we usually have. He was discussing a project that would flood one of the rancherias, were it to be constructed. He said that in making their decision the State of California will abide by the wishes of the rancheria. I hope he is part of a new wave.

Through all of this and through what all of you experts have been saying, it comes down to one thing: We don't own what we should and we don't control what we own. We know the first part, that most of us are poor and we should be rich. We often concentrate too much on that aspect and don't work hard enough on the control part. It is imperative that we begin to control what we own. Some of you are doing that already. Some are not. I think that Joe DeLaCruz will be speaking more to this issue.

The water bill that is being circulated today is another effort to focus our attention on the fact of ownership and to divert our attention from the important business at hand, which is to control what we do own. We don't need to accept the premise that this bill will be a fact of life, and that we must have major meetings and marches on Washington to protest it and combat it. We can adopt very simple legislative strategies that can tie this bill up for years, not just for the remainder of this session or into the next session of the Congress.

We must be very careful when we ask for joint or concurrent jurisdiction to the various committees of Congress that should look at this bill, such as the Judiciary Committee, the Commerce Committee, the Indian Affairs Committee, that we know who the people on those committees are, and who our friends and allies are on this issue. Just because a person has funded your tribally controlled community college doesn't mean that he will be with you on a water issue, or the reverse. We don't have many friends in Congress and we don't have many enemies. We have great apathy and we have only issues.

I understand that Senator Slade Gorton does not wish to introduce his water bill himself, but rather wishes Senators McClure and Wallop to introduce it, because Senator McClure is Chairman of the Senate Energy and National Resources Committee and Senator Wallop is Chairman of the Subcommittee on Public Lands and Reserved Water. The bill is written in such a way as to be referred by the parliamentarian to that committee and to that subcommittee. I also understand that Mr. McClure and Mr. Wallop are not so interested in introducing this bill themselves. It is a situation in which you have many seconds but no one wants to make the motion.

The bill is nothing new: we have all seen it before. It is a rehash of the Charlie Rowe–Lloyd Meeds bill from about four years ago. I understand that Mr. Rowe was at the Department of the Interior about a month ago in the Solicitor's Office, and over in the Bureau of Land Management and Bureau of Reclamation, bragging that Senator Wallop and Senator McClure were already on board, that the fix was in, and that the bill would be introduced immediately and be out of Congress before the end of the session. I admire this optimism. Maybe we should all adopt it and understand that there are two sides to each aisle in each house of the Congress. There are many people who would want to see this bill go through. But there are also many people, who are not Indian and who don't even much care about Indians, who would see it as very unfair.

I want to go back to the premise that we have no enemies and no friends, just issues. Senator Gorton proved to be a valuable ally to us when another Senator, Mr. Grassley of Iowa, had a breakfast meeting with Senators Thurmond and McClure and Secretary Watt, wherein it was discussed and decided that something had to be done about these Indian issues. Mr. Grassley, taking exception to the Omaha water case and the fact that the BIA had funded soil studies, said he wanted to get at that problem. This does not purport to be a verbatim account. Mr. McClure said something like, "You do it, and my Appropriations Committee will back you." So Mr. Grassley put a hold on the Interior appropriation bill so that it would not move forward and proposed a little rider to the appropriation bill, which said, "Provided further that no funds appropriated under this Act or any other Act may be used to enable Indian tribes to retain independent counsel or to finance any aspect of litigation brought by Indian tribes pursuant to the Act of 1921"—the Snyder Act, which he cites incorrectly—"where such court action or litigation is brought by or initiated on the behalf of an Indian tribe."

Before Mr. Grassley had a chance to circulate this to the Appropriations Committee, I took my own poll of Congressional offices, asking if they knew about this. I got a "no" from each office, and a nice sense of outrage or at least surprise in some offices.

The upshot of it was that after the provision was called to the attention of some of our advocates and after some of the people who Mr. Grassley had assumed would go along with him on this—including Mr. Gorton, who said "no," and said "no," very strongly —Senator Baker refused to honor any hold that Mr. Grassley had on the Interior bill on an Indian issue. Prior to that, Senator Cranston had asked Mr. Byrd, the minority leader, to dishonor any time agreement on the bill as a whole if it included this amendment, and this amendment specifically. So we picked up a few advocates there.

This is the kind of amendment that could bring much of Indian litigation to a halt and the kind of thing we should be most concerned about. Wendell Chino talked about the fact that we are in a time when policy is set by economics. That has always been the case. The proposal to cut $1.3 billion from the federal Indian budget was not, I think, an accidental policy decision. We are involved in a time of termination by appropriations.

The McCarran amendment was a rider to an appropriation bill. And after a Supreme Court decision stopping it, Tellico Dam was authorized as a rider to an appropriation bill that said "notwithstanding any other law."

I would like to mention just a couple of things that didn't make it into the appropriation process that would have had considerable impact on policy. There were proposed amendments to the Equal Access to Justice Act that would have, without ever mentioning Indians or Indian tribes, limited funds for attorneys and for supportive cases. In July, prior to the act having gone into effect on October 1, [1981], the amendment to the Equal Access to Justice Act was removed from the Onmibus Budget Reconciliation Act before it hit the House floor.

There was also a proposal to limit venue in the District of Columbia federal court in cases against federal defendants, which would have had significant impact on our cases. That was also taken out. This proposal exists now, not as something that will be put in an appropriation act, but as a freestanding legislative effort.

S.11299 was introduced by Senator McClure by request of the Administration and would permit the Federal Energy Regulatory Commissioners to waive any provision of FERC licensing or the Federal Power Act that they wished, including some very good protective things for Indians. That bill, which still exists as a piece of freestanding legislation, was introduced in June [1981]. In July [1981], the Administration sought to put it into the House version of the Omnibus Budget Reconciliation Act. Fortunately, we were able to excise that provision before the bill made it to the floor. This is the sort of thing that would be law today were it not for a bit of luck and a few leaks.

The Kootenai Indian people in Montana, Idaho, and Canada are working very hard right now to stop a dam that would be placed at Kootenai Falls. Kootenai Falls is the last major falls in the State of Montana. So, of course, there is an effort to dam it up. There was one interesting counterproposal by the people who would like to build the dam, and that was that the falls be converted to a project, except for 10 percent of the falls, which would be concentrated through a pipeline at the very top of the falls and spread out so as to appear like the Kootenai Falls. It would fool the eye. It would have all the visual beauty of the original Kootenai Falls. But it wouldn't fool the berries. It wouldn't fool the bears. And it wouldn't fool the fish. I thought it was an interesting variation on the trickle-down theory, though.

I think it is very important in whatever strategies we adopt for any of our issues not to buy the budget constraint bill of goods. The entire Department of Interior budget does not equal three Trident missiles. The non-Indians have received water welfare for years and do not have the obligations that are owed Indians by the federal government. It is our time. We are due these monies.

In the context of litigation or lobbying, I think it is important that whatever we do and say in the nature of negotiations, we set certain ground rules so that we understand what it is we wish to achieve at the end of the negotiation session. In formal negotiating sessions I think it is important to insist on caucus time, time to go out and figure out what it is you think; and to insist on no interruptions and on reflective time, to ask the non-Indian participants in the negotiation not to touch the silence that may follow a tribal person's statement, because that is, indeed, part of the statement itself. Perhaps, where it is appropriate, tribes should insist on bilingual or translated conduct of the sessions. Ask for some or all of the sessions to be held on tribal turf. If your tribe has a custom and tradition that you cannot speak in a harsh way to someone you have in your territory or at your table, then it is best not to talk about it at lunch or have it in your home. Instead, have it on a tribal turf that is not inhibiting.

Insist on Indian time, which is not, as we all seem to have thought, the stereotype of showing up late, but is time that allows for taking as much time as it takes to conclude the business.

Insist on equal inclusion or exclusion of attorneys or technicians. That is, if it is a lawyers' meeting, it should be a lawyers' meeting. If it is a planners' meeting, it should be a planners' meeting. If it is a meeting of low-level bureaucrats, the low-level bureaucrats, wherever they may be from, should not insist on the tribal chair's presence. Insist on all pertinent data and instantly test all threats, promises, and bluffs. During a negotiation session, call the Senator who allegedly will extinguish your claim, and find out if that is the case. Don't let it pass and don't assume that it is so. This happened to us while we were negotiating the Maine Indian Land Claims Settlement Act. We were told that we had to give in on certain aspects of the claim because the Congress was about to extinguish the claim. We insisted that the Office of Management and Budget in the White House ask President Carter to come out with a statement that he would veto any kind of approach that would wipe out the claim. The OMB said, "No." They said, "Don't be absurd." So we did it another way. President Carter had a town meeting in Bangor, Maine, and a friend of ours asked the question, "Would you veto such a piece of legislation?" And he said, "Absolutely. Because it is not equitable." So, test all threats, promises, and bluffs.

Insist on agreements that seriously oppose extra-negotiation efforts. If the people you are negotiating with are simultaneously lobbying to achieve their end on Capitol Hill or elsewhere, then they are not seriously negotiating. Or you must be at liberty to get an equal club.

Insist on equal self-restraint ground rules. If there is no press, then there is no press for anyone. If there is no discussion of the meeting until the meeting is over, then that goes for everyone. Perhaps that means no telephones at the meeting site.

Insist on the placement of priorities by attorneys being the same as the tribes'. And this includes tribal attorneys. Insist on history and culture lessons, if needed.

Insist on immediate clarification of stereotypes and ask for the other side to point this out, as well. That is, if the Indians are saying, "Oh, the white men are just greedy and liars," and we know that such a statement is not true of everyone, then ask the other side to point this out. Ask for the Indians to point out stereotypes as they occur, and for each side to explain historic inhibitions and the reason for these stereotypes.

Clarify the sense of time and memory. Some injuries may be distant in time from non-Indians, but are immediate and right in our Indian families, and are as if they happened to us today.

Don't be ashamed to discuss money. We should be rich. I hope every Indian in this room can be. Don't be impressed by the photo session, the pat on the head, the hearty handshake. Don't be intimidated by the technological elite. Insist on precision in language. If the terminologist cannot explain what he means by "substantially justified," or such other terms, then perhaps you shouldn't be signing anything that contains a term like that.

"Good faith" is another term to have spelled out very carefully. Always let your ears perk up when someone says, "It's nothing personal, this is strictly business." Let your ears perk up, because the last time you heard that was from Marlon Brando in "The Godfather." In negotiations and dealings on these critical issues, both sides are making value judgments. However diplomatically couched, what often happens in negotiations really means that my children and my children's children are expendable, and that non-Indian children and their children are not. I look to you tribal leaders, and my elders in this room, to see that this does not happen.

Today, we are in the very same position that we were about this time in the previous administration in regard to Griffin Bell. With the exception of many key people who are fair and professional and not mean spirited, this Administration seems to think that there is some trickery in law regarding the Indian cases and that it costs too much. Griffin Bell believed this. Attorney General Griffin Bell, you will recall, wanted to file with the court in *United States v. Maine* a "parameters of the trust responsibility" document. That was stopped. These other efforts can be stopped, too. I think it is critical that, even though this is not a policy-making body, tribal people from this group go to Washington, sit down with the Departments of Interior and Justice, and demand protection, demand hydrological, soil and other kinds of studies, now. Things not funded today will result in inadequate cases two years down the road. Demand that the trustee take actions to benefit the beneficiary and demand that the Administration live up to its promises.

We can have something to do with that end of it, and we just have to do it.

MR. RODNEY B. LEWIS

Tribal Attorney, Gila River Indian Community
Sacaton, Arizona

MR. LEWIS: The first thing I would like to do is comment on some of the remarks that were made last night. I think it is very important that we develop some sort of reasoned reaction to the remarks from the Assistant Secretary. First of all, I was especially impressed by the proposal made by Peter MacDonald. At Gila River we can really identify with big promises and the failures of various kinds of negotiations, contracts, and legislation, and enforcement or lack of enforcement. That is something, I guess, that every Indian tribe in the country has had to face at one time or another.

When we talk about negotiation or legislation, the real problem is the down-side risk for Indian tribes in giving up water rights and expecting something to be provided from the federal government by Congress.

There is a high risk in expecting a lot of things out of any package deal. That is one thing that should concern all of us and one thing of which we are especially wary.

At Gila River we have been in the water business for a long time. We have been through perhaps almost every piece of strategy or tactic that may have been proposed throughout these two days. We have been extremely disappointed on many, many occasions. So we don't expect too much. But at the same time, we still have to keep attempting to preserve and protect our water rights.

What bothered me most about the Assistant Secretary's remarks was the substance, not so much the mode of delivery or anything else like that. The substance was frightening when he spoke about being a team player at the expense of Indian tribes. Here was a person who I think we had thought would be a strong advocate for Indian affairs, for Indians in general, for Pimas and Maricopas in particular, and I am sure each one of your tribal groups had wished the same. But it is something we can see already—the interest of the Indians' team, the interest of Pimas and Maricopas or Papagos or Apaches, simply goes down the drain. It is really disturbing when he speaks of being a team player, being part of the Administration's policy game plan, or whatever you want to call it. That is one thing that is particularly distressing in this whole business.

I would like to sketch some of the problems that Gila River is facing. As I said, the Gila River people have been in the water game for a long time, since the creation of their reservation, and even before. For thousands of years, Pimas and Maricopas have farmed along the Gila River in the Gila Valley in southern Arizona.

In 1865, the reservation was created to protect the farming and irrigation interests of Pimas and Maricopas. Since that time, things have gone downhill. With the influx of settlers in the latter part of the nineteenth century, who settled along the Gila River and who began to divert water,—all of a sudden water ceased to come down the river. Literally, the river dried up. That has been and, I suppose, always will be a serious problem — diversions and the uncertainty of river flow. That is something that many, many people have to live with, especially in the Southwest.

As I mentioned before, Pimas have been through legislation, through negotiation, through litigation. We have been through these three areas, and we still plan to be active in all of these areas in an attempt to quantify and make certain our water rights.

First of all, I would like to describe some of the federal legislation that has affected the Gila River. One was the Coolidge Dam. Now, the Coolidge Dam was authorized in 1925. Let me read from the authorizing legislation: "Coolidge Dam was authorized for the purpose, first, of providing water for the irrigation lands allotted to Pima Indians on the Gila River Indian Reservation, Gila River Indian Community, now without an adequate supply of water. And, second, for the irrigation of such other lands in public or private ownership, as in the opinion of said Secretary, can be served with water impounded by said dam without diminishing the supply necessary for said lands."

Now that was the purpose of the dam. That purpose simply has not been fulfilled. I believe that the gentleman [Guy McMinds] from the Quinault Reservation talked about 85,000 acre-feet passing through his reservation at one point in one day. For any one year that would be, as far as surface flow is concerned, an adequate supply of water, at least adequate for the number of acres that were prepared for that particular year.

Subsequent to Coolidge Dam being built in 1929, the government stipulated to a decree. This is a decree that is the cause of much trouble today. This is a stipulation to which there was no consent, no input from Indians, and was given effect simply because of the fact that the Secretary of the Interior, on behalf of the Pimas, entered into the stipulation.

Let me just read from one part of it, which guarantees "210 acre-feet of natural flow water for 35,000 acres with an immemorial date of priority which may be used at any of the San Carlos Project lands located on the Gila River." But, in the same very complex decree, it later goes on to say—and I will paraphrase the language—in order to allow (1) the upper valley defendants to carry on irrigation of their land, and (2) to let the upper valley have the Coolidge Dam inure to their benefit, and (3) to settle Globe Equity 59, the parties stipulate that when there is stored water available for release through the gates to the Coolidge Dam for diversion and use on the lands of the San Carlos Project, for the irrigation thereof, the upper valley defendants are permitted to divert an amount of Gila River natural flow water equal to such stored water in disregard of the aforesaid prior rights of the plaintiff.

The effect of that phrase was to allow upper valley water users to use Pima water in disregard of our prior immemorial rights. That is the kind of situation that has plagued the attempts of Pimas to develop water and land and resources on the Gila River.

That is an example of the government's stipulation, a stipulation of the Secretary acting on behalf of its wards. And that is another indication of why many Indian tribes, not only Pimas, are very reluctant to settle or enter into any kind of agreement as far as water is concerned.

This sad example has almost single-handedly prevented water development on the reservation, and has left impoverished a group of people who before this time were able to grow foodstuffs for themselves enough to feed neighboring tribes, enough to sell to people coming through the country—a satisfied, viable people with a sound agricultural economic base, turned, virtually, into poverty-stricken people in the late nineteenth century. Now, that is one of the sad aspects of American life. And that is one of the problems that Pimas are attempting to rebound from today.

Going on from that piece of that stipulated decree, what has happened since then? Well, the Gila River Indian Community has attempted to satisfy its water rights through legislation. In 1975, the S.905 bill was introduced in Congress in an attempt to settle the Gila River Indians' water rights. That bill never got off the ground. There was absolutely no interest on the part of Congress to deal with the matter. There was tremendous opposition by the State of Arizona to settle water in central Arizona. What was the risk as far as Arizona was concerned? What did they have to lose? Really, nothing. I think we were fairly naive at that time to think that we had a strong hand, that we had some advantage. We didn't have.

So what has to happen in these kinds of situations is that when we are attempting to negotiate a settlement that is going to be approved by legislation, we are going to have to have some advantage in court. You have to deal from strength. We didn't at that time. How do we deal from strength in 1981? Perhaps really the only viable way of doing this is through litigation. Once people's water rights are on the docket, once there is a possibility of people, industry, towns, and counties losing water or having simply a big zero as far as their water entitlement is concerned, then perhaps that is the only way in which people can come to the negotiating table. At least in Arizona, that is probably the only way we are going to be able to provide any kind of inducement for people to come and settle.

Those are the kinds of things that are being contemplated by the tribe at this point. The tribe is reviewing, investigating, and taking a close look at the possibilities—looking again at the Gila decree, looking at existing water litigation or potential water litigation along the Gila River and its tributaries, the Salt River. Once these suits are filed and these actions are under way, possibly then some negotiations can take place.

This brings me back to the remarks by Ken Smith. He advocates negotiation. Secretary Watt advocates negotiation. But what is going to happen? Are they going to support us in these kinds of things? It is important to have the federal government at your side when you sit down and negotiate with the State of Arizona or the other entities within the state. Whether or not this can be done is speculative, I think, at this point.

That is really the only way in which we are going to protect our water rights. Really, these aren't new strategies; these are things we are all aware of. These are things we have to deal with in our own particular way. Perhaps intertribal efforts can be helpful. But it seems to me that these joint efforts may only be successful within a single state. At least in Arizona, I think we are beginning to recognize this. I think that at some point our joint efforts will provide us with at least some impetus along the way in attempting to identify the strategies that are important in regaining our water rights.

MR. ROBERT N. HARRIS SR.

Chairman, Shoshone Business Council,
Wind River Reservation
Ft. Washakie, Wyoming

MR. HARRIS: Our reservation in Wyoming consists of 2.2 million acres and is the home of 2,200 Shoshones and 3,500 Arapahos. As far as our Shoshone and Arapaho reservation is concerned, we feel it is a classic example of the *Winters* doctrine. It starts with mountains in the west, it comes down across the grazing lands and into the farming lands and mountains to the north. There is water that rises upon the reservation, flows through, and traverses the outside borders of that reservation. It has always been our contention that we will have to place our faith in the *Winters* doctrine and the *Winters* family, as we call it, the family of Supreme Court decisions that more or less supports *Winters.*

The Shoshones and the Arapahos have failed, or maybe have not even attempted, to negotiate in any way with the state or with any other organization. I don't know whether our relation to the State of Wyoming is what it should be. We are with the Billings Area BIA office, which is stationed in Montana. But we are not residents of Montana. So any possibility of negotiation with the State of Montana is strictly out. It's completely out.

As soon as the race to the courthouse started, it started with the Montana tribes. Soon after that, we were sued in the Fifth Judicial Court, by the State of Wyoming, demanding adjudication of the Big Horn River and its tributaries. We tried to appeal to the federal court and asked them to put this in a federal forum. That was denied. The decision of the state was upheld.

So we got busy. With the help of the Justice Department and the Solicitor's Office, two firms—a soils analysis and a hydrology firm—were hired, along with two firms composed of economists and agricultural engineers, and quite a few other experts that took part in this effort.

Since we have prepared for the case, we have been in trial for almost one year. The United States government has rested its case and has come out with a total of 570,304 acre-feet of water per year as a diversion for the historical irrigated land and the future irrigated land on the Wind River Reservation.

The tribes then started their case. The tribal position is that the tribes oppose any quantification of their water rights, particularly in the state court, and affirm that they have paramount rights to all water arising on or flowing through their reservation for both present or future needs. Because they were required by the state to make a statement of their claim for purposes of quantification and the preserving of all objections, the tribes made the following specific claims: The tribes claim all the water claimed by them and by the United States for them as reflected in the proof, which is the number of acre-feet that I just gave you.

Besides that, the tribes asked for additional allotments of acreage, which comes to 880,905 acre-feet of water for a diversion for the Wind River Indian Reservation. Their addition takes in vested rights to be granted to lands that are now in fee status. These lands are in fee status because of government regulations regarding the purchase of land by one Indian from another, and they were not allowed to receive these lands in trust status but must accept them in the fee simple status.

We have ground water. We have also taken in two other areas, Stagner Ridge and Big Horn Flats, which have a total of 997,000 acres and would require 25,000 acre-feet per year.

We feel that our ground water is a replenishable resource when used within the replenished rate, and an unreplenishable resource when used beyond that rate. The tribe's reserved water right assures them the use of a replenishable ground water. Both a reserved right and the ownership of the resources of the reservation assure the tribes of the use of mineral ground water, if they so choose, and of the prevention of the mining of such waters by anybody else.

I might point out that the states are now presenting their cases. We hope that they will be ready. The master, who is appointed by the judge, will take another year to hand down the decree.

We feel this is the only way to go. These are rights that we have. We feel we should litigate first. As Peter MacDonald, I think, said about people on the battlefield—and I think we both have been on the battlefield—we will probably be in a better position to negotiate.

We feel we have one thing that we are going to use in negotiation. The McCarran amendment is adjudication of all water rights, not just Indian rights. So as soon as the Indian water rights are adjudicated on that Big Horn River, we intend to challenge the adjudicated water rights of every white water user within the third division, which might mean a lot in negotiations.

MR. RONNIE LUPE

Chairman, White Mountain Apache Tribe
Whiteriver, Arizona

MR. LUPE: I want to thank the people who are responsible for getting this conference body together, speaking in reference to Indian water rights, the subject we are all very much concerned about.

I want to share with you a little bit of our activity on our reservation, the White Mountain Apache Tribe, in the State of Arizona, regarding these issues. My area is unique. We are up on the high ground. We have an abundance of water and, therefore, we are unique.

Although we ask for help from time to time, we think that we are better, perhaps expert-wise, to challenge their opposition our way than to impose upon other tribes. Historically, you are involved in your own unique area. If I were to bring up another topic, it would only complicate matters more, and I want to lessen some of the burden that you have with respect to Indian water rights with your particular community.

I would like to share with you the sweat, the struggle that we want to take on on our road to protecting the water rights of the White Mountain Apache Tribe in the State of Arizona. Day to day I live an ongoing battle to protect the invaluable life-sustaining *Winters* doctrine rights through the use of water, title to which resides in the White Mountain Apache Tribe, of which I am Chairman. Those rights were exercised by my ancestors long before the advent of the non-Native American culture. Without our rights to the use of water in the Salt River and its tributaries, you may rest assured that the White Mountain Apache Tribe will not survive. Yet, the battle to which I refer, and which goes on from day to day, has a single objective: the seizure of my tribe's rights to the use of water in the Salt River for the benefit of the downstream Salt River Federal Reclamation Project. They are now building this Central Arizona Federal Reclamation Project.

Unquestionably, our rights are prior and paramount on the Salt River. They date from time immemorial. A non-Indian would have no concern that his rights would be protected. That is not true in regard to the White Mountain Apache Tribe.

The mortal enemy of the White Mountain Apache Tribe is now and has been the State of Arizona. It has a single objective, and that is to extend its jurisdiction, power, and authority over our *Winters* doctrine rights by the use of water, depriving my tribe of those rights.

The Secretary of the Interior has, for the last three-quarters of a century, if not before, used every method available to him to frustrate our tribal development and to subordinate our invaluable rights to the Salt River Project. They are now building the Central Arizona Project.

As to the strategies for clarifying our rights to the use of water, I wish to stress this fact: The White Mountain Apache Tribe has consistently refused and continues to refuse to negotiate with the State of Arizona or any of its designated agencies. We have, likewise, refused to permit the Attorney General of the United States to represent us in litigation. Our tribe is all too well aware that the Attorney General frequently acts in concert with the Secretary of Interior, who has only one principal objective: the seizure of the tribe's rights by forcing it into the Maricopa County state court water litigation, which is now in progress. This is the background upon which I address these problems. It is with full knowledge that the Executive Branch of the United States of America is committed to seizing, diminishing, and violating our rights.

In my personal opinion, "quantification" is a catch word used by those with a desire to seize water rights from the Indian tribes in arid and semiarid western states. The term has unfortunately been adopted by some of the friends of the Indian people who, in my personal opinion, do not comprehend its true meaning. It is a term that is part and parcel of another catch word, "negotiate." The same people who use those words do it for the same purpose. Those purposes are: Take from the Indian tribes their rights to the use of water. Never before in history has there been a more concerted effort to seize and violate Indian property rights. Rest assured, when you are advised to quantify, you, the Indian people, are, in effect, being requested to destroy your tribal rights to the use of water.

My tribe, the White Mountain Apache, is being urged to quantify and to negotiate. In the strongest terms we have rejected the request both to quantify and to negotiate. It is our position that the term "quantify" is just as much a fraud on the Indian people as is the word "negotiate."

Repeatedly, an aggressive enemy of my tribe, the Salt River Water Users Association, working closely with the Bureau of Reclamation, has sought to force quantification upon us. The Water Users Association declared that we were entitled only to the water in the Salt River Valley that we could obtain through the process of salvage. Simply stated, the Salt River Valley Water Users Association and the Bureau of Indian Affairs interpreted the word "quantification" to mean zero. They would not at that time and they do not now admit that we have rights to the use of water adequate to meet our needs. We have an abundance of water on my reservation. They continue, however, to speak of quantification and negotiation.

The Attorney General and the Secretary of the Interior are attempting to force us into state court. They are now attempting to quantify our rights to the use of water, and they will next undertake to negotiate away our rights, because we know that they have no intention ever of actually going to trial to protect our rights and interests.

When they found they couldn't quantify our rights to the use of water at zero, they sought to quantify our rights at 36,000 acre-feet annually. Again, the Bureau of Indian Affairs was in the foreground to force the quantification upon us. My tribe told them again and again to go to hell.

Let me tell you how they would quantify our water rights to arrive at 36,000 feet. They told us that if we cut enough trees off of our land and tore up enough of the grazing lands that we had, that would result in salvage water. They would quantify it at 36,000 acre-feet.

This is no joke. In the Bureau of Indian Affair's effort to quantify our water rights, they had the United States Geological Survey measure the quantity of water that ran down the trunks of our juniper trees. They know exactly how much water is involved to totally wet the trunk of a juniper. They refused, however, to tell us exactly how much they would claim for us. Rather, they want us to put a ceiling on our rights. They would then cut it in half. Then they would refer that number to the Department of Justice and negotiate away everything that we have, except, perhaps, 10 percent.

And I repeat, again, we have an abundance of water our reservation. I say these things to you today because I know them to be true based on my own experience.

We know that for the past seventy-five years the Department of Interior has sought to rob us of our Salt River rights. We know that the process is ongoing and has intensified today. We know that the first step in the present plans to take our water rights is to quantify.

The question may properly be asked, "What are we losing if we quantify?" I refer to some history on the subject. As early as the year 1908, the courts announced this principle: Indians are entitled to divert and utilize from the streams that arise upon, border, or traverse their reservations, amounts of water sufficient to meet their present and future requirements.

There is an additional question in regard to quantification, however. How can Indian tribes determine the full amount of water that they will need today and that which they will need tomorrow, when, as a matter of fact, the Secretary of Interior has consistently inhibited and prevented development of water resources on our reservation? We cannot tell what the amount of water is that would be required at this stage if we had been permitted to fully use our water rights for the purposes of industry and agriculture. It is a known fact that the more water you use, the more water you are going to require. Therefore, we are of the opinion that the request now to quantify is simply for the purpose of being deprived of the opportunity fully to ascertain the extent of the rights that we must exercise if we are to achieve full economic development.

The most recent effort to quantify our rights is most interesting. The Department of Interior recently published a report declaring that we should not have any water rights by reason of the fact that the downstream white man can make better use of it. To demonstrate that we could not use our water rights and that we should be quantified at zero, we were, the White Mountain Apache Tribe, accused of being prone to alcoholism, homocide, and suicide. It is the first time in history that those words were utilized in an effort to quantify our rights in the manner proposed.

As you can see, water rights, when you ask each and every one of us to participate, are quite lengthy and complicated. To say what I want to say and the feeling of my people in a matter of five minutes, I have to take more time so that you and I at least can comprehend what we are up against, we as the White Mountain Apache Tribe, along with all of you.

This conference was convened apparently to discuss Indian water rights in a so-called changing environment. I seriously question whether the environment is changing, especially where Indian water rights are concerned. The environment has always been hostile and continues to be hostile to Indian water rights. The only change I see now is that the federal government through its agencies—the Bureau of Reclamation, the Secretary of Interior, the Attorney General of the United States—have become openly opposed to Indian water rights. Although they still pay lip service to Indian water rights, their conduct exposes their fake promises to us.

The greatest problem facing these agencies is how to make legal their illegal taking of Indian water—water reserved to the White Mountain Apache Tribe by the *Winters* doctrine. For at least seventy-five years the Salt River Project has illegally appropriated water from the White Mountain Apache Tribe, hoping and doing everything in its power to hinder our own development, while using every means at its disposal to enhance its own development.

My observation is nothing new. I quote to you from a statement issued in 1973 by the National Water Commission from its paper "Water Policy for the Future": "In the water-short West, billions of dollars have been invested, much of it by the federal government, in water resources projects benefiting non-Indians, but using water in which the Indians have a priority of right if they choose to develop projects of their own in the future. In short, the nation faces a conflict between the rights of Indians to develop their long-neglected water resources and the impairment of enormous capital investments already made by non-Indians in the same water supply. To resolve that conflict is not an easy task."

Four years later, on October 12, 1977, Forrest J. Gerard, then Assistant Secretary of the Interior for Indian Affairs, made the following statement: "I think it is essential for us to participate if we expect the national water policy to reflect accurately the unique nature of Indian water rights and the federal government's fiduciary duty to protect those rights. Moreover, after years of disregard, Indian water rights are being taken seriously."

Yes, after nearly a century of misappropriation, Indian water rights are being taken seriously. The federal government is greatly concerned about how to gracefully, without shame and disgrace, give Indian water to non-Indians, as it has always done. This government concern resulted in the establishment of an Indian Water Policy Review begun during the Carter administration and that continues today.

The Indian Water Policy Review was and is an important and essential part of a national water resources management policy. Its purpose is to solve the problem of reserved Indian water rights. My research tells me that there were three objectives of the Indian Water Policy Review: (1) to preserve, protect, and assert the water rights of the Indian people; (2) to develop appropriate methods to determine the present and future water requirements of the Indian people, i.e., quantification; and (3) to develop and implement a program to ensure that a dependable water supply will be made available to support these requirements.

Following these three, several recommendations were made to carry out these objectives. They are as follows: (1) The government should make a firm commitment to develop Indian water resources; (2) the federal courts should have exclusive jurisdiction over the adjudication of Indian water rights; (3) Indian tribes should participate in the water resource planning process; (4) the possibility of regional or basinwide legislative solutions of controversies involved in Indian water rights should be explored; (5) methods should be examined for facilitating negotiated settlements between tribes and competing parties for the use of water; (6) an effective tribal scheme should be developed for regulation of water use on the reservation; and (7) the federal government should clarify its responsibilities in the area of Indian water rights.

Some of these objectives and recommendations seem to carry out, as I read it, past history, for instance, the recommendation of the National Water Commission, made in 1973, that the federal government assist the tribes in developing the water supplies that are "legally as well as morally theirs." The country's obligations plainly mandate such a commitment, and I agree wholeheartedly that the neglect and deliberate obstruction of the last seventy-five years cannot be undone without a significant commitment of resources to Indian tribes.

Only one objective has been emphasized since, and that is quantification. Only one recommendation has been emphasized since, and that has been to foster negotiations between tribes and competing parties.

Despite the formidable body of law deriving from the *Winters* rights, which are legally and morally ours, there is a push for us to go to the negotiating table. The State of Arizona and the Salt River Project are opposing parties to negotiations with our tribe, not the Secretary of Interior, who represents the United States government.

Hand in hand with the government's emphasis on negotiation, there is a crippling attack on our own water development. I have had to struggle, beg, threaten, and fight for every penny for our own Canyon Day Irrigation Project on my reservation, while millions are being made available to non-Indian irrigation projects.

As mentioned by my friend Peter MacDonald last night, the Navajo brothers have suffered in the past in their Navajo Indian Irrigation Project from lack of funding, while the companion non-Indian diversion project, the San Juan–Chama, which is for the benefit of non-Indian water users, has prospered. The Secretary of the Interior committed to the non-Indian project huge quantities of the San Juan River, upon which the Navajos must entirely rely and which are the Navajo's water rights.

On July 13, 1978, the National Tribal Chairman's Association and the National Congress of American Indians met with the Assistant Secretary for Land and Water Resources, and at that historic meeting and confrontation, we opposed the effort to treat federal and Indian water rights in the same paper. We objected strenuously to the proposal to subject Indian water rights issues to public review and comment.

In response to that position, the Assistant Secretary for Land and Water issued this statement: "The Secretary of the Interior is fully aware of the unique status of the Indians as beneficiary of the trust responsibility owing to them by the United States. Indians are the owners of the beneficial right to the use of either surface water or ground water related to the reservation. The trustee, the United States, is obligated to protect Indian rights to the use of water." The statement went on to say that "Indian water rights are not the same as federal rights and, therefore, cannot be included in a policy statement involving federal rights."

Had it not been for the alertness of Indian leaders at that time, federal water rights would have been characterized as identical to Indian water rights. It would have paved the way for state courts to more easily bring the tribes into state court and seize their water rights under the McCarran amendment and the ill-advised *Akin* case.

It is clear that the McCarran amendment did not waive tribal sovereign immunity in state courts. Therefore, tribes cannot be joined in state court proceedings. Yet the United States continues to drag the tribes into state court proceedings in an unfriendly forum where their *Winters* rights may be forever extinguished.

It has been recognized by the Department of Interior and by the Congress that the federal government, because of conflicts between its own interest and those of the tribes or because of conflicting tribal interests, have experienced difficulty in adequately representing Indian interests. But the National Water Commission in 1973 stated that exclusive federal jurisdiction was required "to avoid the suspicion of bias that might attend adjudication by elected state officials."

Mr. Forrest Gerard, former Assistant Secretary of the Interior for Indian Affairs, speaking for our trustee, the Secretary of Interior, stated in 1977 that the most critical aspects of defending Indian water rights in state courts are: "(1) the difficulty of adequate preparation by the United States and the tribes, given the heavy competition among tribes for relatively scarce funds required for the crucial and technical studies needed to support Indian claims, and (2) the fact that the appellate courts cannot review the trial court's findings of fact, which is the most critical stage of *Winters* rights adjudication." "These factors," he added, "may allow state courts to restrict Indian water entitlements."

To my tribe what the message is—and the message is very clear to me—is that the United States government is not going to put its money where its mouth is. It is using scare tactics to say to the tribes, "We can't stop from going into state court and you're going to lose there because we don't have the money to defend you and, therefore, you are going to have to quantify and negotiate."

This is the same type of reasoning that the federal government used over seventy-five years ago when it chose not to go into federal court to stop the white farmers from seizing the federally protected waters of the Gila River Tribe. Their excuse was that a federal court order would be too difficult to enforce against the non-Indians of Stafford, Arizona, and Thatcher, Arizona, upstream.

Is this then, I ask, the conduct of a responsible advocate or of a conscientious trustee? No money is available for Indian irrigation and no money is available for an adequate defense of our rights in the states, which are dead set on seizing our water. The Secretary of Interior and the Attorney General of the United States are immorally attempting to strip the White Mountain Apache Tribe of its water rights.

In order to carry out its program of quantification, the Department of Interior has conducted a study against our will. That study included quantification of water rights. At the same time, the Attorney General of the United States, who represented the Secretary of Interior, has made an appearance in the Maricopa County Superior Court for the State of Arizona for the White Mountain Apache Tribe—again, against our will. Our tribe has not made an appearance; and we have refused.

Let me relate to you, for your information, a list of the parties claiming water and being represented by the Justice Department. Mind you, we are also represented by the Justice Department. For the United States Department of Interior: (1) Bureau of Land Management; (2) Water and Power Resources Service; (3) National Park Service; (4) Fish and Wildlife Service. For the Department of Defense: the United States Air Force and Army; for the Department of Agriculture: the National Forest Service. Getting down to Indian tribes: the San Carlos Apache Reservation, White Mountain Apache, Tonto Apache, Fort McDowell Indian Reservation, Yavapai Prescott Indian Reservation, Salt River Indian Reservation, the Gila River Indian Reservation,

Gila Bend Papago Reservation, Ak Chin Indian Reservation. All of these opposing parties are in court represented by the same attorney, one attorney.

It has been said that no man can serve two masters. Here we have the Justice Department representing several conflicting interests against the Bureau of Reclamation's pet project, the Salt River Project. I am told by my attorneys that such conduct in private practice would result in a lawyer being disbarred.

The Justice Department lawyer said this in the Arizona state court, and this is the most immoral statement of all: "The United States will file claims for the Indian reservations for the United States' legal interest as a trustee of the water rights of the respective reservations. The Indian tribes have separate equitable interests in the water rights of the reservations. The United States believes that certain of the Indian tribes may file claims in this proceeding which may differ from the claims that the United States will make for its interests as trustee."

Such double talk is not new to the White Mountain Apache Tribe; it is a method they use, an excuse to represent us in the state court. As a result of that outrageous legal proposition, we have initiated suit against the Secretary of Interior and the Attorney General of the United States in the District Court for the District of Columbia, challenging their arbitrary and capricious act of submitting our precious water rights to a state court, when it is clear, and they have even admitted to us, that the McCarran amendment is not proper or applicable to the Phoenix lawsuit.

Let me back up a little to give you some idea just what we live with back home. The hostility of the states and the territories was so great against Indian tribes years ago that the federal government decided it was best for the tribes to have exclusive and full power over Indian affairs. Territories such as Arizona and other western states at that time were required to disclaim any control over Indian tribes or land when they joined the union. The states were stripped of all authority in regard to Indian affairs. The primary status of the *Winters* rights of the White Mountain Apache Tribe arises from the fact that the character, nature, and extent of our rights to water spring from the supreme law of the land.

The agreements of the tribes with the United States of America enjoy a legal status far beyond and above any relationship that could be created within the State of Arizona. Because the State of Arizona entered the union subject to the disclaimer as to the Indian rights and property, and also because it does not own rights to the use of water, it cannot enter into an agreement that is binding on the Indians. Since the state has no jurisdiction in regard to Indian properties, any negotiation or agreement with Arizona would be a waste of time.

The Salt River Project is simply the Salt River Federal Reclamation Project being administered by a state-created public corporation. The real party in interest is the United States of America. The trustee, the U.S.A., must make some arrangements to resolve the conflict of interest with regard to claims of the Salt River Project and the Arizona tribes. The conflict within the Department of Interior is irreconcilable, and the claims asserted by the Bureau of Reclamation through the Salt River Project create a wall in regard to any negotiations.

Historically, the United States, through the Bureau of Reclamation or the Corps of Engineers, has violated every river system in the western United States on which an Indian reservation is situated, and will continue to violate Indian rights. Those violations have been very frequent and intentional, and the damages suffered by the Indians have been beyond repair.

The negotiations should be conducted with the trustee, not the states. There should be as their purpose two objectives: (1) a guarantee to the Indians of their *Winters* doctrine rights and that there will be no further encroachment upon those rights, and (2) there should be determined the extent of money damages that the United States will be forced to pay for the violation of Indian rights.

Perhaps I appear cynical to you here today, but I can imagine that there will be an Indian Water Claims Commission Act, like Peter MacDonald stated, created some day that will hear all of the tribes' claims against the United States government who, by conspiring, design, and neglect, allowed the wrongful taking of the tribes' water rights. A new generation of land claims attorneys will become rich, and the conscience of the United States will be soothed when the tribes are legally paid pennies for their water worth billions.

The assertion of the *Winters* rights poses a severe threat to the economics of the State of Arizona, which is already dependent on the water from streams and underground aquifers in which the White Mountain Apache Tribe and other Arizona tribes have extensive rights.

Certainly, many of those who are competing with us for the use of water are increasingly seeking to discover the extent of our entitlement. Energy companies, land speculators, corporations of every kind tend to view Indian water as the last remaining source of uncommitted water. I do not intend to satisfy their curiosity as Chairman of the White Mountain Apache Tribe in the near future by quantifying our water needs. The State of Arizona and the Salt River Project have nothing to give us.

I have referred to the efforts to quantify my tribe's water rights in the Salt River, and to seize those rights by negotiation. That my tribe has refused to adopt that course of conduct is beyond question and free from doubt. I have watched with great concern what is happening to the Navajo in the San Juan River Valley. We are witnessing there the intentional violation by the principal agent of the trustee, the United States. The unconscionable seizure of Navajo rights to the use of water by the devices referred to simply evidences the magnitude of the efforts now being made by the Secretary of the Interior and others to seize, for the benefit of non-Indian projects and purposes, the last Indian rights to the use of water in the western United States.

I can speak for the White Mountain Apache people and safely say that we will not negotiate with the State of Arizona or the Salt River Project for what is rightfully ours. Even now, the Salt River Project is attacking our agricultural irrigation project and lobbies extensively against any further monies for its future development.

Nevertheless, we have tremendous water needs for irrigation, domestic use, livestock, municipal, industrial, and public services, fish and wildlife, outdoor recreation, mineral production, aesthetic and religious needs, hydroelectric power, and many other uses for which our waters can be utilized for the benefit of our people, now and in the future.

In conclusion, I sincerely believe that there will be two final battles to be fought by the Indian tribes in the western United States. The first will be for water, without which our people cannot survive, and the second will be for the very reservation land itself, for one follows the other.

As soon as the United States government and the non-Indian users strip the tribes of their water, they will say that there is little need for us Indian people to have such large areas of land. Then you and I will meet here again in Oakland or some other city, and strategies will be outlined as to how to negotiate with the states to retain some of our land for some of our people.

CONVENING ORGANIZATIONS

Symposium on Indian Water Policy

AFFILIATED TRIBES OF NORTHWEST INDIANS

The Affiliated Tribes of Northwest Indians are an unincorporated association of Indian tribes in the states of Washington, Oregon, Idaho and Montana. Their primary purposes are to preserve Indian traditions and cultures and to enlighten the public about the rights and concerns of Indian tribes and their members.

AMERICAN INDIAN BAR ASSOCIATION

The American Indian Bar Association (AIBA) is a non-profit corporation established in 1977 to promote unity, cooperation and the interchange of ideas among its members and to strive for justice and effective legal representation for all Indian people. AIBA's membership includes Indian attorneys, tribal judges, law students and Indian legal paraprofessionals.

AMERICAN INDIAN LAWYER TRAINING PROGRAM, INC.

The American Indian Lawyer Training Program, Inc. (AILTP) is a non-profit, tax-exempt corporation founded in 1973 to provide access to the increasingly vast and complex legal developments that affect Indian tribes and their members; to contribute toward the development of Indian law through publication of resource materials which focus on those areas of law most vital to the Indian community; and to promote tribal sovereignty and Indian self-determination through training programs designed to develop the skills of members of the Indian legal community.

CALIFORNIA TRIBAL CHAIRMEN'S ASSOCIATION

The California Tribal Chairmen's Association (CTCA) is a non-profit association reorganized in 1977 under the concepts of the Indian Self-Determination and Education Assistance Act (P.L. 93-638). CTCA's purposes are to advocate and obtain contracts and grants on behalf of its 38-member tribes and to provide for the economic, educational, cultural, social and legal advancement of its membership.

INTER-TRIBAL COUNCIL OF ARIZONA, INC. (ITC)

The Inter-Tribal Council of Arizona, Inc. (ITC) functions as an association of tribal governments for nineteen tribes in Arizona. Its primary purpose is to analyze and present united and coordinated responses to public policy changes affecting Indian tribes. ITC performs policy research in a broad number of areas, disseminates information and provides technical assistance to tribes, and coordinates inter-tribal responses on matters of common concern.

NATIVE AMERICAN RIGHTS FUND

The Native American Rights Fund (NARF) is a national Indian interest law firm which was established in 1970. NARF has been representing Indian tribes and individuals in cases of major significance for the past eleven years. Major emphasis is placed upon cases involving the preservation of Indian tribal existence and resources and fulfillment of the nation's long-standing obligations to Indian people.

PART III

SELECTED BIBLIOGRAPHIES

SELECTED BIBLIOGRAPHY OF ARTICLES AND ESSAYS AFFECTING INDIAN WATER RIGHTS

The following is a sampling of articles, essays, cases and bills pertaining to Indian water rights.

Aboriginal Water Rights. James L. Merrill, 20 *Natural Resources Journal* 45 (1980).

Adjudication of Indian and Federal Water Rights in the Federal Courts. 46 *Colorado Law Review* 555 (1975).

Adjudication of Indian Water Rights: Implementation of the 1979 Amendments to the Montana Water Use Act. Michael F. Lamb, 41 *Montana Law Review* 73 (1980).

Alaska Native Water Rights as Affected by the Alaska Native Claims Settlement Act. Kerry Stoebner, Vicky Camerino and Steve Nickeson, 4 (No. 3) *American Indian Journal* 2 (1978).

American Indian Reservation Economic Development Retarded or Thwarted Through Abridgement or Loss of Indian Titles to Land and Rights to the Use of Water by Policies, Agencies and Personnel of Federal Government. William H. Veeder, Memorandum and Implementation (1969).

American Indian Water Law Symposium. Robert S. Pelcyger, Reid P. Chambers, John Vance and Ralph Keen, 15 *University of Tulsa Law Journal* 699 (1980).

Analysis of November 16, 1967 Opinion to the Extent that It Relates to the Rights of the Crow Indians in the Big Horn River. William H. Veeder, Opinion, B.I.A. (1967).

A Proposal for the Quantification of Reserved Indian Water Rights. Susan Millington Campbell, 74 *Columbia Law Review* 1299 (1974).

Application of the Winters Doctrine: Quantification of the Madison Formation. Michael M. Hickey, 21 *South Dakota Law Review* 144 (1976).

Central Arizona Indian Tribal Water Rights Settlement Act of 1976. Papago Tribe of Arizona, Congressional Testimony, submitted to Senate Committee on Interior and Insular Affairs (1976).

Comments on Indian Water Rights. 41 *Montana Law Review* 39 (1980).

Confiscation of Indian Winters Rights in the Upper Missouri River Basin. William H. Veeder, 21 *South Dakota Law Review* 282 (1976).

Conflicts of Interest Proceedings Before the Supreme Court of the United States: A Preface to Disaster for the American Indian People. William H. Veeder (1971).

Congressional Quantification of Indian Reserved Water Rights: A Definitive Solution or a Mirage? Charles DuMars and Helen Ingram, 20 *Natural Resources Journal* 17 (1980).

Considerations and Conclusions Concerning the Transferability of Indian Water Rights. Jack D. Palma II, 20 *Natural Resources Journal* 91 (1980).

Crow Indian Rights to the Use of Water in the Big Horn River and Its Tributaries. William H. Veeder, Memo, BIA (1969).

Damming the West: Ralph Nader's Study Group Report on the Bureau of Reclamation. Richard Berkman and W. Kip Viscusi, Center for the Study of Responsive Law (1973).

Declaration of the Indian Rights to the Natural Resources in the Northern Great Plains States. Report prepared by member tribes in the Native American Natural Resources Development Federation of the Northern Great Plains in conjunction with Native American Rights Fund, Bureau of Indian Affairs and private consultants. Native American Natural Resources Development Federation of the Northern Great Plains (June 1974).

Energy Development and Conservation Policies Affecting Indian Reservations. Carole Ann Heart, U.S. Commission on Civil Rights, Energy Resources Development: Implications for Women and Minorities in the Intermountain West (1978).

Extent of Indian Water Rights on Reservations in the West: *Northwestern Bands of Shoshone Indians v. United States*, 65 Sup. Ct. 690. John Patterson, 18 *Rocky Mountain Law Review* 427 (1946).

Federal Groundwater Rights: A Note on *Cappaert v. United States* 15 (No. 2) *Public Land and Resources Law Digest* 204 (1978).

Federal Indian Water Rights: A Retrogression to Quasi-Riparianism? Harry B. Sondheim and John R. Alexander, 34 *Southern California Law Review* 1 (Fall 1960).

Federal Protection of Indian Resources. Hearings before the Subcommittee on Administrative Practice and Procedure of the Committee on the Judiciary, U.S. Senate (1971–1972).

Federal Reserved Rights and Interstate Allocation of Water. Catherine L. Dirck, 13 *Land and Water Law Review* 813 (1978).

Federal Reserved Rights in Water: The Problem of Quantification. Carol S. Leach, 9 *Texas Tech Law Review* 89 (1977).

Game, Water, and People Up for Grabs: A Review Essay. Robert H. Keller, Jr., 5 (No. 5) *American Indian Journal* 2 (1979).

Government Ownership and Trusteeship of Water. Frank J. Trelease, 45 *California Law Review* 638 (1957).

Indian Claims to Groundwater: Reserved Rights or Beneficial Interest? Gwendolyn Griffith, 33 *Stanford Law Review* 103 (1980).

Indian Control and Use of Water for Mineral Development. Glen A. Wilkinson, Rocky Mountain Mineral Law Foundation, Indian Land Development: Oil, Gas, Coal and Other Minerals (1976).

Implied Reservation Claims After *Cappaert v. United States*. C. Steven McMurry, 1977 *Arizona State Law Journal* 647 (1977).

Indian Giving: The White Man Still Speaks With a Lying

Tongue. Eris Treisman, 246 *Harpers* 79 (1973).

Indian Government Relations on Water Utilization in the Salt and Gila River Valleys of Southern Arizona, 1902–1914. Terrence J. Lamb, 10 (No. 3) *Indian Historian* 38 (1977).

Indian "Paramount" Rights to Water Use. Paul L. Bloom, 16 *Rocky Mountain Mineral Law Institute* 669 (1971).

Indian Prior and Paramount Rights to the Use of Water. William H. Veeder, 16 *Rocky Mountain Mineral Law Institute* 631 (1971).

Indian Prior and Paramount Rights Versus State Rights. William H. Veeder, 51 *North Dakota Law Review* 107 (1974).

Indian Reserved Water Rights: The *Winters* of Our Discontent. 88 *Yale Law Journal* 1689 (1979).

Indian Rights to Land Underlying Navigable Waters: State Jurisdiction Under the Equal Footing Doctrine v. Tribal Sovereignty. 55 *North Dakota Law Review* (1979).

Indian Water Rights. Sharon M. Morrison, 41 *Montana Law Review* 39 (1980).

Indian Water Rights: A Compilation of Federal Treaties, Agreements, Executive Orders, and Statutes Relating to Indian Water Rights. Idaho Dept. of Water Resources Legal Affairs, Rep. #1 (1978).

Indian Water Rights: A State Perspective After Akin. Jack D. Palma II, 57 *Nebraska Law Review* 295 (1978).

Indian Water Rights: A Study of the Historical and Legal Factors Affecting the Water Rights of the Indians of the State of Idaho. Phillip J. Rassier, Idaho Department of Water Resources, Legal Affairs Report No. 1 (1978).

Indian Water Rights and the Energy Crisis. William H. Veeder, U.S. Commission on Civil Rights, Energy Resource Development: Implications for Women and Minorities in the Intermountain West (1978).

Indian Water Rights and the National Water Commission. William H. Veeder, 6 (No. 1) *Civil Rights Digest* 28 (1973).

Indian Water Rights and the States: Looking from Both Sides. Robert S. Pelcyger and D. Craig Bell, 6 (No. 6) *State Legislatures* 20 (1980).

Indian Water Rights as They Relate to State Jurisdiction. William H. Veeder, Conference of Western Attorney Generals (1977).

Indian Water Rights in the Upper Missouri River Basin. William H. Veeder, 48 *North Dakota Law Review* 617 (1972).

Indian Water Rights in Theory and Practice: Navajo Experience in the Colorado River Basin. Monroe E. Price and Gary D. Weatherford, 40 *Law and Contemporary Problems* 97 (1976).

Indian Water Rights: Some Emerging Frontiers. Robert S. Pelcyger, 21 *Rocky Mountain Mineral Law Institute* 743 (1975).

Indian Water Rights—Today and in the 1980's. Dan Israel, Colorado Bar Association (1979).

Indian Water Rights—The Winters Doctrine Updated. Robert D. Dellwo, 6 *Gonzaga Law Review* 215 (1971).

Indians, Water, and the Arid Western States—A Prelude to the Pelton Decision. Gerald R. Miller, 5 *Utah Law Review* 495 (1957).

Interagency Conflicts of Interest: The Peril to Indian Water Rights. Ronald T.L. Young, 1972 *Law and the Social Order* 313 (1972).

Inventory of Rights to the Use of Water on the Flathead Indian Reservation. William H. Veeder, Memo, BIA (1969).

Legal Issues in Indian Jurisdiction. Committee on the Office of the Attorney General, National Association of Attorneys General (December 1974).

Memorandum Relative to the Titles to Rights to the Use of Water and the Authority to Control and Administer Them on the Flathead Indian Reservation. William H. Veeder, Memo, BIA (1969).

Navigability in the Missouri River Basin. Alvin E. Bielefeld, 4 *Land and Water Review* 97 (1969).

Navigation Servitude and Reserved Indian Property: Does the Rule of No Compensation Apply? *Utah Law Review* 57 (1979).

Navajo Water Rights: Pulling the Plug on the Colorado River? William Douglas Back and Jeffery S. Taylor, 20 *Natural Resources Journal* 71 (1980).

Objections to Proposed Rules and Regulations: Part 417—Procedural Methods for Implementing Colorado River Water Conservation Measures with Lower Basin Contractors and Others. William H. Veeder, Memo, Department of the Interior (1969).

Paleface, Redskin, and the Great White Chiefs in Washington: Drawing the Battle Lines Over Western Water Rights. Belinda K. Orem, 17 *San Diego Law Review* 449 (1980).

Perspectives on Water and Energy in the American West and in Indian Country. Charles F. Wilkinson, 26 *South Dakota Law Review* 393 (1981).

Procedures for Evaluating the Effects of Federal Water Projects That Impact Upon Indian Reservations. U.S. Department of the Interior, Office of the Assistant Secretary for Indian Affairs (March 28, 1980).

Pueblo Indian Water Rights: Who Will Get the Water? *New Mexico v. Aamodt*. A. Patrick Maynez, 18 *Natural Resources Journal* 639 (1978).

Pueblo Water: The More Things Change, The More They Stay The Same. Steve Nickeson, 5 (No. 13) *Race Relations Reporter* 13 (1974).

Recent Developments in the Northwest Regarding Indian Water Rights. Robert D. Dellwo, 20 *Natural Resources Journal* 101 (1980).

Report of Environmental Factors by the Department of the Interior and the La Jolla, Rincon, San Pasqual, Pauma, and Pala Bands of Mission Indians submitted in support of Interior's Recapture Recommendation and the Indian Bands' Application for a Non-Power License. Report to the Federal Power Commission, Secretary of the Interior, La Jolla, Rincon, San Pasqual, Pauma and Pala Bands of Mission Indians (1974).

Report on the Protection of Pueblo Indian Rights to the Use of Water in the Rio Grande Basin: A Discussion on Pending Litigation. Daniel Rosenfelt (1969).

Reserved Water Rights for Federal and Indian Reservations: A Growing Controversy in Need of Resolution. Elmer B. Staats, Report to the Congress from the Comptroller General of the United States, CED-78-176 (November 16, 1978).

Res Judicata—Will It Stop In-Stream Flows from Being the Wave of the Future? Harold A. Ranquist, 20 *Natural Resources Journal* 121 (1980).

Sale and Lease of Indian Water Rights. Bill Leaphart, 33 *Montana Law Review* 266 (1972).

Should Rivers Having Running? Toward Extension of the Reserved Rights Doctrine to Include Minimum Stream Flows. Scott W. Reed, 12 *Idaho Law Review* 153 (1976).

Special Considerations Involving Indian Rights. Edward H. Clyde, 8 *Natural Resources Lawyer* 237 (1975).

State Jurisdiction to Adjudicate Indian Reserved Water Rights. Jeff Taylor and Duane Birdbear, 18 *Natural Resources Journal* 221 (1978).

Supplement to Solicitor Opinion No. M-36914, on Federal Water Rights of the National Park Service, Fish and Wildlife Service, Bureau of Reclamation and the Bureau of Land Management. Clyde Martz, U.S. Department of the Interior, Office of the Solicitor (January 16, 1981).

The Dark and Bloody Ground of Indian Water Rights: Confusion Elevated to Principle. Norris Hundley, Jr., 9 *Western Historical Quarterly* 455 (1978).

The Effect of Changes in Place and Nature of Use of Indian Rights to Water Reserved Under the *Winters* Doctrine. Harold A. Ranquist, 5 *Natural Resources Lawyer* 34 (1972).

The Importance of Water Supply to Indian Economic Development. David M. Dornbusch, Office of Water Research and Technology (1977).

The Indian Water Wars. Steve Nickeson, 5 (No. 9) *Race Relations Reporter* 10 (1974).

The Irrigable Acres Doctrine. Rebecca E. Wardlaw, 15 *Natural Resources Journal* 375 (1975).

The Navajo Agricultural Products Industry: Subsistence Farming to Corporate Agribusiness. Tom Barry, 5 (No. 7) *American Indian Journal* 2 (1979).

The Navajo Irrigation Project. William H. Veeder, Memo, BIA (1965).

The Navajo Tribe's Water Rights in the Colorado River Basin. Daniel H. MacMeeking (1971).

The Navigation Servitude and Reserved Indian Property: Does the Rule of No Compensation Apply to Indian Interests in Navigable Waters? Robert J. Ericsson, 1979 *Utah Law Review* 57 (1979).

The Pelton Decision: A Symbol—A Guaranty That the Development and Conservation of Our Nation's Resources Will Keep Pace with Our National Demands. William H. Veeder, 27 *Montana Law Review* 27 (1965).

The Political Economics of Arizona Water. Steve Nickeson, 5 (No. 17) *Race Relations Reporter* 15 (1974).

The Reemergence of Tribal Nationalism and Its Impact on Reservation Resource Development. Daniel H. Israel, 47 *Colorado Law Review* 617 (1976).

The Right to Remain Indian: The Failure of the Federal Government to Protect Indian Land and Water Rights. U.S. Commission on Civil Rights Report prepared by the All Indian Pueblo Council (1972).

The Southwest Indian Report. U.S. Commission on Civil Rights (May 1973).

The Use of Out-of-Court Means for Resolving Indian Conflicts. Preliminary Report, Indian Law Resource Center, Washington, D.C. (1980).

The Water Rights of Indian Tribes. U.S. Department of Justice, 12 *Land and Natural Resources Division Journal* 189 (1974).

The Winters Doctrine and How It Grew: A Memorandum on the Origin, Scope and Application of Reserved Rights to the Use of Water for the Benefit of Indian Reservations and Other Reserved Lands and Enclaves of the United States. Harold A. Ranquist, Memorandum, Office of the Solicitor, Department of the Interior (February 1975).

The Winters Doctrine and How It Grew: Federal Reservation of Rights to the Use of Water. Harold A. Ranquist, 1975 *Brigham Young University Law Review* 639 (1975).

The Winters Doctrine and the Greening of the Reservation. 4 *Journal of Contemporary Law* 19 (1977).

The Winters Doctrine: Seventy Years of Applications of Reserved Water Rights to Indian Reservations. University of Arizona, Office of Arid Lands Studies (1977).

The *Winters* Rights of Reservations Unaffected by Projects Authorized by Congress Under the 1902 Reclamation Act as Amended, Unless Specifically Authorized. Ralph F. Keen, U.S. Department of the Interior, Office of Trust Responsibility, Bureau of Indian Affairs (1975).

Uneasy Federalism: State Water Laws and National Water Uses. Frank J. Trelease, 55 *Washington Law Review* 751 (1980).

United States v. New Mexico and the Course of Federal Reserved Water Rights. Alan E. Boles, Jr. and Charles Elliott, 51 *University of Colorado Law Review* 209 (1980).

United States v. New Mexico: Purposes That Hold No Water. James F. Elliott, 22 *Arizona Law Review* 19 (1980).

Water and Water Courses—Limiting the Reservation Doctrine: *Mimbres Valley Irrigation Co. v. Salopek*, 564 P.2d 615 (N.M. 1977) *cert. granted*, 46 U.S.L.W. 3426 (No. 77-510). John E. Masters, 13 *Land and Water Law Review* 501 (1978).

Water for Non-Indians on the Reservation: Checkerboard Ownership and Checkerboard Jurisdiction. Philip W. Dufford, 15 *Gonzaga Law Review* 95 (1979).

Water Law: Pueblo Indians' Water Rights, *New Mexico v. Aamodt*, 537 F.2d 1102 (10th Cir. 1976). Wendy J. Busch, 54 *Denver Law Journal* 302 (1977).

Water Laws—Procedural Inconsistencies and Subsistence Issues in the Federal Reserved Water Rights Doctrine, *United States v. Akin*, 504 F.2d 115 (10th Cir. 1974). Timothy O. Beppler, 10 *Land and Water Law Review* 477 (1975).

Water Resources on the Public Lands—PLLRC's Solution to the Reservation Doctrine. Frank J. Trelease, 6 *Land and Water Law Review* 89 (1970).

Water Rights in the Coal Fields of the Yellowstone River Basin. William H. Veeder, 40 *Land and Contemporary Problems* 77 (1976).

Water Rights of Various Levels of Government—States' Rights v. National Powers. Frank J. Trelease, 19 *Wyoming Law Journal* 189 (1965).

Water Rights on Indian Allotments. David H. Getches, 26 *South Dakota Law Review* 405 (1981).

Water Rights Protection From A Tribal Point of View. Thomas W. Fredericks, Federal Bar Association, Indian Law Seminar (May 1976).

Water Rights: The McCarran Amendment and Indian Tribes' Reserved Water Rights. Elizabeth McCallister, 4 *American Indian Law Review* 303 (1976).

Water Rights: The *Winters* Cloud Over the Rockies: Indian Water Rights and the Develoment of Western Energy Resources. Michael S. Laird, 7 *American Indian Law Review* 155 (1979).

Winters Doctrine Rights, Keystone of National Programs for Western Land and Water Conservation and Utilization. William H. Veeder, 26 *Montana Law Review* 149 (1969).

SELECTED BIBILIOGRAPHY OF CASES AFFECTING INDIAN WATER RIGHTS

Alaska Public Easement Defense Fund v. Andrus, Cecil D. Calista Corporation v. Andrus, Cecil D. Sealaska Corporation v. Secretary of Interior, 435 F. Supp. 664 (D. Alas. 1977). Public easements under the Alaska Native Claims Settlement Act were reserved to permit access to public lands, not to provide the public rights to use native lands for recreation purposes.

Anaya, Henry P. v. Public Service Company of New Mexico, No. 43347 (Dist. Ct. 1971). Suit to enjoin Public Service Company from interfacing with water rights to the Santa Fe stream system and its underground basin for Indian land use.

Arizona v. California, No. 8, original (U.S. Sup. Ct. 1982). A joint motion by California, Arizona and Nevada to set present perfected rights to the use of mainstream water for specific needs of certain tribal lands.

Capitan Grande Band of Mission Indians v. Helix Irrigation District, 514 F. 2d 465 (9th Cir. 1975); *cert. denied,* 423 U.S. 874, 96 S. Ct. 143, 46 L.Ed.2d 106 (1975). Public Law 280 did not make the California state statute of limitations applicable to cut off a cause of action in trespass to tribal land brought by a federally-recognized Indian tribe against a private irrigation district.

Citizens League for Civil Rights, Inc. v. Baker, Odric, 464 F. Supp. 1389 (W.D. Wisc. 1978). Court dismisses suit by nonmembers of tribe who own property on and around reservation against tribal governing board charging that the tribal conservation and court codes infringed upon plaintiff's hunting, fishing and riparian rights.

Colorado River Water Conservancy District v. United States, United States v. Akin, Mary, 424 U.S. 800, 96 S.Ct. 1236, 47 L.Ed.2d 483 (1976). State courts have jurisdiction under the McCarran Amendment to adjudicate federal and tribal water rights as part of a general stream adjudication.

Daly, Shirley A. v. Natural Resources Board of the State of Wisconsin, 60 Wisc.2d 208, 208 N.W.2d 839 (1973); *cert. denied,* 414 U.S. 1137, 94 S.Ct. 883, 38 L.Ed.2d 763 (1974). State Natural Resources Department hearing concerning dam construction on terminated reservation was conducted with adequate notice and due process to Indians whose interests were affected by the project.

Fallon, City of v. Secretary of Interior, No. R-74-101 BRT (D.Nev. 1981). Action alleging that the implementation of Secretary's rules for Newlands Reclamation Project constitutes major federal action requiring an environmental impact statement.

Fort McDowell Mohave-Apache Indian Community v. Salt River Valley Water Users Association, No. CA80-5219 (9th Cir. 1982). Suit to determine whether state has jurisdiction to adjudicate the Fort McDowell Indian Community's federal reserved water rights pursuant to the McCarran Amendment, in light of the jurisdictional disclaimer over Indian lands in the Arizona constitution and enabling act.

Jicarilla Apache Tribe v. United States, 657 F. 2d 1128 (10th Cir. 1981). Court rules that neither the Bureau of Reclamation nor the city may store water in violation of congressional directives, and that the judgment of the district court declaring the contract between parties invalid is affirmed.

Nevada v. United States, cert. denied, ___ U.S. ___, ___ S.Ct. ___, 68 L.Ed.2d 195 (1981). United States is immune from Nevada action to quiet title to bed of Pryamid Lake located on Indian reservation, since government did not waive its immunity, and Quiet Title Act does not apply to trust or restricted lands.

New Mexico ex. rel. S.E. Reynolds v. United States, No. 75-184 (Dist. Ct. 1976). Suit to settle federal, state and Indian water rights in the San Juan River in New Mexico.

Northern Cheyenne Tribe v. Adsit, Thomas Ralph, United States v. Tongue River Water Users Association, (9th Cir. opinion of February 22, 1982). Dismissal of federal court action to adjudicate Indian water rights is reversed because the circumstances of Montana water rights litigation did not mandate dismissal based upon *Colorado River Conservation District v. United States,* 424 U.S. 800 (1976) *(Akin).*

Paug-Vik, Inc. v. Wards Cove Packing Company, (Alas. Sup. Ct., opinion of September 25, 1981). Wards Cove Packing Company is entitled to continued water appropriations from Seagull Lake, a non-navigable lake claimed by aboriginal title by natives of the village of Naknek and included in lands patented to Paug-Vik, Inc., under the Alaska Native Claims Settlement Act.

Puget Sound Power and Light Company v. Federal Energy Regulatory Commission, Puget Sound Power and Light Company, Before the Federal Power Commission, 644 F. 2d 785 (9th Cir. 1981); *cert. denied,* November 16, 1981, 50 U.S.L.W. 3402. Court upheld Federal Energy Regulatory Commission's ruling that the White River is a navigable stream, and therefore, power company's hydroelectric facility on the river is subject to the licensing jurisdiction of the Commission pursuant to the Federal Power Act.

Pyramid Lake Paiute Tribe v. Hickel, Walter J., Pyramid Lake Paiute Tribe v. Morton, Rogers C. B., (D.C. Cir. 1974); *cert. denied,* 420 U.S. 962, 95 S.Ct. 1351, 43 L.Ed. 2d 439 (1975). Secretary violated his fiduciary obligations to tribe by failing to minimize diversions from river feeding reservation lake, which resulted in continued diminishment of lake and its fisheries, but tribe was not entitled to award of attorneys' fees.

Rincon Band of Mission Indians v. Escondido Mutual Water Company, (S.D.Cal., decision and order of December 10, 1980 on motion for partial summary judgment). Action by tribes to recover damages from and prevent further diversion and appropriation of river water in violation of Indians' paramount water rights.

Salt River Pima-Maricopa Indian Community v. Salt River Project Agricultural Improvement and Power District, (D.Ariz., settlement agreement of December 20, 1976). Action for damages and a declaration that water projects within the reservation are owned by the United States exclusively for tribe's benefit is resolved by Boundary Settlement Act of 1978.

Schonchin, Evangeline v. Sexson, James A., No. 78-294 (D.Ore., 1981). Proceeding to determine federal reserved water rights of the Klamath Indian allottees.

Sierra Pacific Power Company v. Federal Energy Regulatory Commission, Pyramid Lake Paiute Tribe of Indians v. Sierra Pacific Power Company, No. 80-7453 (9th Cir. 1982). Tribe seeks confirmation of Federal Power Commission determination that the Truckee River is a navigable river, and thus four hydroelectric facilities located on it are subject to the licensing jurisdiction of the Federal Power Commission.

South Dakota ex. rel. Mark V. Meierhenry v. Rippling Water Ranch, Inc., (D.S.D., opinion and order of January 19, 1982). Suit brought to determine whether state or federal court is proper forum to adjudicate all rights to use water and water rights on the Missouri River system in the State of South Dakota.

Trinity, County of v. Andrus, Cecil D., 438 F.Supp. 1368 (E.D. Cal. 1977). Secretary of Interior did not violate the Anadromous Fish Act in failing to insure the preservation and propagation of the Trinity River fishery.

Truckee-Carson Irrigation District v. Secretary of Interior, No. R-74-34-BRT (D.Nev. 1982). Plaintiff seeks a judicial determination of (1) its rights and duties under the federal government's rules for the use of water on the Newlands Reclamation Project, and (2) the legality of the notice of termination by the U.S. of the 1926 contract.

United States v. Adair, Ben, (9th Cir. 1982). Tribe contends the Klamath Treaty reserved water sufficient to maintain tribal hunting and fishing rights.

United States v. Alpine Land and Reservoir Company, (9th Cir. 1981). Court denied tribe's motion to intervene in action by the government to quiet title to rights to water for a federal reclamation project, and court later holds that water rights of federal reclamation project are not limited by virtue of state law or contracts between Secretary of Interior and project water users.

United States v. Anderson, Barbara J., (E.D.Wash., memo opinion and order of July 23, 1979). Tribe is entitled by federal reserved water rights doctrine to injunctive relief to prevent stream water from dropping to level which threatens tribal fishery enterprise.

United States v. Bel Bay Community and Water Association, (W.D.Wash., order of September 26, 1978, setting aside partial summary judgment). Suit to determine whether the State of Washington has authority to issue appropriation permits, or to manage water or the rights to the use of water within the Lummi Indian Reservation.

United States v. District Court in and for the County of Eagle, 401 U.S. 520, 91 S.Ct. 998, 28 L.Ed.2d 278 (1971). The Eagle River and its tributaries constitute a "river system" within the meaning of statute which grants consent to join United States as a defendant in suits for adjudication of water rights, including water reserved for use and benefit of federally reserved lands.

United States v. District Court in and for Water Division No. 5, 401 U.S. 527, 91 S.Ct. 1003, 28 L.Ed.2d 284 (1971). Intervention by tribe as interested party in action to prohibit state court from asserting jurisdiction over water dispute.

United States v. Nevada and California, 412 U.S. 534, 93 S.Ct. 2763, 37 L.Ed.2d 132 (1973). In litigation in the original jurisdiction of U.S. Supreme Court to establish a prior water right against all upstream uses to maintain Pyramid Lake, court ruled that suit was not within its exclusive jurisdiction because there was no controversy between the two states and that it would decline to exercise its original discretionary jurisdiction.

United States v. Truckee-Carson Irrigation District, 649 F.2d 1286 (9th Cir. 1981). Suit seeks judicial allocation of Truckee River waters between the Pyramid Lake Tribe for its fishery and the other Truckee River water users in Nevada.

ANNOTATED INDEX OF PENDING LITIGATION AFFECTING INDIAN WATER RIGHTS

ARIZONA

In the Matter of the Determination of Conflicting Rights to the Use of Water from the Gila River, Below its Confluence with the San Francisco River, Chase Creek and Eagle Creek.
Phelps Dodge Corporation, petitioner, is a copper producer operating in the Gila River watershed. It contends that the Gila River tributaries were unadjudicated in *United States v. Gila Valley Irrigation District,* Globe Equity No. 59 (D. Ariz., June 29, 1935) (Gila Decree). Involves water rights of Gila River Indian Community & San Carlos Apache Tribe.

In the Matter of the Determination of Conflicting Rights to the Use of Water from the San Pedro River and the Tributaries of the San Pedro River, including Aravaipa Creek.
ASARCO, Inc., petitioner, is a copper producer operating in the San Pedro watershed, a tributary of the Gila River. ASARCO takes the position that the San Pedro was unadjudicated by the Gila Decree. Affects reserved rights of the Gila River Indian Community.

Gila River Indian Community v. ASARCO, et al.
Plaintiff tribe seeks only a declaration of its paramount rights in the waters of the San Pedro River watershed, including ground water; it does not seek an adjudication of other claimants on the system *inter se.* As in the ASARCO and Phelps Dodge proceedings, the tribe takes the position that Gila River tributaries were not adjudicated by the Gila Decree.

In the Matter of the Determination of Conflicting Rights to the Use of Water from the Salt River Above Granite Reef Dam and Its Tributaries Including Tonto Creek, Excluding the Verde River and Its Tributaries.
Salt River Valley Water Users' Association, Petitioner. Affects rights of the White Mountain Apache, San Carlos Apache, Salt River Indian and Gila River Indian Reservations.

Salt River Pima-Maricopa Indian Community v. Arizona; San Carlos Apache Tribe v. Arizona; Payson Community of Yavapai Indians v. Arizona.
Simultaneously, with the filing of removal petitions, the three tribes filed these actions for declaratory relief. The tribes contend that the state proceeding is inapplicable to them and should be dismissed.

San Carlos Apache Tribe v. Arizona.
This suit seeks a declaration that the San Carlos Apaches have prior and paramount rights to water in the Salt River watershed ahead of all other defendants. The suit is not a general adjudication.

Fort McDowell Mohave-Apache Indian Community v. Salt River Valley Water Users Association, et al.
The Fort McDowell Tribe makes a claim similar to the one of the San Carlos Apache Tribe on the Verde River. It is an affirmative proceeding seeking a declaration that the tribe's right is ahead of all other claimants on the stream. The Verde River is a tributary of the Salt River and flows through the Fort McDowell Reservation.

Navajo Nation v. United States, et al.
Tribe seeks declaration of its rights as against all water users in the Little Colorado River. Involves Navajo and Hopi rights.

United States v. Gila Water Commissioner, Globe Equity Number 59.
Adjudication of the main stem of the Gila River involving rights of the San Carlos Apache Tribe and the Gila River Indian Community.

Hurley v. Abbott.
Rights to the Salt River below Granite Reef Aqueduct Dam were determined in 1910 and rights to apply for Salt River Project water established. Issues in case concern validity of water source contracts and abandoned waters, among others.

United States v. City of Tucson.
General adjudication of ground water rights involving claims of the Papago Indian Tribe. Suit raises issue of reserved rights in ground water. Major defendants include Tucson, mines and large agricultural interests.

Babbit v. Andrus.
Action by Governor of Arizona to challenge allocations made by Secretary of Interior of water from Central Arizona Project to Indian tribes and seeking injunction to prevent Secretary from entering into water contracts with tribes.

CALIFORNIA

United States v. Escondido Mutual Water Co.
Suit to determine the validity of contracts limiting the water rights of the Rincon, La Jolla, San Pasqual, Pala and Pauma Indian Bands, the respective water rights as between the Indians, the Escondido community and the Vista Irrigation District, and for money damages.

In the Matter of Escondido Mutual Water Co.
Application by private company for renewal of power licenses to convey water across federal and Indian lands. Broad issues of first impression are presented concerning (1) respective authority of Secretary and FERC under Federal Power Act, and (2) interrelations of Secretary's other statutory authority with Federal Power Act.

In the Matter of Southern California Edison Company.
Southern California Edison Com any seeks a new license for a small hydroelectric project which diverts the headwaters of White River from the Coachella Basin to the San Gorgonio River Basin. The Agua Caliente Band of Mission Indians intervened to oppose the license renewal on the grounds that the diversion of water impairs the band's ground water rights.

Arizona v. California.
The Supreme Court's landmark ruling is reported at 373 U.S. 546 (1963). At present the United States is before the Court claiming additional water rights for the Colordo River, Fort Mojave, Chemehuevi, Quechan and Cocopah Indian Tribes for (1) lands which subsequent to the trial in the original case have been determined to be part of the reservations, and (2) for lands which were omitted from the claim of the United States in the prior proceeding.

COLORADO

In the Matter of the Application for Water Rights of the United States of America, Water Division 7, State of Colorado.
General stream adjudications involving reserved water rights of the Ute Mountain Ute and Southern Ute Indian Reservations.

MONTANA

United States v. Aageson, et al.
General adjudication of all water rights on the Milk River and St. Mary River systems within the State of Montana, including reserved water rights for the Blackfeet, Rocky Boy's, Fort Belknap and Fort Peck Indian Reservations, Glacier National Park, BLM lands, and several wildlife refuges and waterfowl production areas.

United States v. Ams Ranch, Inc., et al.
General adjudication of all water rights on the Marias River system, including reserved water rights for the Blackfeet Indian Reservation, Glacier National Park, the Lewis and Clark National Forest and BLM lands.

United States v. Abell, et al.
General adjudication of all water rights within the Flathead River Basin, which is that area encompassing the Flathead River and its tributaries from their sources to the place where the Flathead River flows into the Clark Fork River. This proceeding involves reserved water rights for the Flathead Indian Reservation, the National Bison Range, Glacier National Park, wild and scenic river purposes, and several wildlife refuges, national forests and tribal and federal power sites.

United States v. Aasheim, et al.
General adjudication of all water rights on the Poplar River and its tributaries, Big Muddy Creek and its tributaries, and the tributaries of the Missouri River which arise in or flow through the Fort Peck Indian Reservation. This case involves reserved water rights for the Fort Peck Reservation, the Medicine Lake National Wildlife Refuge and BLM lands.

United States v. Big Horn Low Line Canal, et al.
General adjudication of all water rights on the Big Horn River, the Little Big Horn River, Pryor Creek, Sage Creek, Tullock Creek and Sarpy Creek, within the State of Montana, and all tributaries thereto. This adjudication involves reserved water rights for the Crow Indian Reservation, the Custer National Forest, the Pryor Mountain Wild Horse Range, and the Big Horn Canyon National Recreation Area.

United States v. Tongue River Water Users Association.
General stream adjudication of all water rights in the Tongue River system. This proceeding involves the reserved water rights of the Northern Cheyenne Indian Reservation and, to a lesser extent, the Crow Indian Reservation.

In the Matter of Montana Power Company, Kerr Project No. 5.
Competing applications by Montana Power Company and the Confederated Salish and Kootenai Tribes for the future operation of Kerr Project No. 5.

In the Matter of Northern Lights, Inc., Kootenai River Project No. 2752.
Application to construct and operate hydroelectric power project at Kootenai Falls in Montana. Involves off-reservation treaty-guaranteed fishing rights of Confederated Salish and Kootenai Tribes of Montana.

NEVADA

Truckee-Carson Irrigation District v. Secretary of the Interior.
In 1973, the Department of the Interior adopted operating criteria and procedures for the Newlands Reclamation Project, which the Truckee-Carson Irrigation District refused to follow. The TCID operates the Newlands Reclamation Project under contract entered into with the Secretary of the Interior in 1926. After notice, the Department cancelled the 1926 contract and contemplated taking over operational control of the project. TCID responded with this suit. The suit seeks to void cancellation of the 1926 contract; to prevent a government take-over of the project; and to avoid implementation of the Department's operating criteria and procedures.

United States v. Truckee-Carson Irrigation District, et al.
General stream adjudication by the United States against all water users in the Truckee River Basin. The United States, and the Pyramid Lake Paiute Tribe of Indians as intervenors, claim a reserved water right sufficient in amount to preserve the level of Pyramid Lake and to reestablish the tribe's fishery in the lake and in the Truckee River.

City of Fallon, et al. v. Secretary of the Interior.
City alleges that United States cannot take over the Newlands Reclamation Project or enforce the Department of the Interior's operating criteria without preparing an environmental impact statement.

United States v. Alpine Land and Reservoir Company, et al.
This case centers on the question of an appropriate water duty for lands within the Newlands Reclamation Project which are served by the Carson River. This action has been underway since 1925. The final decree in this case will be an adjudication of the surface flows of the Carson River against all other water users.

Carson-Truckee Water Conservancy District, et al. v. Secretary, et al.
The plaintiffs, Carson-Truckee Water Conservancy District, State of Nevada, and Sierra Pacific Power Company claim entitlement to water stored in Stampede Reservoir for municipal and industrial purposes. The Department of the Interior has responsibility under the Endangered Species Act to conserve an endangered and threatened species of fish which are dependent upon Truckee River water for survival. The Department also seeks to preserve the fishery of Pyramid Lake given the government's fiduciary responsibility to the Pyramid Lake Paiute Tribe of Indians.

Nevada v. United States.
The State of Nevada, through this suit, claims ownership of the bed of Pyramid Lake. By its claim the state would seek to exert jurisdiction over the Pyramid Lake fishery.

Petition of the Watermaster in United States v. Orr Watch Ditch Decree in Equity.
In 1976, the Department of Justice wrote to the Federal Watermaster insisting that he enforce the terms of the 1944 Orr Ditch decree with respect to diversion of water from the Truckee River. The Watermaster responded by filing a petition with the court for instructions.

Truckee-Carson Irrigation District v. United States.
The TCID claims monetary damage for breach of an alleged implied contract between the District and the United States. The District claims entitlement to recover revenues allegedly lost as a result of the District foregoing the sale of winter power as part of Newlands Project operations.

United States v. Truckee-Carson Irrigation Project.
Quiet title action by the United States against the District to regain control of the 64-acre parcel of land located at Lake Tahoe. The District received custody of the land under terms of its 1926 contract with the United States. The District now refuses to recognize United States' revocation of that custody.

United States v. Orr Water Ditch Company, et al.
The United States, on behalf of the Pyramid Lake Paiute Tribe, has petitioned the court for a change in place and purpose of use of water rights decreed to the tribe under the 1944 Orr Ditch decree.

In the Matter of Sierra Pacific Power Company.
Pyramid Lake Paiute Indian Tribe and Secretary of the Interior filed complaint alleging that Sierra Pacific's four hydroelectric developments on the Truckee River in Nevada must be licensed by the Federal Energy Regulatory Commission.

NEW MEXICO

New Mexico v. Lewis.
General stream adjudication of Pecos River involving rights of the Mescalero Apache Indian Reservation.

United States v. Aamodt.
General adjudication of the Rio Pojoaque and Rio Tesuque, tributaries to the Rio Grande, involving the rights of the Pueblos of San Ildefonso, Pojoaque, Tesuque and Nambe.

State of New Mexico v. Abbott.
General adjudication of the rights of the Santa Clara, San Juan and San Ildefonso Pueblos on tributaries to the Rio Grande.

State of New Mexico v. Aarellano.
General adjudication of the Rio Hondo involving rights of the Taos Pueblo.

State of New Mexico v. Abeyta.
General stream adjudication of the Rio Grande del Rancho and Rio Pueblo de Taos involving water rights of the Taos Pueblo.

State of New Mexico v. Aragon.
General stream adjudication of the Chama River involving the water rights of San Juan Pueblo and the Jicarilla Apache Indian Tribe.

State of New Mexico v. United States.
General stream adjudication of the rights of the Jicarilla Apache, Ute Mountain and Navajo Indian Tribes.

OREGON

United States v. Ben Adair.
General stream adjudication of the Williamson River system involving rights of the Klamath Indian Tribe and Klamath Indian allottees.

In the Matter of Portland General Electric Company, Pelton Dam Project No. 2030.
Proceeding to determine methodology for paying annual charges for the use of tribal natural resources in connection with company's hydroelectic project on the Warm Springs Indian Reservation.

SOUTH DAKOTA

State of South Dakota v. Rippling Water Ranch, Inc.; United States, as Trustee for and on behalf of the Standing Rock Sioux Tribe, the Cheyenne River Sioux Tribe, the Lower Brule Sioux Tribe, the Crow Creek Sioux Tribe, the Oglala Sioux Tribe, the Rosebud Sioux Tribe, et al.
General water rights adjudication among all water claimants along the Missouri River and its major tributaries.

WASHINGTON

Confederated Tribes and Bands of the Yakima Indian Nation v. United States, et al.
This proceeding is a class action brought to determine the priority and quantum of the water rights of the Yakima Indian Reservation.

State of Washington, Department of Ecology v. Acquavella, et al.
General stream adjudication of the waters of the Yakima River drainage basin situated in Benton, Kittitas, Klickitat and Yakima Counties, Washington. It involves reserved water rights for the Yakima Indian Reservation and national forest lands.

United States v. Barbara J. Anderson.
Adjudication of rights to the use of waters of the Chamokane Creek and its tributaries brought by the United States on behalf of the Spokane Indian Tribe.

United States v. Bel Bay Community and Water Association.
Suit to determine State of Washington's regulatory jurisdiction over non-Indians within the Lummi Indian Reservation and the respective rights of the Indian and non-Indian users.

United States v. Walton; Colville Confederated Tribes v. Walton.
General stream adjudication of the No Name Creek within the Colville Indian Reservation. The Ninth Circuit issued its decision in June, 1981.

In the Matter of Washington Water Power Company, Spokane River Project No. 2545.
Proceeding to determine whether hydroelectric projects within boundaries of Spokane Indian Reservation in Washington and Coeur d'Alene Indian Reservation in Idaho must be licensed by Federal Energy Regulatory Commission, and, if so, extent of annual charges which company must pay to tribe.

High Ross Dam Project No. 553.
Application by city of Seattle to raise height of its dam by 122 feet. Secretary of Interior intervened to protect downstream Skagit River fishery to which Swinomish, Upper Skagit and Sauk-Suiattle Tribes have treaty protected rights.

WISCONSIN

Chippewa Reservoir Project No. 108.
Relicensing application by Northern States Power Company for project partially within Lac Courte Oreilles Indian Reservation.

WYOMING

In re the General Adjudication of All Rights to Use Water in the Big Horn River System and All Other Sources.
United States is a party with respect to all federal reserved and appropriative rights claimed for federal users including Wind River Shoshone and Arapaho Reservation, national forests, wildlife refuges, parks and public lands.

COMPENDIUM OF BILLS BEFORE CONGRESS AFFECTING INDIAN WATER RIGHTS

Following is a tabulation of bills before the U.S. Congress (both House and Senate) affecting Indian water rights, including date of introduction, principal sponsor, and congressional committee to which the legislation has been referred:

SENATE

S. 407
FLANDREAU SANTEE SIOUX FEASIBILITY STUDY

(Intro. Feb. 5 by Abdnor, R-S.D.) A bill to authorize a study of the feasibility of federal development of the water resources of the I'Santi Unit of the Missouri River Basin located on the Flandreau Santee Sioux Reservation in South Dakota. Referred to the Senate Environment and Public Works Committee.

S. 545
ROSEBUD SIOUX FEASIBILITY STUDY

(Intro. Feb 24 by Abdnor, R-S.D.) A bill to authorize a study of the feasibility of federal development of the water resources of the Little White River Unit located on the Rosebud Sioux Reservation in South Dakota. Referred to Senate Select Committee on Indian Affairs.

S. 563
TRIBAL-STATE COMPACT ACT OF 1981

(Intro. Feb. 24 by DeConcini, D-Ariz.) A bill to authorize the States and the Indian tribes to enter into mutal agreements and compacts respecting jurisdiction and governmental operations in Indian Country. Referred to Senate Select Committee on Indian Affairs.

S. 712
SOIL CONSERVATION ACT OF 1981

(Intro. Mar. 13 by Jepsen, R-Iowa) A bill to further local and state efforts to conserve, protect and enhance the nation's soil, water and related resources for a sustained agriculture, and for other purposes. Referred to Senate Agriculture Committee.

S. 874
STEELHEAD TROUT PROTECTION ACT

(Intro. Apr. 2 by Gorton, R-Wash.) A bill to provide for additional protection of steelhead trout as a game fish, and for other purposes. Referrred to Senate Select Committee on Indian Affairs.

S. 944
WATER AND WASTE DISPOSAL

(Intro. Apr. 8 by Helms, R-N.C.) A bill to increase the interest rates for loans made or insured under the Consolidated Farm and Rural Development Act for water and waste disposal and essential community facilities. Referred to Senate Agriculture Committee.

S. 1088
NATIVE AMERICAN PROGRAMS ACT

(Intro. Apr. 30 by Denton, R-Ala.) A bill to promote the goal of economic and social self-sufficiency for American Indians, Hawaiian Natives and Alaska Natives which provides for $28,000,000 in annual appropriations and a repeal of the Native American Programs Act of 1974. Referred to Senate Select Committee on Indian Affairs.

S. 1095
WATER RESOURCES PLANNING ACT OF 1981

(Intro. May 4 by Abdnor, R-S.D.) A bill to amend the Water Resources Planning Act. Referred to Senate Environment Committee. Ordered reported May 8 by Water Resources Subcommittee. Ordered reported May 13 by Senate Environment Committee. Report filed in Senate May 18 by Environment Committee.

S. 1244
ENERGY IMPACT ASSISTANCE ACT OF 1981

(Intro. May 20 by Hart, D-Col.) A bill to amend section 601 of the Powerplant and Industrial Fuel Use Act of 1978 to provide comprehensive assistance to states, local governments, and Indian tribes to mitigate the adverse social and economic impacts caused by major energy developments (including water related developments) and for other purposes. Referred to Senate Committee on Energy and Natural Resources.

S. 1370
SHIATOOK LAKE DEVELOPMENT

(Intro. June 16 by Boren, D-Ok.) A bill to authorize the Secretary of the Army to acquire, by condemnation proceedings, or otherwise, such interests in the oil, gas, coal, or other minerals owned by the Osage Tribe of Indians needed for Skiatook Lake, Osage County, Oklahoma. Referred to Senate Select Committee on Indian Affairs.

S. 1553
SOUTH DAKOTA WATER PROJECTS

(Intro. July 30 by Abdnor, R-S.D.) A bill to authorize the Interior Secretary to proceed with the development of the WEB pipeline, to provide for the study of

South Dakota Water Projects to be developed in lieu of the Oahe and Pollock-Herreid irrigation projects, and to make available Missouri Basin pumping power to projects authorized by the Flood Control Act of 1944 to receive such power. Referred to Senate Agriculture Committee.

HOUSE

H.R. 1815
INDIAN SELF-DETERMINATION ACT AMENDMENTS

(Intro. Feb. 6 by Lee, R-N.Y.) A bill to amend the Indian Self-Determination Act to provide that grants under such Act may not be made to a tribal organization for proceedings the tribal organization initiates based on the claim that land was acquired without compliance with the laws of the United States relating to conveyances by an Indian, Indian Nation, or tribe of Indians. Referred to House Committee on Interior and Insular Affairs.

H.R. 2329
ARKANSAS RIVER NAVIGATION SYSTEM CLAIMS

(Intro. Mar. 4 by Synar, D-Ok.) A bill to confer jurisdiction on certain courts of the United States to hear and render judgment in connection with claims of the Cherokee Nation of Oklahoma related to and arising from construction of the Arkansas River Navigation System. Referred to House Committees on Interior and Insular Affairs and the Judiciary.

H.R. 2914
DROUGHT MITIGATION

(Intro. Mar. 30 by Whitehurst, R-Va.) A bill to provide temporary authorities to the Secretary of Commerce to facilitate emergency actions to mitigate the impacts of the current drought and promote water conservation. Referred to House Banking Committee.

H.R. 3167
LICENSING OF HUALAPAI DAM

(Intro. Apr. 8 by Stump, D-Ariz.) A bill to authorize the licensing of Hualapai Dam and for other purposes. Referred to House Interior Committee.

H.R. 3388
CONSOLIDATED FARM AND RURAL DEVELOPMENT ACT INTEREST RATES

(Intro. May 1 by Wampler, R-Va.) A bill to increase the interest rates for loans made or insured under the Consolidated Farm and Rural Development Act for water and waste disposal, and essential community facilities. Referred to House Agriculture Committee.

H.R. 3432
EVALUATING WATER RESOURCES PROJECTS

(Intro. July 17 by Howard, D-N.J.) A bill to amend the Water Resources Development Act of 1974 relating to planning and evaluating water resources projects and for other purposes. Referred to House Agriculture Committee which filed a report.

H.R. 3686
CIVILIAN CONSERVATION CORPS II ACT

(Intro. May 21 by Roybal, D-Ca.) A bill to establish the Civilian Conservation Corps II to perform such projects on public or Indian lands or water as the Secretary of the Interior may authorize, and for other purposes. Referred to House Education and Labor Committee.

H.R. 3760
INDIAN TRIBAL GOVERNMENTAL TAX STATUS ACT OF 1981

(Intro. June 4 by Jones, D-Ok.) A bill to amend the Internal Revenue Code of 1954 to extend certain tax provisions to Indian tribal governments on the same basis as such provisions apply to the states. Referred to House Ways and Means Committee.

H.R. 3824
URBAN JOBS AND ENTERPRISE ZONE ACT OF 1981

(Intro. June 4 by Kemp, R-N.Y.) A bill to amend the Internal Revenue Code of 1954 to provide certain community development, employment, and tax incentives for individuals and businesses in depressed areas (including Indian reservations). Referred to House Ways and Means Committee and concurrently for consideration in part to the House Banking, Finance and Urban Affairs Committee.

H.R. 4347
SOUTH DAKOTA WATER PROJECTS

(Intro. July 30 by Roberts, R-S.D.) A bill to authorize the Interior Secretary to proceed with development of the WEB Pipeline, to provide for the study of South Dakota water projects to be developed in lieu of the Oahe and Pollock-Herreid irrigation projects, and to make available Missouri Basin pumping power to projects authorized by the Flood Control Act of 1944 to receive such power. Referred to House Interior Committee.

H.R. 4363
SOUTHERN ARIZONA WATER RIGHTS SETTLEMENTS ACT

(Intro. July 31 by Udall, D-Ariz.) A bill to provide water to the Papago Tribe of Arizona and its members, to settle tribal and individual water rights claims in portions of the Papago Reservations, and for other purposes. Referred to House Interior Committee.

CONTRIBUTORS' BIOGRAPHIES

John A. Folk-Williams is the president and founder of the Western Network, a communications program studying conflicts over resource use in the western states. Western Network, based in Santa Fe, New Mexico, analyzes the interaction of Indian and non-Indian constituencies in the context of specific decision-making and dispute resolution processes as these groups compete for control of important resources, particularly water. Before founding Western Network, he spent twelve years as a field representative and consultant to several private foundations with special interests in Indian and natural resources issues.

Charles N. Estes, Jr. is an Assistant City Attorney in Albuquerque, New Mexico. During the period 1976–1980, he was an Assistant United States Attorney for the District of New Mexico. He was a staff attorney in the Justice Department's Land and Natural Resources Division and served as an Administrative Assistant to the Chairman of the All Indian Pueblo Council. He received his Bachelor of Arts and law degrees from Harvard University.

Barbara W. Fritzemeier is editor of the *Indian Law Reporter* published by the American Indian Lawyer Training Program. She received her Bachelor of Arts degree from Wittenberg University and her law degree from the University of California, Hastings College of Law. She is a member of the California State Bar.

Patricia Zell is a staff attorney with the Select Committee on Indian Affairs in the United States Senate. Before joining the Select Committee, she was a staff attorney with the American Indian Lawyer Training Program and was instrumental in developing and coordinating the symposium on *Indian Water Policy in a Changing Environment.* She served as research director for the American Indian Policy Review Commission and was a staff assistant for the Department of the Interior's Office of Land and Water Resources. She also served as a hearing team member for the U.S. Civil Rights Commission. She received her bachelor's degree from Washington University and her law degree from Georgetown University School of Law.